Art History Versus Aesthetics

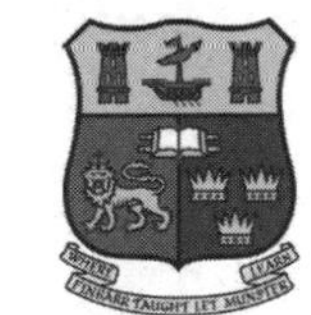

The Art Seminar

VOLUME 1
ART HISTORY VERSUS AESTHETICS

VOLUME 2
PHOTOGRAPHY THEORY

VOLUME 3
IS ART HISTORY GLOBAL?

VOLUME 4
THE STATE OF ART CRITICISM

VOLUME 5
THE RENAISSANCE

VOLUME 6
LANDSCAPE THEORY

VOLUME 7
TRANSCENDENCE

Sponsored by the University College Cork, Ireland; the Burren College of Art, Ballyvaughan, Ireland; and the School of the Art Institute, Chicago.

Art History Versus Aesthetics

EDITED BY

JAMES ELKINS

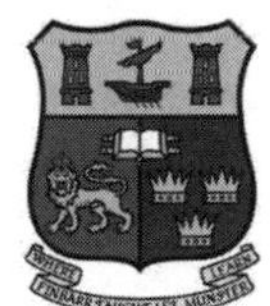

University College Cork
Coláiste na hOllscoile Corcaigh

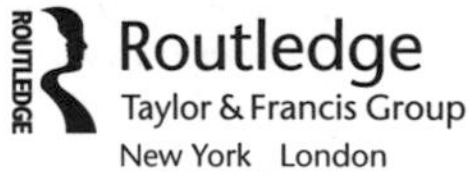

Published in 2006 by
Routledge
Taylor & Francis Group
270 Madison Avenue
New York, NY 10016

Published in Great Britain by
Routledge
Taylor & Francis Group
2 Park Square
Milton Park, Abingdon
Oxon OX14 4RN

Printed in the United States of America on acid-free paper
10 9 8 7 6 5 4 3 2 1

International Standard Book Number-10: 0-415-97688-X (Hardcover) 0-415-97689-8 (Softcover)
International Standard Book Number-13: 978-0-415-97688-6 (Hardcover) 978-0-415-97689-3 (Softcover)
Library of Congress Card Number 2005013494

Library of Congress Cataloging-in-Publication Data

Art history versus aesthetics / edited by James Elkins.
p. cm. -- (The art seminar ; vol. 1)
Includes bibliographical references and index.
ISBN 0-415-97688-X (978-0-415-97688-6) -- ISBN 0-415-97689-8 (978-0-415-97689-3)
1. Art--Historiography--Congresses. 2. Aesthetics--Congresses. I. Series.

N7480.A776 2005
701'.17--dc22 2005013494

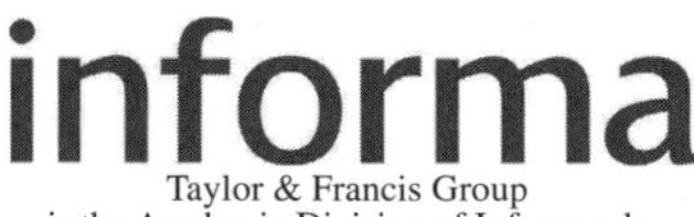

Taylor & Francis Group
is the Academic Division of Informa plc.

Visit the Taylor & Francis Web site at
http://www.taylorandfrancis.com

and the Routledge Web site at
http://www.routledge-ny.com

Table of Contents

Series Preface

James Elkins

It has been said and said that there is too much theorizing in the visual arts. Contemporary writing seems like a trackless thicket, tangled with unanswered questions. Yet it is not a wilderness; in fact it is well posted with signs and directions. Want to find Lacan? Read him through Macey, Silverman, Borch-Jakobsen, Žižek, Nancy, Leclaire, Derrida, Laplanche, Lecercle, or even Klossowski, but not—so it might be said—through Abraham, Miller, Pontalis, Rosaloto, Safouan, Roudinesco, Schneiderman, or Mounin, and of course never through Dalí.

People who would rather avoid problems of interpretation, at least in their more difficult forms, have sometimes hoped that "theory" would prove to be a passing fad. A simple test shows that is not the case. Figure 1 shows the number of art historical essays that have terms like "psychoanalysis" as keywords, according to the *Bibliography of the History of Art*. The increase is steep after 1980, and in three cases—the gaze, psychoanalysis, and feminism—the rise is exponential.

Figure 2 shows that citations of some of the more influential art historians of the mid-twentieth century, writers who came

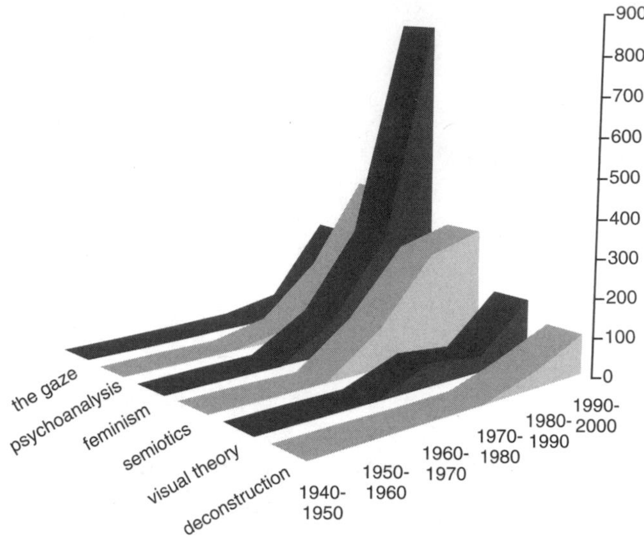

Figure 1 Theory in art history, 1940–2000.

before the current proliferation of theories, are waning. In this second graph there is a slight rise in the number of references to Warburg and Riegl, refl ecting the interest they have had for the current generation of art historians: but the graph's surprise is the precipitous decline in citations of Panofsky and Gombrich.

Most of art history is not driven by named theories or individual historians, and these graphs are also limited by the terms that can be meaningfully searched in the *Bibliography of the History of Art*. Even so, the graphs suggest that the landscape of interpretive strategies is changing rapidly. Many subjects crucial to the interpretation of art are too new, ill-theorized, or unfocused to be addressed in monographs or textbooks. The purpose of *The Art Seminar* is to address some of the most challenging subjects in current writing on art: those that are not unencompassably large (such as the state of painting), or not yet adequately posed (such as the space between the aesthetic and the anti-aesthetic), or so well known that they can be written up in critical dictionaries (the the-

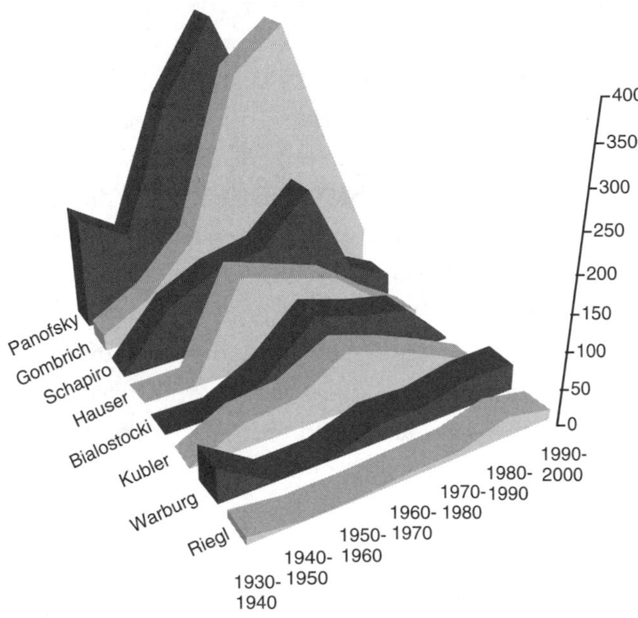

Figure 2 Rise and fall of an older art history, 1930–2000: Citations of selected writers.

ory of deconstruction). The subjects chosen for *The Art Seminar* are poised, ready to be articulated and argued.

Each volume in the series began as a roundtable conversation, held in front of an audience at one of the three sponsoring institutions—the University College Cork, the Burren College of Art (both in Ireland), and the School of the Art Institute of Chicago. The conversations were then transcribed, and edited by the participants. The idea was to edit in such a way as to minimize the correctable faults of grammar, repetitions, and lapses that mark any conversation, while preserving the momentary disagreements, confusions, and dead-ends that could be attributed to the articulation of the subject itself.

In each volume of *The Art Seminar*, the conversation itself is preceded by a general introduction to the subject and one or more "Starting Points," previously published essays that were distributed to participants before the roundtable. Together the "Introductions" and "Starting Points" are meant to provide the essential background for the conversation. A number of scholars who did not attend the events were then asked to write "Assessments"; their brief was to consider the conversation from a distance, noting its strengths and its blind spots. The "Assessments" vary widely in style and length: some are highly structured, and others are impressionistic; some are under a page, and others the length of a commissioned essay. Contributors were just asked to let their form fit their content, with no limitations. Each volume then concludes with one or more "Afterwords," longer critical essays written by scholars who had access to all the material including the "Assessments."

The Art Seminar attempts to cast as wide, as fine, and as strong a net as possible, to capture the limit of theorizing on each subject. Perhaps in the future the ideas discussed here will be colonized, and become part of the standard pedagogy of art: but by that time they may be on the downward slide, away from the centers of conversation and into the history of disciplines. At the moment they are unresolved, and their irresolution has much to tell us.

1
Introduction

The Border of the Aesthetic

Robert Gero

The border of the aesthetic is a contested space—a multiply defended zone of discourses occupied by theorists working within the disciplines of philosophy and art history. Theoretical maneuvers and countermaneuvers occur within the domain of each discipline. In both disciplines, theorists battle over the definition of the aesthetic. On one side, theorists claim that aesthetic encounters with artworks involve immediate, noninferential sensory responses that are refined by sustained contemplation alone and not by appeal to such extraphenomenal factors as facts about art theory, art practice, or art history. This is a subjectivist position that is usually framed as the view that aesthetic judgments are autonomous. On the other side, the claim is that theory and practice are logically implicated in aesthetic judgment because they are logically implicated in the artwork itself. This position makes possible a coherent basis for talk of "true" and "false" in aesthetic judgment and art criticism—or at least talk of "better" and "worse." In general, theorists are divided by whether they count aesthetic encounters with artworks to be logically independent of their theoretical properties or necessarily constrained by them.

Since the eighteenth century, writers within philosophy have worked to reconcile these extremes. Alexander Baumgarten, who first introduced the term "aesthetics" in 1735, defined it as sensitive cognition.[1] In discussing poetry, he distinguished the category of sensitive discourse, with its suggestive flood of densely packed imagery and ideas, from the category of intellectual discourse, with its network of clear and distinct abstract ideas. David Hume, in 1757, argued that aesthetic responses were spontaneous, subjective states that could be informed by reason as well as sense. Hume supported this by appeal to the intrinsically reflective structure of the aesthetic response. The possibility of informed reflection was the ground on which Hume delineated true critics from pretend critics even though he continued to maintain that aesthetic judgments were subjective reports of feeling and lacked truth value. According to Hume, true critics of "the finer arts" must subject their aesthetic responses to training: they must be translocal, engaging with artworks of "different nations and ages" in order to make informed comparisons; they must be transpersonal, calibrating their responses to the point of view of the intended audience; and they must be analytical, using reason to judge how well the work realized its calculated ends or was "confined by rules of art, discovered to the author either by genius or by observation."[2]

Since the beginning of the modernist period, the field of combat has been Kantian: in the *Critique of Judgment* (1790), Kant introduced or developed most of the critical terms in play in modernist art analysis—beauty and the sublime, reflective judgment, the presence of an intellectual pleasure in aesthetic appreciation, the presence of a "free play" of cognitive and imaginative elements in aesthetic appreciation, the absence of determinate concepts in aesthetic judgment, the role of artworks as productive exemplars in art making, and the crucial, regulating function of the *sensus communis* in training artists, critics, and other art viewers. For this reason, all contemporary art theorists can be viewed as negotiating a position in relation to Kant. Consequently, a review of Kantian aesthetics will be a helpful aid in reading Section 3, "The Art Seminar."

In the *Critique of Judgment*, Kant analyzed the formal structures of both aesthetic judgment and art making in terms of the "free play" of imagination and understanding. This is the "free play" of the beautiful where the imagination can endlessly play at forming and the understanding can endlessly play at describing. For Kant, artworks are an imaginative array of representations, "a multiplicity of partial representations," what he calls "aesthetic ideas" that "strain" to approximate an objective presentation of a rational idea.[3] Rational ideas are not determinate concepts but are ways of trying to think about, or somehow represent, what lies beyond human experience or what is mysterious and ineluctable within it. Aesthetic ideas are not determinate concepts either, nonetheless, as disciplined imaginative insights, they have cognitive content. Aesthetic appreciation is the entertaining of indeterminate and partial concepts that never coalesce into one privileged, conceptual "closure." In Kant's aesthetic, this rush of thought stimulates intellectual pleasure when it somehow satisfies the spectator in spite of resisting crystallization into a fixed or definite thought. In fact, Kant claims that the reason artworks can stimulate such enjoyable floods of thought is *because* that thought is not narrowly constrained within the boundary of a particular determinate concept. Aesthetic pleasure is the harmonic play of the understanding and the imagination as they work together to organize meanings.

For Kant, such a free play is possible only if the artwork is a dynamic mechanism operating according to a kind of complex internal logic that both invites and eludes interpretation. Kant claimed that artists can isolate and extract this mechanism from another artist's artwork and either directly appropriate it or re-work it in their own artworks. For Kant, no worked structure is an artwork unless it creates and maintains the free play necessary for a purely intellectual or cognitive enjoyment. Consequently, art production necessarily involves the invention of works that have sufficient complexity and sufficient openness to stimulate a rich train of thought, a set of plausible readings that must always remain indefinite.

Kant's work has been appropriated to advance differing accounts of the aesthetic. Some define the aesthetic as the experiencing of a sensible object of any sort—natural or artifactual—when it is framed as *an irreducibly singular event*, disconnected from any determinate purpose, function, or art-historical situation. On this account, the aesthetic is tied to the perceptual: every perceptual object could be viewed aesthetically, for example, an aerial night bombing or a makeshift memorial shrine, but not every artwork. Pablo Picasso's *Guernica* (1937), for example, would be included in the scope of the aesthetic; but not Andy Warhol's *Brillo Box* (1964) or Paul McCarthy's *Bossy Burger* (1991).

This narrowed bracketing of the aesthetic is the application to art of the disciplinary project of the Enlightenment—what Jürgen Habermas calls "the project of modernity ... to develop objective science, universal morality and law, and autonomous art according to their inner logic."[4]

The autonomy of art has been variously viewed. It has been mourned as "aesthetic alienation": "the experience of art as *aesthetical* is the experience of art as having lost or been deprived of its power to speak the truth ... modernity is the site of beauty bereaved."[5] A cultural position or set of concerns, later organized under the term "anti-aesthetic," emerged in the late 1950s and early 1960s and attacked the aesthetic as the mark of art. They attempted to "change the object itself," "the very nature of art," and "the object of criticism":

> "Anti-aesthetic" also signals that the very notion of the aesthetic, its network of ideas, is in question here: the idea that aesthetic experience exists apart, without "purpose," all but beyond history, or that art can now effect a world at once (inter)subjective, concrete and universal—a symbolic totality. … More locally, "anti-aesthetic" also signals a practice, cross-disciplinary in nature, that is sensitive to cultural forms engaged in a politic ... or rooted in a vernacular—that is, to forms that deny the idea of a privileged aesthetic realm.[6]

J. M. Bernstein notes that theories of art that view artworks as historical constructions, "attempt[ing] to interrogate art historically,"[7] necessarily understand artworks "in non-aesthetic terms."[8] On the other hand, the aesthetic has been valued as a subversive zone of experiencing because it is not compromised by the instrumentality of political and economic negotiations. Theodor Adorno sees art or the "aesthetic mode of conduct" as "a reservoir of critique … because it alone can block the repressive authority—instrumental rationality (perfected under capitalism)":[9]

> Aesthetic experience becomes living experience only by way of its object, in that instant in which artworks themselves become animate under its gaze. ... Through contemplative immersion the immanent processual quality of the work is set free. ... This immanent dynamic is, in a sense, a higher-order element of what artworks are. If anywhere, then it is here that aesthetic experience resembles sexual experience, indeed its culmination.[10]

Many writers practicing or avoiding philosophical aesthetics share this sense-based interpretation of the aesthetic. Arthur Danto has claimed that Warhol's *Brillo Box* is an anomalous artwork that exposes the basic theoretical dimension of art and forces the abandonment of the aesthetic theory of art. According to Danto, *Brillo Box* refutes the theoretical claim that the only significant properties of an artwork are aesthetic properties that supervene on the sense-based properties of the work. He claims "aesthetic considerations have no essential application to … art produced from the late 1960s on":[11]

> For me, the interesting feature of the *Brillo Box* was that it appropriated the philosophical question of the relationship between art and reality and incorporated it into the *Brillo Box* and in effect asks why, if it is art, the boxes of Brillo in the supermarket, which differ from it in no interesting perceptual way, are not. At the very least the *Brillo Box* made plain that one cannot any longer think of distinguishing art from reality on perceptual grounds, for these grounds have been cut away. … What makes the one art may be something quite invisible, perhaps how it arrived in the world and what someone intended it to be.[12]

For Danto, when an artwork can have significant nonperceptual properties, art is revealed as nonaesthetic. For this reason, he concludes that the project of interpreting and appreciating art cannot be confined by the terms of the aesthetic.

In contrast, the aesthetic has been defined as referring exclusively to the experiencing of an object *when framed as an artwork*. On this account, every artwork, even one possessing insignificant or no perceptual qualities is aesthetic, while most perceptually discriminated objects are not. Thierry de Duve shares this reading of the aesthetic:

> The sentence "here is some art" produces a case of art, but it is not a case of theory; it is a case of feeling. The experience is not repeatable, which is to say, experimental; it is singular, which is to say aesthetic.[13]

Other theorists in this group have redrawn the boundary of the aesthetic far beyond the liminal border of the perceptual. Stephen Davies counts as aesthetic *all* the complex semantic properties of an artwork necessary for its appreciation as an artwork.[14] He claims that Duchamp's *Fountain* (1917) possesses the property of "referring to the history and technique of sculpture" because it has gained aesthetic properties "as a result of attaining art status."[15] Noël Carroll has challenged this use of "aesthetic" to cover a diverse set of properties ranging from the sensuous to the semantic. However, he agrees that the formal properties of an artwork are aesthetic, defining them as "the ensemble of choices that realize the point or purpose of the work."[16] Consequently, Carroll concludes that conceptual artworks such as John Cage's *4'33"* have nonperceptual aesthetic properties:

> With respect to *4'33"*, the form of the work crucially involves the choice of notational silence—the pianist enters, opens the score, and does nothing—thereby virtually compelling the audience to attend to whatever ambient sounds occur in the ensuing interval of four minutes and thirty-three seconds. The point of the work—Cage's great project, one might say—is to deconstruct the privileged position of music in the music/noise couplet and to alert the listener to the aural richness that surrounds her at any given moment.[17]

Carroll points out that this move also entails another attack on a modernist aesthetics: he claims that one can grasp the artistic form of John Cage's *4'33"* without ever attending a performance of the work.[18] Here Carroll extends Malcolm Budd's attack on "the acquaintance principle" by concluding that some aesthetic properties themselves, and not just knowledge of them, can be grasped on the basis of their reliable description, without requiring any experiencing of them directly. [19]

Recently, James Shelley has advanced a new aesthetic theory of art using Frank Sibley's notion of aesthetic perception understood as noninferential perception. According to Sibley, aesthetic perception is necessary for aesthetic judgment and is impossible without a direct encounter with the artwork:

> People have to *see* the grace and unity of a work, *hear* the plaintiveness or frenzy in the music, *notice* the gaudiness of a color scheme, *feel* the power of a novel, its mood, or its uncertainty of tone. They may be struck by these qualities at once, or they may come to perceive them only after repeated viewings, hearings, or readings, and with the help of critics. But unless they do perceive them for themselves, aesthetic enjoyment, appreciation, and judgment are beyond them. Merely to learn from others, on good authority, that the music is serene, the play moving, or the picture unbalanced, is of little aesthetic value; the crucial thing is to see, or hear, or feel. To suppose that one can make aesthetic judgments without aesthetic perception, say, by following rules of some kind, is to misunderstand aesthetic judgment.[20]

Shelley argues that noticing the cognitive contents of artworks is sufficient to support aesthetic experience.[21] He claims that ideas or thoughts can be affective, that is, "thoughts [can] move us perhaps as much as sensuous forms do. They strike us with daring and wit, and with power and beauty":

> There is a notion of the aesthetic on the table—Sibley's—according to which daring, impudence, and wit are no less aesthetic than grace, elegance and beauty … [consequently] there is a notion of the aesthetic … according to which *Fountain*, *L.H.O.O.Q.*, and *Erased DeKooning Drawing* are no less aesthetic than are the Trevi Fountain, the *Mona Lisa*, and the DeKooning drawing that Rauschenberg erased.[22]

On this account, aesthetic properties can depend on semantic properties of artworks just as they depend on perceptual properties. Consequently, all artworks are aesthetic, even nonperceptual works with significant cognitive content and irrelevant perceptual properties. Interestingly, Shelley claims that this move is properly termed an "aesthetic" theory of art since it is in line with Francis Hutcheson's treatment of the aesthetic in his *Inquiry Concerning*

Beauty, Order, Harmony, Design (1725), a work Shelley describes as "a founding text of modern aesthetics." In it, Hutcheson analyzes the idea of beauty as "an 'internal' or 'mentalsensation,' received by means of an 'internal' or 'mental' sense."[23] Hutcheson also defends, at length, the claim that "powerful yet economical" theorems can strike us with their beauty.[24]

The preceding is offered as a summary to help frame the terms of conversation that follow in Section 3, "The Art Seminar." Within art history, there are differing accounts of whether art history constrains aesthetic judgment or is constrained by it. Some theorists have claimed that art historians identify vital stylistic elements in artworks by detecting the aesthetic significance of those elements. Others have argued for a stronger claim: no stylistic element or subcomponent of an artwork can be articulated unless that element's aesthetic significance within the work has first been determined:

> No doubt the painter Ingres drew his exquisite lines and did not use a ruler, but whereas the use of unruled lines is a vital stylistic element in Barnett Newman, it is not one we would mention in connection with Ingres. Why is this? It is because Newman has introduced those unruled lines with a special formal effect in mind, and this formal effect forms a large part of the aesthetic significance of a Newman canvas. Ingres presumably did not ever consider the use of a ruler: no aesthetically significant choice was involved in his use of unruled lines.[25]

In contrast, other scholars have argued that aesthetic evaluation is impossible without first determining the history of the artwork, its particular positioning within art history. Erwin Panofsky is perhaps the preeminent example:

> But that we grasp [aesthetic] qualities in the fraction of a second and almost automatically must not induce us to believe that we could ever give a correct pre-iconographical description of

> a work of art without having divined, as it were, its historical "locus." While we believe that we are identifying the motifs on the basis of our practical experience pure and simple, we really are reading "what we see" according to the manner in which objects and events are expressed by forms under varying historical conditions ... we subject our practical experience to a corrective principle which may be called the history of style.[26]

Kendall Walton reinforces this claim; for him, historical facts about the origination of an artwork are essential to determining the aesthetic properties of an artwork. Aesthetic evaluation is possible only if such facts as the artist's intention or the existence of particular "well-established and well-recognized" categories of art production within the art world of the artist (such as impressionist painting and twelve-tone music) have been determined in advance:

> We could not possibly tell by staring at [the work], no matter how intently and intelligently, whether it is coherent, or serene, or dynamic, for by staring we cannot tell whether it is to be seen as a sculpture, a *Guernica*, or some other exotic or mundane kind of work of art. (We could attribute aesthetic properties to it in the way we do to natural objects, which of course does not involve consideration of historical facts about artists or their societies. But to do this would not be to treat the object as a *work* of art.) ... And of two works which differ *only* in respect of their origins—that is, which are perceptually indistinguishable—one might be coherent or serene, and the other not.[27]

Others have taken art-critical practice in general to constrain the aesthetic judgment of particular artworks. Denis Dutton indexes the artist's creatively realized intention to complicate "enabling" or "regulating" background conditions that include, for poetic works, "the background of the vocabulary, grammar, syntax, conventions, associations and history of language."[28] This move has been attacked on the grounds that it fails to discriminate between fixed background conditions that *explicitly* enter into the artwork's design and those that do not.[29]

If background conditions surrounding the production of a particular artwork are read in the broadest sense, the artwork becomes a condensed representation of a particular sociohistorical context and discourse. Its dominant function is to be an interpreted moment of a cultural time-space. Here the specificities of art history and aesthetics are lost in the generalities of institutional display. Jacques Rancière has observed that artworks have been historicized by art museums in the very act of framing *qua* aesthetic display:

> Our museums of fine arts don't display pure specimens of fine art. They display historicized art: Fra Angelico between Giotto and Masaccio, framing an idea of Florentine princely splendor and religious fervour; Rembrandt between Hals and Vermeer, featuring Dutch domestic and civic life, the rise of the bourgeoisie, and so on. They exhibit a time-space of art as so many moments of the incarnation of thought.[30]

According to Rancière, art making is no longer "subject to a set of intrinsic norms: a hierarchy of genres, adequation of expression to subject matter, correspondence between the arts, etc."[31]: now it is possible for "everything to play the part of the heterogenous, unavailable sensible."[32] Rancière claims that this romantic construction of the heteronomy of the art object as a form of life, what he calls "the plot of the spirit of forms," is, in fact, the construction of a mode of experience that projects the properties of the aesthetic experience onto the art object yet paradoxically recognizes the object as art only on the condition that it is nonart.[33] Rancière claims that the current aesthetic regime operates via a Romantic poetics that regards art and life to be permeable. As a result, both formalism in art and normativity in art have been overthrown.

In Section 3, "The Art Seminar" and Section 4, "Assessments," a very wide range of opinions regarding the aesthetic becomes evident: some writers reject the role of the aesthetic in art criticism in favor of historically-bounded criteria; others attempt to redesign or return the aesthetic to a concept compatible with the historical. Others begin with assumptions that reject any confluence between art history and aesthetics; this places them outside of arguments that can contain both aesthetics and history, including the literature I have reviwed here. These positions, in sum, comprise a large portion of the spectrum of conceptual possibilities as I see it. Most of the terms of art history, considered as a discipline, are at least influenced, if not determined by, fundamental issues such as the ones I have outlined. I will bring this introduction to a close by sketching my own position in relation to these issues.

I believe that Kantian aesthetic theory remains applicable to the category of contemporary artwork classified as "nonaesthetic." A reading of Kant's formalism demonstrates an essential connection to postmodernist art practice and appreciation. *Contra* Clement Greenberg, Kant's account of aesthetic appreciation is not formalist in a narrow sense. To conclude otherwise is to neglect Kant's account of art making as a species of intellectual play: "production through freedom, i.e., through an act of will that places reason at the basis of its action."[34]

To view a work as art is to enjoy shifting levels of interplay: seeing how the artist has merged imagery, sounds, cultural icons, found objects, sometimes even another artist's work, into new representations that express meaningful ideas; seeing how the artist's selection of, and treatment of, a medium fits into the art-historical record of media treatment; seeing how the artist's work is positioned with earlier works of that artist and other artists in history; seeing how the artist's work plays in relation to other disciplines and the social dimension of life. Rosalind Krauss notes that art practice regarded as "eclectic" from a modernist point of view can be seen as "rigorously logical" from a postmodern perspective:

> Within the situation of postmodernism, practice is not defined in relation to a given medium—sculpture—but rather in relation to the logical operations on a set of cultural terms, for which any medium—photography, books, lines on walls, mirrors, or sculpture itself—might be used.[35]

Instead of conclusions—which would, given the complexity of the subject and the brevity of this exposition, be premature—I would like to advance another theory of the aesthetic. My model incorporates and extends theoretical moves advanced by several of the theorists under discussion in this essay:

1. The Sibley/Shelley move: No property of an artwork counts as aesthetic unless it can generate a noninferential judgment in a trained, sentient spectator. I would extend this: any property of an artwork counts as aesthetic if its virtual "viewing" is sufficient to generate noninferential judgments.
2. Davies's move: Aesthetic properties are not just sensuous properties; they include such art-historically indexed properties as "referring to the history and techniques of sculpture." I would both narrow and broaden this claim. First, only art-historical descriptions of works that generate perceptual/sensory experiences count as aesthetic properties of artworks. Second, art-historical descriptions can sometimes generate new properties and even new works.
3. Carroll's move: Artistic form is the set of choices that realize certain purposes or points. I would extend this: some artworks are strategic structures. Because certain artworks utilize theory strategically, they can be "seen" only by trained spectators who are aware of other artworks and the

ways theoretical commitments and moves within the art world can generate aesthetic properties.

This, in outline, seems a promising way to define the aesthetic since it is informed by the spectrum of theory and by the encounter with a class of contemporary artwork that has generally frustrated and confounded aesthetic analysis. Here I follow Adorno:

> [T]he concrete historical situation of art registers concrete demands. Aesthetics begins with reflection on them: only through them does a perspective open up on what art is. . . . The principle of method here is that light should be cast on all art from the vantage point of the most recent artworks, rather than the reverse, following the custom of historicism and philology, which, bourgeois at heart, prefers that nothing ever change. If Valéry's thesis is true that the best in the new corresponds to an old need, then the most authentic works are critiques of past works. Aesthetics becomes normative by articulating such criticism. This, however, has retroactive force, and from it alone is it possible to expect what general aesthetics offered only as a hope and a sham.[36]

Notes

1. Alexander Baumgarten, *Theoretische Ästhetik,* trans. H. R. Schweitzer (Hamburg: Felix Meiner, 1988). Originally published in 1750 /1758 as Aesthetica.
2. David Hume, "Of the Standard of Taste," in *Essays Moral, Political, and Literary,* ed. Eugene Miller (Indianapolis, IN: The Liberty Fund, 1987), 235. Originally published in 1757.
3. Immanuel Kant, *Critique of Judgment,* trans. Werner S. Pluhar (Indianapolis, IN: Hackett, 1987), Part I, Book II, 49:316. Originally published in 1790 as *Kritik der Urtheilskraft.*
4. Jürgen Habermas, "Modernity: An Incomplete Project," in *The Anti-Aesthetic: Essays on Postmodern Culture*, ed. Hal Foster (Port Townsend, WA: Bay Press, 1983), 9. Originally delivered in 1980 as a talk.
5. J. M. Bernstein, *The Fate of Art: Aesthetic Alienation from Kant to Derrida and Adorno* (University Park: Pennsylvania State University Press, 1992), 4.
6. Hal Foster, "Postmodernism: A Preface," in *The Anti-Aesthetic*, x, xv.

7. The Fate of Art, 4.
8. The Fate of Art, 3.
9. Josef Früchtl, "Adorno and Mimesis," in *Encyclopedia of Aesthetics*, ed. Michael Kelly (Oxford: Oxford University Press, 1998), 1:25.
10. Theodor W. Adorno, *Aesthetic Theory*, trans. Robert Hullot-Kentor (Minneapolis: University of Minnesota Press, 1997), 175–6. Originally published in 1970 as *Äesthetische Theorie*. Adorno's position is complex: his notion of the autonomy of art is derived from psychoanalysis and historical materialism, not the disciplinary project of modernity. For Adorno, artworks are "immanently dynamic" in relation to the spectator and to other artworks (176). He claims "history is inherent to aesthetic theory. Its categories are radically historical" (359).
11. Arthur Danto, *After the End: Contemporary Art and the Pale of History* (Princeton, NJ: Princeton University Press, 1997), 25. Danto regards his work in *The Transfiguration of the Commonplace* (Cambridge, MA: Harvard University Press, 1981) and *The Philosophical Disenfranchisement of Art* (New York: Columbia University Press, 1986) as demonstrating this philosophically.
12. Arthur Danto, "Pop Art: Aesthetics of Andy Warhol," *Encyclopedia of Aesthetics*, 1:42, 44.
13. Thierry de Duve, *Kant after Duchamp* (Cambridge, MA: MIT Press, 1996), 50–51.
14. Stephen Davies, *Definitions of Art* (Ithaca, NY: Cornell University Press, 1991), 108.
15. Ibid., 67.
16. Noël Carroll, "Non-Perceptual Aesthetic Properties: Comments for James Shelley," *British Society of Aesthetics* 44 no. 4 (October 2004): 416–17.
17. Ibid., 415.
18. Ibid.
19. Ibid., 416–17; Malcolm Budd, "The Acquaintance Principle," *British Journal of Aesthetics* 43 no. 4 (October 2003): 386–92.
20. Frank Sibley, "Aesthetic and Non-Aesthetic," Philosophical Review 74 (1957): 137.
21. James Shelley, "The Problem of Non-Perceptual Art," British Journal of Aesthetics 43, no. 4 (October 2003): 373–78.
22. Ibid., 378, 373.
23. Ibid., 376; Francis Hutcheson, *Inquiry Concerning Beauty, Order, Harmony, Design*, ed. Peter Kivy (The Hague: Martinus Nijhoff, 1973), §I, art. X, § III, arts. I, II, V.
24. Hutcheson, Inquiry, § III.
25. Jenefer M. Robinson, "Style and Significance in Art History and Art Criticism," *The Journal of Aesthetics and Art Criticism*, 40 (1981): 11.
26. Erwin Panofsky, "Iconography and Iconology: An Introduction to the Study of Renaissance Art," in *Meaning in the Visual Arts* (Garden City, NY: Doubleday, 1955), 34–35.
27. Kendall Walton, "Categories of Art," *The Philosophical Review*, 79 (1970): 334–67.

28. Denis Dutton, "Kant and the Conditions of Artistic Beauty," *The British Journal of Aesthetics* 34 (1994): 235.
29. Robert Wicks, "Dependent Beauty as the Appreciation of Teleological Style," *The Journal of Aesthetics and Art Criticism* 55 (1997): 396–97.
30. Jacques Rancière, "The Aesthetic Revolution and Its Outcomes," *New Left Review* 14 (March–April 2002): 141.
31. Ibid., 135.
32. Ibid., 135, 144–45.
33. Ibid., 141, 135–36.
34. Kant, *Critique of Judgment*, Part I, Book II, 43:163.
35. Rosalind Krauss, "Sculpture in the Expanded Field," in *The Anti-Aesthetic: Essays on Postmodernism* (New York: New Press, 2002), 41. Originally published in October 8 (Spring 1979).
36. Adorno, *Aesthetic Theory*, 359.

2
Starting Points

Exorcising the Dreariness of Aesthetics[1]

Joseph Margolis

I

A little more than 50 years has passed since J. A. Passmore's much-admired paper, "The Dreariness of Aesthetics," made its appearance in *Mind*.[2] There is, of course, no point in hurrying now to defend aesthetics against the charges Passmore leveled then. The truth is, Passmore believed that aesthetics need not be dull. A good part of his paper was occupied with showing why opinions to the contrary (John Wisdom's, for instance) were not compelling. Passmore made it clear, by tactful induction, that he was generally opposed to "woolliness" in thought. (Who is not?) Unfortunately, though, he happened to find woolliness disconcertingly widespread and thriving. In one prescient passage he ventured to say that

> books on artistic "goodness"... often try to provide a substitute for individual judgment; they are dull for the same reason that

> books on scientific method are often dull; they set out to destroy spontaneity and speculation, and to substitute for them the application of a mechanical method.

Passmore could not have known, when he wrote this, that the "unity of science program" would be placed in mortal peril by the time we, on the occasion of the fiftieth anniversary of the American Society for Aesthetics, would be reviewing our own field in order to assess just what it has accomplished in its first half-century. The fact remains that Passmore's advice about aesthetics has been followed, more or less, both in recent aesthetics and the philosophy of science. Premature generalizations about "beauty," "aesthetic goodness," and the "value" of art pretty well match the vacuity of talk about "scientific reason," "scientific method," "scientific values," and "science" *tout court*.

In Anglo-American philosophy, for instance, it was undoubtedly the appearance of Thomas Kuhn's *The Structure of Scientific Revolutions* that, in a largely unintended way, started a radical turn toward the historical contingencies of scientific practice. By now, it has put the idea of a changeless, uniform, comprehensive, and adequate method of science pretty well on the defensive (perhaps even at a point beyond defense).[3] The analogous development in aesthetics is considerably more halting. Passmore's sensible advice about overcoming the "dullness" of aesthetics recommends only abandoning global generalizations and favoring "an intensive special study of the separate arts, carried out with no undue respect for anyone's 'aesthetic experiences,' but much respect for real differences between the works of art themselves." The point is well taken. I must add only that Passmore nowhere explains why, once we have attempted these scrupulous studies, we should not also risk returning to the "metaphysics" of art and "meta-" generalizations about beauty, goodness, criticism, and the like, if we find them promising. Also, I personally find (I must admit) no benefit at all in the technical use of the term "aesthetic" in any of its combinations: it is nothing but a catch-all for discourse about the arts (which, of course, was not what Kant had in mind or what that genial army of contemporary Kantians may still have in mind perseverating about the "aesthetic"). (I recommend its complete dismissal.) Passmore himself betrays (if that is the right word) his keenness about the arts and something of his own grasp of literature. It would be entirely fair to say that aesthetics need not be dull, in the sense that most regular contributors to the field may now be counted on to be quite well informed about particular runs of art. (That, of course, hardly touches on drearinesses of the human sort.)

In fact, in aesthetics (as in the philosophy of science), genuinely fruitful speculations do not require an expert's grasp of the pertinent materials. What is needed, rather, is an appreciation of some reasonably salient practices of the sciences, the arts, criticism, and history, pointed enough to recommend a change in our way of conceiving strategic questions. The many specialists who identify themselves as philosophers of science for instance are, for the most part, only distantly familiar with, say, the close work of quantum physicists—and that has hardly damaged the usefulness of their reflections. A literate grasp of the state of the field is ordinarily enough to make their contributions worth considering. There is no reason why the same should not be true in aesthetics. It is also worth remarking that, at the present time, both of these specialties are enormously more interesting and useful than, say, epistemology or moral philosophy, disciplines with which they are usually rather closely paired and (unfavorably) compared. Neither of these has taken Passmore's advice to heart: that is, that we should have a reasonably detailed familiarity with part of what is *actual* in the domain being explored—possibly even *actuel,* in the French sense.

No, the dreariness of aesthetics is the dreariness of normalized professional practice that endorses the unexamined impression that the themes of the greatest philosophical invention have already been largely mapped (usually in the eighteenth century or in antiquity) and that we can do no better than follow the lead of one giant thinker or another, by filling in the missing pieces or making some polite adjustments. Academic aesthetics, I'm sorry to say, is strenuously skewed in the direction of this sort of enthusiasm. I have nothing against the great pioneers in aesthetics or the philosophy of science, for that matter: in the case of Hume and Kant, they are the same figures. But it cannot fail to be dreary to suppose that our best beginnings (in Aristotle, in Hume, in Kant) have pretty well hit very near to the fixed and essential mark. That sort of thinking does a great disservice to the originality we mean to honor. It is easily demonstrated that the master themes of late twentieth-century aesthetics (and philosophy of science) are either completely absent from, or have only barely been glimpsed in, the work of our eighteenth-century cousins. (How could it be otherwise?) If we see that, we see that we must begin with *actualites*—and must always begin thus. We must then also see that, with every important change in our history, it would be hopeless to suppose that any grand master of the past could possibly lead us *now*. Only the unspoken, the more than dubious thesis that art (or any human practice: science) has already revealed its own timeless essence (and that we, of course, have been fortunate enough to have grasped it), could also explain why Plato, Aristotle, St. Thomas, Hume, Kant, Hegel and similar figures should not rightly form, increasingly with time, the genteelly receding background of the best of our present reflections. That is the situation in the philosophy of science. Without being impolite: even quite recent theorists like Hempel and the principal figures of the Vienna Circle—Popper and, progressively, younger contemporaries of these—are regularly relegated to an honored but plainly limited station no longer at the cutting edge. The same is true (in the philosophy of art) regarding Croce, Bergson, Dewey,

Collingwood, Santayana, and more recent figures. There can be little doubt that a considerable part of current Anglo-American aesthetics is simply superannuated. It does no good to insist that parallels with science are inappropriate here. No doubt a greater tolerance and a certain redundancy are needed in our reflections about the arts, but that hardly shows that, at given stages in professional work, certain favored lines of inquiry may not be superseded—not merely by dialectical cleverness, but by the *Zeitgeist*'s ushering in more effective conceptual schemes.

I suggest that Passmore was ultimately wrong about the cause of the dreariness of aesthetics. It is *not* due to generalizations made over all the arts at once, as opposed, say, to generalizations made over literature or music or sculpture. For one thing, Passmore's advice assumes that it is reasonable to generalize over literature and the other "separate" arts, whereas it actually signifies the same kind of essentialism or hasty abstraction as the other; and, for another, even generalizations over the extension of a single predicate raise the same worry about uniformity as the most ambitious conjectures! Otherwise, there would be no point in pursuing the laws of nature (which, of course, is not to say there *are* any). No. The dreariness issues from not understanding that every pertinent generalization—even those that aspire to *de re* and *de dicto* necessities—is hostage to the horizonal limitations of our historically oriented powers: its exposé is not an invitation to abandon generalization (of course we cannot) or to restrict its scope (of course there is no timelessly right criterion by which to define its correct extension) but an invitation to admit the inherent (the comic) contingency of its best work.

The single most compelling philosophical theme that takes its essential energy from reflecting on the meaning of the French Revolution (hence, at a time well after most of the "classical" theorizing of the eighteenth century was completed) and that has grown noticeably more insistent from that time to our own (and that pointedly bears on the fortunes of aesthetics) is this: *thinking has a history;* to think, to conceive, to reason, to argue, to understand, are, in some incompletely fathomable regard, artifacts of the changing conditions of social existence and survival in which thinking appears. The great figures of Western philosophy—Aristotle and Kant especially, as far as the fortunes of aesthetics and the philosophy of art are concerned—*never seriously entertained that notion.* Furthermore, there is no plausible sense in which contemporary theorists are genuinely "Aristotelian" or "Kantian" if they compromise with Aristotle's or Kant's insistence in this regard. These are themes distinctly muted among contemporary Aristotelians—as in the otherwise interesting (but subversive) speculations of figures like Martha Nussbaum and Alasdair MacIntyre.[4] They are matched, in Kant's case, in the work of such different theorists as Hilary Putnam and Rudolf Makkreel.[5]

There is no question that Aristotle was well aware of the contingent variety of the norms and modes of thinking of different societies within the Greek world; and certainly Kant considers the variety of social customs and the inventive possibilities of the conceptual imagination. But Aristotle is quite clear about the invariance of nature, the interconnection between the valid forms of reason and such invariance, and our human aptness for grasping the real invariances of nature.[6] For his part, Kant insists on the symbiosis of the mind's conceptualizing power and the intelligible structure of the experienced world, which sets the invariant (species-wide) constraints under which (as Kant believes) invention and improvisation make sense. Those who would soften the Aristotelian inflexibility feature *Eudemian Ethics* over *Nicomachean Ethics,* and those who would soften the Kantian feature the third *Critique* over the first.

The theme of the historical nature of thinking belongs principally to Hegel and the German Idealists, and we are as much indebted to Hegel in this regard as we are to Kant for the increasingly radicalized sense of the symbiotic theme: for instance, along the lines of incommensurable conceptual schemes (as with Thomas Kuhn and Paul Feyerabend)[7] and of the deep contingency of our historically shifting *epistemes* (as with Michel Foucault).[8] In fact, the ubiquitous theme of late twentieth-century thinking is just that of the (Kantian) *symbiosis historicized* (in the Hegelian sense), *set in the context of a world of flux* (which Aristotle explicitly opposed). If all this be granted, then it may be fair to say the dreariness of contemporary aesthetics is largely due to the profession's resistance to the implications of the general dictum just formulated.

It is true that current literary theory, literary criticism, and literary history in particular have adopted a sometimes suicidal stand on traditional issues in the philosophy of art. But we need not favor such examples, in favoring the theme being urged. What can be coherently managed under the new terms being offered is hardly obvious. The new orientation is bound to alter the reliability of our philosophical intuitions born of the earlier insistence on invariance. We shall simply have to see what is possible. Coming to terms with the new theme would go a great distance toward reducing the dreariness of aesthetics. The odd fact is that, in Anglo-American analytic philosophy, the new theme has made its best inroads in the philosophy of science, not in the philosophy of art. That is an irony.

II

It does no good to rail against those in the philosophical trenches. The trick is to *say* what, at the present time, the most promising lines of theorizing regarding the arts are, as well as how they connect aesthetics to the stronger currents of the day and stand against a tired canon. What is wanted is a recommendation, a piece of advice—not an argument—in the plain sense that no author intruding on the supposed uncertainties and misdirected steps of his peers would want to claim flatly that his own arguments were right and theirs were wrong. The suggestion is a friendlier one: the work of the philosophy of art, it says, would be instantly more relevant and more lively if it brought the profession's talent into accord with the theme announced. That's all! A certain dreariness would fall away at once. Of course, there's no prospect that everyone would instantly drop their favorite philosophical garden tools and rush to buy the latest conceptual gear. But it would be heartening to believe that a cohort of younger minds might be attracted to the newer practice—supposing, that is, that they had never really had an opportunity to consider its prospects and advantages. What we need is a kind of compendium of the resources of the newer theme.

Let us proceed by stages—beginning at some distance—by first defining an inclusive conceptual space not yet restricted to the arts themselves. There is, in fact, a set of notions collecting our theme, the separate items of which are shared by nearly all the most distinctive late twentieth-century philosophical currents, both Anglo-American and continental European. It gives a good sense of the scope of what is being suggested: any move in its direction may lighten some patch of dreariness.

It includes the following:

1. symbiosis: that there is no principled disjunction between what the "brute" world contributes and what the cognizing mind contributes to the salient intelligible structures of the experienced world;
2. intransparency: that whatever we take to be the objective structures of the world cannot be discerned by way of any cognitively assured or privileged or direct perception of the way the world is;
3. historicity: that human thinking—reasoning, conception, argument, understanding—is, in some measure, an artifact preformed by the enculturing processes of historical soci-

eties and alterable as an effect of exercising those cognizing capacities;

4. constructivism: that human agents—persons, selves—are themselves socially constituted, lack intrinsically fixed natures, have, or are, only histories, or have historied natures.

These themes have made a considerate bid by now to sweep all the philosophical specialties. They color our largest conceptual resources. For example, they disallow strict *de re* and *de dicto* necessities, but they do not disallow the sense in which seeming necessities may be admitted under the constraints of (1) – (4) or relativized to our historical horizon. Thus, excluded middle may be judged by some to be an ineluctable logical principle—Aristotle certainly thought it was;[9] but there is no knockdown argument to guarantee it. On the other hand, the paradoxes that physics has generated with regard to the spatial location of particles appear to be artifacts of our conceptual horizon and local notion of physical necessity.[10] Quine, in effect, opposed the presumption of the first;[11] and, in a general way, Foucault has given us a modest understanding of how something like the second might arise (without ever broaching the special puzzle of quantum physics).[12]

The price of changing philosophical visions should be reassuring, therefore: it does not preclude "necessities" we feel we must acknowledge, but it alters their conceptual standing. It brings them into closer accord with the theme announced and suggests how to reclaim difficult and contested dogma. In doing that, it prepares the ground for a more tolerant range of choices among logics, say, than the familiar canon would be willing to allow. For example, it permits abandoning bivalence—at least piecemeal—wherever it proves useful, as it surely does among critical, appreciative, interpretive judgments regarding the arts. Under the pressure of conforming to bivalence, many an aesthetician has felt obliged to deny or attenuate the cognitive standing of critical judgments altogether.[13] It encourages spendthrift solutions, but it is an unnecessary extravagance. There's no strict necessity in the canon. Similarly, if noncontradiction remains vacuous or inoperative when uninterpreted, and if determinate contradictions depend on the entrenched use of particular descriptive terms, then (as the paradoxes of classical mechanics make clear) we may relieve such burdens by redefining and reinterpreting the domain in question. (This need not be an arbitrary maneuver.)

The same is true of reference and predication. There is, for instance, only one remotely plausible conceptual strategy for eliminating reference in favor of predication. It's the one offered by Quine (and known to Leibniz but not espoused by him): that is, that referring expressions—proper names, "Socrates" or "Pegasus," say—may be reparsed as unique predicates ("socratizing" or "pegasizing") that, if true of anything, are uniquely true of their intended referents.[14]

The point of the recommendation (Quine's) is to bring all the informal discourse of whatever discipline we might care to name—art history for instance—into strict accord with a systematic extensionalism, so that aesthetics or the philosophy of art might prepare a vocabulary logically superior to any other: in the double sense that, on the argument, it would not sacrifice any descriptive or explanatory distinctions of importance, and it would thereafter be plainly and advantageously in accord with the marks of rational rigor therein recommended. But it is easy to see that any concession to historical relativity, encompassing context, intentional complexities, and the like, would pose insuperable difficulties for the recommended program. For example, Nelson Goodman's interesting and influential semiotic model of the arts pretty clearly eliminates—finds unnecessary—the historical dimension of musical scores. Goodman supposes (but nowhere demonstrates) that a reading of a score that was historically informed (informed about whatever in the culture at large would instruct us as to the right rendition of the piece notated) could always be perspicuously rendered by a fully extensional notation of the predicable properties of the music. In short, in Goodman's view, every musically significant notation may (when suitably adjusted) be read as specifying with precision and without reference to any larger considerations not similarly open to such notation, the choice of sounds, rhythms, style, and the like that accurately capture the defining features of the piece in question.[15] But that claim rests on a favorable resolution of the problem of reference: for reference, it is supposed, is otherwise fatally infected in intentional ways that, if not appropriately constrained, subvert the extensional ideal.

Here you see the direct bearing of the contest between a now well-entrenched philosophical canon and the upstart doctrine being recommended. I must say that there *is* no prospect of effectively retiring natural-language reference (or referring acts) in favor of a thoroughly extensionalized account of predicates. If Quine's proposal fails, then, as a quite incidental consequence, so must Goodman's regarding musical notation. That is not a negligible discovery.

The full argument is not our concern here: it's the conceptual strategy that counts. But, for what it's worth, we may note the fact that Quine's solution nowhere addresses the essential cognitive question: that is, just *how* to specify, under real-world conditions, the unique predicates matching *any*—hence, *every*—particular that we successfully identify referringly in the context of a society's remembered predicative and referential practice. This means that, for the most strenuous logical, conceptual, alethic concerns we can imagine, there need be no embarrassing incoherences that arise simply because we have construed such principles as noncontradiction, excluded middle, numerical identity, and such ineliminable linguistic practices as reference and predication, in accord with (1) – (4). That is a large gain at very little cost.

Having come this far, we may offer some collateral distinctions to improve and enlarge our conceptual resources regarding the theory of the arts. The arts, we may say, are preeminently "folk-theoretical" concerns. That is, they engage us at the same level of discourse at which we reflect on ourselves as intelligent, cognitively apt, active, purposive agents (persons or selves). It is conceivable that that "level" of discourse may be eliminated or reduced by way of suitable physicalist strategies. Many suppose that such a move is possible. It is also true that there is no known *reductio* that shows such projects to be impossible; on the other hand, there is no known conceptual strategy that shows us specifically how, under real-world conditions, to meet the objective. The matter is really the subject of an intellectual bet: we are at a stalemate on the ultimate question; but the fact remains that even the most sanguine eliminative and reductive accounts of "folk-psychological" discourse (for instance, those offered by Stephen Stich and Paul Churchland) are noticeably parasitic on the conceptual resources of the "folk-psychological" in a way they have no prospect of ever discharging.[16] Of course, we have no ideas what a reductive idiom for analyzing the arts would be like if we *abandoned* our "folk-theoretical" idiom.

The reductionists are typically guilty of an elementary oversight: they wrongly suppose that the social, the cultural, the historical, the collective dimension of human existence—the conceptual "space" in which the phenomena of language, art, economic production, political behavior, and the like make sense is reducible to the terms of the "folk-psychological" (which, in turn, they suppose they can reduce in physicalist terms). They seem completely unaware of the fundamental difference between the mind/body problem and the culture/nature problem. Think, for instance, of trying to reduce the linguistic to the mental (which, one might claim, marks the elementary blunder of Chomsky's theory of language[17]).

I argue that *intentionality*—the intentionality that, in the arts, we associate with the representational, the expressive, the stylistic, the significant, the symbolic, the semiotic, the meaningful, the rhetorical, the purposive, the historical, the interpretable, the rulelike, the institutional, the traditional—belongs to the *cultural dimension* of human life, not to the *mental* (or, not to the mental primarily, should it prove necessary to admit the mental [as it very likely does]—in the course of instantiating collective aptitudes like the linguistic). The opponents of the "folk-psychological" have, therefore, offered nothing as yet against what I have deliberately christened the "folk-theoretical" (beyond the merely mental—or "folk-psychological"); for, by the latter term, I mean specifically to feature all those intentional complexities that belong, along the lines just sketched, to the collective life of human societies. There *is* no known strategy for eliminating or regimenting the "intentional" in the second sense; and all the best-known arguments in the pertinent literature, putatively against intentionality, somehow assume that an attack on the first ("mentalese") would, in principle, eliminate the intentional everywhere.[18]

The fear that some such reversal is in the offing, that we must bring our idiom *in aesthetics and the philosophy of art* into anticipatory accord with that imminent change has misled many theorists to curb the free play of intentional complexities or to discount the work of those who resist reining in their interpretive inventions. For example, why, we may ask, does Goodman introduce a semiotic model of the arts without any attention to the interpretive complexities of artworks? Suppose it were the case (as, indeed, seems reasonable) that the syntactic features of literature and music cannot be convincingly separated from the semantic and even *extralinguistic* concerns of historical agents and societies? If that were true, it would call into question an entire strategy of philosophical analysis.

Similarly, why does Danto never address the metaphysics of the relationship between culture and physical nature—that he himself so tantalizing introduced by contrasting the " 'is' of artistic identification" and the " 'is' of numerical identity"?[19] Danto has always avoided directly challenging the reductive physicalist model he himself invokes (but does not quite adopt) in broaching an analogy between the treatment of physical movements and (interpretable) action and colored canvasses and (interpretable) paintings.[20] The result is that, drawing on his considerable expertise, he keeps entirely *separate* the informed interpretation of particular paintings and the conceptual conditions linking nature and culture *on which* the disciplined assessment of particular interpretations would depend. I am not challenging any critical observations of Danto's here. I draw attention only to the lacuna in his philosophy of art which keeps us from understanding *how* to construe or confirm the truth-claims of interpretive critics. We may for instance wish to invoke some sort of cultural realism regarding the intentional phenomena of an actual artwork. But you will not find among Danto's accounts of art, history, action, or knowledge any sustained clue to integrate our discourse about culture and physical nature.

The trouble is that, in an ethos in which a deep suspicion of the mental, the intentional, the cultural, the historical, the interpretive, the nonphysical is as vigorous as (we know) it is, Danto's longstanding shyness about the matter encourages, among those who need a firmer assurance, a tendency to judge that admitting the "intentional" signifies a conceptual weakness that had better be left inexplicit. That conclusion is completely groundless—though influential. Unfortunately, it produces a dreariness that Passmore might have noticed.

III

I come now to a number of narrower recommendations regarding the philosophy of art. The upshot of the preceding section was to endorse the viability of some suitably generous form of *cultural realism:* a realism of intentional complexities. Our tally (1) – (4) signifies that all discourse about the natural world is an abstraction (not, for that reason, objectionable) *from* the symbiotized space of the whole of intelligible reality—which cannot itself be inhospitable to the "folk-theoretical" stance here advocated.

Once we put matters thus, we may bring to bear on the theory of art and criticism the distinctions already collected, as well as others of the same stripe. A number of strategic doctrines might then be championed, all of which depend on and exploit the difference between physicalist and cultural realism. That difference is plain enough: the first disallows the forms of intentionality that the second embraces. Where the eliminative and reductive programs fail (or at least do not succeed), where the "folk-theoretical" is in the ascendent, we need make no apologies for an aesthetics or philosophy of art keyed to cultural realism.

It is a fact, however, that in Anglo-American aesthetics there are only a few sustained efforts to address the puzzles of cultural realism. In the European tradition, cultural realism is largely assumed without being announced—though it is true enough that the epithet is hardly favored. The "logic" of history and criticism hangs in the balance, nevertheless. One sees this in the philosophically slack but critically astute interpretive efforts of the hermeneuts, the genealogists, and the deconstructionists. The entire question of the "logic" of interpretation is strangely absent from a good portion of analytic aesthetics. There, once again, you have the sign of philosophical dreariness.

The most strategic of the doctrines hinted at are linked to the treatment of predicables. I have already remarked that reference and predication, which enter into all natural-language speech acts, are thoroughly "folk-theoretical." In particular, reference cannot be regimented extensionally because of the cognitive impossibility of actually denoting particulars by way of uniquely instantiated predicates. In failing to isolate such predicates, we are forced back to contextual considerations, to extending our practice slowly and in accord with consensual memory. This signifies that reference is insuperably intentional. The so-called causal theory of reference faces a similar difficulty: for, first of all, what functions as the singular cause of a particular's being identified as what it is is itself a referential question; and secondly, successful reference cannot fail to implicate other intentional complications (for instance, those regarding the division of labor and the correction of error).[21]

Even if, for the sake of the argument, we allowed the replacement of reference by suitably unique predications, we should have to face the corresponding intentional difficulties bedeviling predication. For the extensionalists—Donald Davidson and Jerry Fodor, for instance[22]—believe that a predicate expression can be treated extensionally by simply determining the set (extension) of all those things to which the predicate rightly applies. The obvious trouble is that, cognitively considered, there is no way to determine that extension except in terms of the consensual habit and tolerance of an historical community of natural-language speakers judging whether, in the spontaneous extension of predicates to new instances not covered by the paradigms of such predicates, the similarities in question are good enough or not. The famous problem of universals cannot be resolved by logical syntax alone, and no successful supplementary strategy has ever been devised. If so, then predication is hopelessly intentional. This cannot possibly fail to affect the logic of interpretation, but it is largely ignored.

Now then, when the predicates we need are intensionally stubborn (that is, when they behave nonextensionally) *and* when they are intentionally complex in the cultural sense supplied (not merely "intentional" in the sense favored by Brentano and Husserl), *and* when what we predicate of cultural phenomena we predicate as belonging to the real world, we are bound to admit all the peculiarities that accrue. (I call such predicables "Intentional," meaning by that that "Intentional" = "cultural" and that Intentional phenomena are at once indissolubly "intentional" and "intensional.")[23]

One consequence of so speaking is this: particular artworks cannot be said to have precise boundaries or precisely defined properties, if they are distinguished by such (Intentional) properties as representational, expressive, symbolic, metaphoric, or stylistic properties. Their contours, as the particular things they are, will be hostage to whatever vagaries affect our fixing their Intentional properties. For instance, if they are interpretable (as they obviously are), they may change (their "natures" and properties may change) under the conditions of actual interpretation, or they may be alternatively specified (not arbitrarily and still realistically) in accord with different interpretive intuitions, or they may be construed as determinate only insofar as they are consensually so determined. These are distinctly radical possibilities. So also is the corollary that the reidentification of artworks and other cultural entities can be made to depend on historical consensus rather than invariant natures. But the practice of criticism and the description and interpretation of art would be greatly altered. You will look in vain among the strongest analytic aestheticians for an acknowledgment of thc conceptual puzzles such admissions would entail (or the compelling reasons why such possibilities may be safely dismissed). There's another source of dreariness.

I think it's clear that many other such possibilities could be added.

Notes

1. This essay first appeared in the *Journal of Aesthetics and Art Criticism* 51 no. 2 (1993): 133–140. Reprinted by permission of the author.
2. Passmore, "The Dreariness of Aesthetics," Mind 60 (1951); reprinted in *Aesthetics and Language,* ed. William Elton (Oxford, 1954).
3. Kuhn, *The Structure of Scientific Revolutions* (Chicago: University of Chicago Press, 1963); 2nd enlarged edition, 1970.
4. Nussbaum, *Love's Knowledge: Essays on Philosophy and Literature* (Oxford: Oxford University Press, 1990); MacIntyre, After Virtue: *A Study in Moral Theory,* 2nd edition (Notre Dame, IN: University of Notre Dame Press, 1984); and MacIntyre, *Three Rival Versions of Moral Enquiry: Encyclopedia, Genealogy, and Tradition* (Notre Dame, IN: University of Notre Dame Press, 1990).

5. Putnam, *The Many Faces of Realism* (LaSalle, IL: Open Court, 1987); Makkreel, *Imagination and Interpretation in Kant: The Hermeneutical Import of the Critique of Judgment* (Chicago: University of Chicago Press, 1990).
6. See Aristotle, *Metaphysics*, Book IV.
7. See Kuhn, "Reflections on My Critics," in *Criticism and the Growth of Knowledge,* eds. Imre Lakatos and Alan Musgrave (Cambridge: Cambridge University Press, 1970); and Feyerabend, Against Method (London: Verso, 1975), chap. 17.
8. Foucault, *The Order of Things: An Archaeology of the Human Sciences* (New York: Random House, 1970).
9. Aristotle, *Metaphysics*, Book γ.
10. Putnam, "Quantum Mechanics and the Observer," *Philosophical Papers*, vol. 3 (Cambridge: Cambridge University Press, 1983).
11. Quine, "Two Dogmas of Empiricism," *From a Logical Point of View* (Cambridge, MA: Harvard University Press, 1953).
12. Foucault, *The Order of Things*, chap. 10, particularly regarding the "historical a priori."
13. Scruton, *Art and Imagination: A Study in the Philosophy of Mind* (London: Methuen, 1974); Colin Radford and Sally Minogue, The Nature of Criticism (Sussex, England: Harvester, 1981).
14. Quine, *Word and Object* (Cambridge, MA: MIT Press, 1960), 9–37; also, The Leibniz-Clarke Correspondence, ed. H.G. Alexander (Manchester, England: Manchester University Press, 1956), especially Leibniz's third paper.
15. Goodman, *Languages of Art: An Approach to a Theory of Symbols* (Indianapolis, IN: Bobbs-Merrill, 1968), chap. 4.
16. Stich, *From Folk Psychology to Cognitive Science: The Case against Belief* (Cambridge, MA: MIT Press, 1983); and Paul M. Churchland, A Neurocomputational Perspective: The Nature of Mind and the Structure of Science (Cambridge, MA: MIT Press, 1989).
17. Chomsky, *Knowledge of Language: Its Nature, Origin, and Use* (New York: Praeger, 1986).
18. This seems, for instance, to be the assumption in Daniel Dennett's *Content and Consciousness* (London: Routledge and Kegan Paul, 1969), chap. 2; and Dennett, *The Intentional Stance* (Cambridge, MA: MIT Press, 1987).
19. Danto, "The Artworld," *Journal of Philosophy* 61 (1964).
20. See, for instance, Danto, *The Transfiguration of the Commonplace: A Philosophy of Art* (Cambridge, MA: Harvard University Press, 1981), chap. 1, 3.
21. Kripke, "Naming and Necessity" in *Semantics of Natural Language*, 2nd ed., eds. Donald Davidson and Gilbert Harman (Dordrecht: Reidel, 1972).
22. See Davidson, "Semantics for Natural Languages," *Inquiries into Truth and Interpretation* (Oxford: Clarendon, 1984); Fodor, *Representations: Philosophical Essays on the Foundations of Cognitive Science* (Cambridge, MA: MIT Press, 1981), chap. 10.
23. See my *Texts without Referents: Reconciling Science and Narrative* (Oxford: Basil Blackwell, 1989), chap. 6–8.

Why Don't Art Historians Attend Aesthetics Conferences?

James Elkins

This was a talk given at the 1996 American Society for Aesthetics conference. It was a second attempt to talk to aestheticians about the two disciplines.

— Chicago, July 2004

In October last year, in the St. Louis meeting, I gave a talk on Jay Bernstein's book *The Fate of Art: Aesthetic Alienation from Adorno to Derrida*. At the time I had a number of things I wanted to say about his book, but I soon found myself unsure about how I could address the issues in a way that would seem sensible to any art historians who might also attend the session. That problem proved debilitating. As the conference approached, I realized my prefaces and parentheses were growing more rapidly than the arguments they were supposed to protect, until finally I noticed that what I found most intriguing about Jay's book was that it was somehow unrepresentable to art history. I started paring away my comments on Jay's reading of Derrida, in order to make room for a kind of art historical explanation of Jay's concern with Kant. I tried framing my dwindling remarks in such a way that what Jay had written could sound less like a philosophy of history and more like a history of philosophy—in other words, so it would be an historiographic study of a certain episode in the reception of Kant, rather than a theory about art in any less constrained sense. In doing that, I began to wonder about the very idea of rearranging someone's philosophic genealogy so it could make sense as history: that is not part of what most art historians would say that they do. Eventually, the few art historians in my imaginary audience divided themselves into two factions: one group interested in using Kant to speak about the anti-aesthetic, and another concerned with the heritage of the late eighteenth century in Germany—in other words, people who specialized in the two periods most fully represented in Jay's footnotes. At that point I more or less gave up writing about *The Fate of Art*, and I started trying to write directly about the differences between our two disciplines.

The talk I ended up giving was really pretty unmodulated. I think I began by saying something like this:

> It is notoriously true that art historians virtually never look at the *Journal of Aesthetics and Art Criticism*, the *British Journal of Aesthetics*, or the *Zeitschrift für Aesthetik*—not to mention the twenty-odd other aesthetics journals published throughout the world. Most developments of interest to art history are reported in its own journals, and when artists are discussed in the pages of aesthetics journals, the essays are not consistently cited in subsequent art historical literature.

And so forth. The idea was to make a survey of some of the more readily apparent differences between the disciplines in order to see if they might lead toward a single kind of explanation. All I knew for sure was that I did not want to settle for the kinds of answers my colleagues in art history had offered when I asked why they did not go to aesthetics conferences—they had said, for example, that aestheticians don't talk about artworks, and that they don't care about history. Those observations have some truth to them, but it isn't the kind of truth that can help get conversations started.

Eventually I settled on an explanation that is two thirds philosophic argument and one third historical objection. Today I am going to recap it briefly, and offer some responses and addenda that couldn't fit in last year's conference. I have two excuses for reviving the same argument: first, because I still think it is the best way to pose the difference between the two disciplines, and also because it seems like a project worth working at: I can't imagine two disciplines that are better suited to one another, more securely historically intertwined, than art history and aesthetics. The two share common traditions regarding the ways that artworks create meaning, and they even share notions of rebellion against some of those meanings. It may be a good sign that there are some very interesting art historians in this room (Michael Holly, Keith Moxey, Stephen Bann, Anne Wagner, Thierry de Duve, and Tim Clark were present, among others) but I would say, without sounding too curmudgeonly, that I am not sure if that constitutes a trend, or even if it means anything in particular. It is important not to lose sight of the fact that we art historians are a small minority here. The two disciplines really have relatively little academic life in common: our conferences, our journals, and our departments remain disjoint. My hunch is that the best way to address that is to try to find a subject on which we could agree to disagree, and that is the purpose of the argument I am going to recapitulate.

The argument concerns the nature of what is taken to be either irreducibly visual or ungeneralizably singular about artworks. Art history would then be the discipline that clings to either or both possibilities, and aesthetics the discipline that abstracts or otherwise generalizes them. It's true that the words for what counts as singularity or uniqueness are variable between the disciplines. What art historians might call the uniqueness of the object, or its detail or specificity, philosophers might call its nonidentity, or its quiddity, or its ontological status. (They would not, technically speaking, call the property I have in mind *particularity*, which is opposed to generality in the Kantian philosophy. But I am talking here about vernacular usages, where uniqueness slides into particularity.) What art historians might call an object's visuality or uncoded form, philosophers might refer to as its aesthetic dimension, or its immanent materiality. Here, for the sake of this argument, I am going to take it that translations are usually not difficult; the root problem is not so much differences of vocabulary as a difference of differences.

Nor is it the case that the differences between alternate senses of what is inherently visual about a work of visual art, or what is unique about a given visual object, are notations of difference that can be assigned to one or the other discipline. Just because a text confines itself to concepts such as "the object *qua* object" or the *Ding–an–sich*, rather than the sticky details of Pollock's gestural marks, does not mean it is somehow further from whatever might count as the particularities of the visual. Art-historical texts that bristle with details can still depend on the most broad assumptions about artworks; and conversely, aesthetics texts that keep to the language of metaphysics can still turn on unique encounters with unique works. Hence, I don't mean to propose anything about the true or accurate description of artworks, but rather about the perception of disciplinary distances.

So here is the argument, in a form I hope is clearer than the one I gave last year. Imagine two societies that live on distant islands—call them Ah and Ae. ("Ah" for art history, "Ae" for aesthetics.) Although they are neighbors in their archipelago, they are very far apart, so that they are just barely visible to one another in good weather. One day, a trader arriving from Ah carries with him a request from the people on Ah for a picture of their own island as it appears from Ae, and he brings with him a picture that had been made on Ah, purporting to show the island Ae. No one on Ae recognizes the odd shapes in the drawing, but they comply anyway, and after a time the trader returns with the message that no one on Ah recognized their island in the strange picture sent over from Ae. People on the two islands study the drawings, and conclude that it is probably best to stay where they are, since the people on the other island clearly can't draw, and they may not even be able to see straight. For diplomacy's sake they even send some letters back and forth, arguing about whose representation is worse, and they end up deciding that the members of the opposite tribe have no idea how to talk about pictures to begin with.

I find this to be a fair allegory of my own experience as an art historian speaking to aestheticians about the gap between the disciplines. In my parable, the people on Ah have different ideas about what makes a picture naturalistic than do people on Ae, but the differences between their differences are such that no one on either island has a theory that encompasses the practices on the other. The central problem, both in the parable and in universities, is why accounts of the difference seem different to the two sides. If the natives of Ae and Ah were on either end of a long telescope, then a single account—a single optical equation—could explain both distortions, and satisfy both sides. As it is, there is disagreement on the nature of the difference between the two representations.

Last year I quoted a passage from Jay's book in which he is concerned with what he calls the "threefold departure from theory" current in the practice of art:

> [B]ecause art authorizes unique, individual items, it tendentially works against the hierarchy of universal and particular; because art is bound to the life of particulars, it tendentially celebrates the claims of sensuousness and embodiment;

> because its practices are tendentially governed by the claims of sensuousness and particularity, it instigates an alternative conception of acting, one which binds doing and making, *praxis* and *poiesis*, together (p. 12).

Where is a philosophy, I asked in response to this passage, when it can theorize these concerns, but only by mentioning them as philosophic constructs or as moments in other philosophic texts? What does it mean to occupy a position that knows the need to say what it lacks, and even—as it transpires in the course of the book—that knows lack as a necessary aspect of the position allegedly most different from it, but that does not experience the necessity of "embodying" even a single "tendentially particular," sensuously unique object? How does the ongoing exclusion of actual examples of tendential uniqueness, as opposed to references to the concept and existence of tendential uniqueness, affect an argument that defines itself as an act of hybridization, as Jay's does?

That was the gist of the paper I read last year, which was partly about nonvisuality in Jay's book and in Derrida. In his response, Jay said that my reading treated his and Derrida's failures to engage visual specificity as if they were "flatly failures of will or intellect, failures to find the right mode of filling a space just there to be filled." On the contrary, he said, "there isn't any space yet that can be routinely filled." The aporia, in his view, is a "categorical disposition of universal and particular governing everyday life," so that "the difficulties of art and philosophy token and repeat that aporia, they do not make it."

Thinking of things that way, it can seem as if misunderstandings between the disciplines might ultimately be due to the ways the aporia is negotiated. But I am not sure that the gap can even be addressed as such—as an aporia within or between existing ways of talking. If it were, then it should be possible to imagine interdisciplinary texts that discuss, for instance, whether the aporia is best described in a philosophic manner as a categorical disposition of universal and particular governing everyday life, or in some other, less orderly way. In other words, no matter what was believed about the solubility, origins, meaning, or significance of the aporia, it would be open to discussion. It might turn out to be a practical matter, or it might not; it might be assigned to Western metaphysics, or it might not. Whatever the terms of the debate, such a conversation would follow the model of the two islanders on either end of a long telescope—they would disagree, but they wouldn't disagree on *how* they disagree. But I don't know any discussion of that sort, and so I have come to doubt that the aporia is a single object to both sides.

Luckily, because of the format of these sessions, I have had a year to think about what I could say in answer to Jay's response. And it is essentially this: that the problem is not the truth of what he claims, but that it is a claim. When writers like Jay, whose work entails the existence and nameability of the aporia, approach questions of particularity or uniqueness and discern an abyss between the immanent object and the domain of conceptualization, they tend to assume that the configuration is available as a logical proposition—something like: "Immanent materiality is separated from the conceptual by an aporetic gap." Once it's put that way, any number of propositions might follow as logical inferences.

I think this is where much of art history parts company with aesthetics. Individually, and in different contexts, the three elements of the proposition—"immanent materiality," the aporia, the "domain of concepts"—might find places in historical and critical discussions. But together they form a sentence that art historians might regard with suspicion. By definition, the "domain of concepts" is amenable to logical argument, but *ex hypothesi* the aporia (or the "abyss" or the "gap") is not a concept but a marker of an undefined absence. And what about "immanent materiality"? Since it is, by definition, the complement to the "domain of concepts," how are we to understand what it means in the proposition "Immanent materiality is separated from the conceptual by an aporetic gap," given that the proposition is grammatical and does, after all, consist of fairly ordinary words? "Immanent materiality" is not a concept analogous to "illogic" or even "deviant logic." What would it mean to say—as the proposition implies—that the uniqueness, or the particularity, or the nonverbal, undescribed, inenarrable, "purely visual" portions of an artwork are conceptualized in the same sense as the phrase "domain of concepts"?

From a philosophic standpoint, what is at stake here is a relation (aporia) between two things (immanence and concepts). That is the picture of Ah, as it might be drawn by someone on Ae. Since the relation itself is in question, the proposition seems entirely open to rival interpretations. But I think things look very different from the standpoint of the history of art. It is not clear that a phrase such as "immanent materiality" does justice to what happens in the studio or in the viewing of a work, when an artist is just plain confused about the work, or when an art historian is absorbed in a single object, or that it captures those experiences in the same way as a phrase like "domain of concepts" captures whatever analytic tools may be applied. The two are not conceptualized in an analogous fashion. For one thing, "domain of concepts" is an example of the class it names, while "immanent materiality" is a concept borrowed from the "domain of concepts"—that is, from the very reservoir of philosophemes that it ostensibly counterbalances. Its analytic purchase is uncertain since it is used to name the very domain of experience that excludes it. What's more, the act of borrowing itself is suspicious, and so, I think, are the critical consequences. If we begin to doubt the conceptual pedigree of "immanent materiality," the proposition disintegrates into a deeper uncertainty: without a name for the first thing, there can be no relation, even an aporetic one. Instead of an unknown relation (aporia) between two things (say, materiality and concepts), we have an unknown relation (aporia) between something known (the domain of concepts) and something *else* unknown, and that other thing cannot be understood without giving up what is known. That, I propose, is the picture of Ae, as it might be drawn by someone on Ah.

This may seem an unlikely point on which to lay the entire miscommunication between the disciplines, but I think it is at the heart of the differences between the disciplines. If there is truth in it, it may help explain why conversations and conferences have not brought the disciplines closer together. At least I think this is a step forward from the usual explanations, and I propose it as a way of thinking why people might want to identify themselves as art historians or aestheticians: it would depend, in this light, on what they might make of the proposition.

In order, for example, to value the chronicling of that act, it is necessary *not* to see the relation as such; so artists who begin to take some version of the proposition as philosophers do, might be tempted to give up art and start doing philosophy. And conversely, aestheticians who start to perceive the problems entailed in claiming that the proposition is a well-formed sentence might be likely to begin writing something that resembles art history, at least in its skepticism about the value of the proposition as a logical claim.

I'd like to close with an observation about the level of noise at last year's conference. I was startled then by the number of lunchtime and dinner conversations that were given over to *arguments*: people were scrapping, in a good-natured way of course, over various positions and theories held by their colleagues. The same is true of journals like the *Journal of Aesthetics and Art Criticism*: to borrow some of the common language of philosophy, art historians don't often find themselves "compelled to admit" that they are "trying to have it both ways," or are "blocked" from saying what they think they ought to say, or "committed" to some "position" that might end with an "–ism." Now I wouldn't want to say art historians don't argue, but there was something about the pervasiveness, the naturalness, and the inexhaustibility of some of the arguments that I heard that struck me as very different from the somewhat less deliberate conversations I've heard over the years at art history conferences. I wonder if that phenomenon might be connected to the general tacit acceptance of propositions per se, and perhaps especially the proposition I have been considering.

In my experience few art historians have articulated ways of thinking about the relation between particularity and conceptualization. They haven't made up their minds, and they probably haven't thought much about the problem—or thought of it *as* a problem. To some degree, art history does not seem to want answers to these questions: or to put it more exactly, it may depend on not seeing them *as* questions.

— Montreal, October 1996

After the session in Montreal, Michael Kelly, who was in the audience, said that I might consider that my probem was, in fact, solved. He mentioned The Encyclopedia of Aesthetics *(New York: Oxford University Press, 1998), which he was editing, and which has a number of art historians as contributors. He also noted that the audience included a number of art historians, including Thierry de Duve. We counted about eight. I asked him where the other 13,992 were — because the College Art Association has about 14,000 members.* The Encyclopedia of Aesthetics *has an unusual collection of authors (just as this book does): I think both are exceptions that prove the rule.*

At the 1995 conference, Jay Bernstein read a response that included a very specific description of a work of installation art. Part of the idea was that "there isn't any space yet that can be routinely filled." In 1999, his response appeared in a strangely modified form, in a footnote to his essay "Aporia of the Sensible:

Art, Objecthood, and Anthropomorphism," in Interpreting Visual Culture: Explorations in the Hermeneutics of the Visual, *edited by Ian Heywood and Barry Sandywell (London: Routledge, 1999), 235–36.*

I think these issues remain unsolved.

— Chicago, June 2005

3
THE ART SEMINAR

This conversation was held July 11, 2004, at the University College Cork, Ireland, at the close of a conference called "Rediscovering Aesthetics." The participants were: Diarmuid Costello (Oxford Brookes University), Arthur Danto (Columbia University), Nicholas Davey (University of Dundee), Anna Dezeuze (University of Manchester), Martin Donougho (University of South Carolina at Columbia), Thierry de Duve (Université de Lille 3), James Elkins (University College Cork / School of the Art Institute of Chicago), Francis Halsall (University College Cork), John Hyman (Oxford University), David Raskin (School of the Art Institute), Dominic Willsdon (Royal College of Art / Tate Modern), and Richard Woodfield (Nottingham Trent University).

James Elkins: Let's take as our starting point that art history, considered as a discipline, is largely disconnected from aesthetics, and that that disconnection is not well theorized by either discipline. And so let me suggest that we talk about different models for the relation between the fields: let's try to gather some models, and see what features they have in common.

Let me start with something Arthur Danto said yesterday: that aesthetics can now find a place in art history as a *means* to a nonaesthetic understanding of artworks. In the wake of deconstruction and theory (as he put it), beauty could be said to be "internal" to the meaning of the work, and aesthetics could become "grist" for the reconfigured humanities. An art history which is focused on subjects such as identity theory and institutional history might find *in* aesthetics things that it might use.

What I wondered about was under what conditions art historians might be interested in importing terms from aesthetics, and whether those terms might then be perceived as being embalmed, or encased, in another discourse. That second point raises interesting problems about how such a practice of art history might *look*.

Arthur Danto: I don't think that there is a particularly technical vocabulary in aesthetics. Probably any term in the language can be given an aesthetic inflection, but there are a handful of terms that people have mostly talked about. The beautiful is the canonical one, which has this to single it out, that of all the aesthetic predicates, beauty is the only one that is a value in addition to being a descriptive predicate. Beauty is a value like goodness or truth, and that distinguishes it from *pretty, delicate,* and so on.

My suggestion was that one pick an aesthetic property out of a work of art, and ask what it means that the work has that property. Why, for example, is a work beautiful? Then it seems to me that one might get a deeper view of the work. The example I used yesterday was the beauty with which David depicted Marat in *Marat assassiné;* I thought that the reason David thought it was important that his body be beautiful is because the pose is that of the Deposition. The beauty is intended first to facilitate that comparison between Marat and Jesus, and to imply that Marat's suffering was like Jesus's, and second to do what seventeenth-century paintings did, which was to create an identification with the subject on the part of the viewer, in order to reinforce faith. (Or in the case of the French Revolution, to raise the level of revolutionary fervor.)

So that would be an historical explanation of why David decided to make Marat beautiful, instead of gory. But *gory,* too, could be an aesthetic predicate, and the same question could be asked.

If you tend to think of aesthetic properties as governed by reasons, and if those reasons are guided by the effects the artists wished the works to have on viewers, then I think aesthetics can be a valuable adjunct to the practice of art history, leading into the historical meanings of works. The initial aesthetic response would then be part of the interpretive project of art history.

Richard Woodfield: I think that raises a very important point, which is the limited job that words conventionally associated with aesthetics can do. Arthur first talked about the painting's beauty, and then about how it was constructed; I find that process of talking about the construction of artistic properties much, much more interesting than using words drawn from aesthetics.

JE: Could it be said that Arthur's use of *beauty* in that example is already historicized, because it is a beauty of a particular sort, understood *by means of* the history of Depositions and analogous figures?

RW: Yes; there is a debate about the feminization of the masculine body in painting of David's generation, and so you could unpack this particular notion of beauty.[1]

JE: Perhaps then there is a problem: an historian wouldn't be *using* aesthetics, but rather using an historically constrained model: the historian would, in effect, already be within art history. The question of the intersection of the disciplines seems to be folded into a discussion that takes place within history.

AD: I think there is something that mediates between aesthetics and art history, which would be art criticism. What you are doing as a critic is trying to explain why things are as they are in a work, and that mediates between an aesthetic response and an historical explanation.

The example I used in *The Abuse of Beauty* was the beauty of Motherwell's paintings of *Elegy to the Spanish Republic;* I found them beautiful before I knew they were elegies.[2] Once I knew they were, it raised an interesting question: Why was it important for an elegy to be beautiful? That led me to ask about the relation between beauty and death. The politics of the situation called for an elegy because there was nothing to be done about the Spanish Republic except mourn the fact that it was aborted. Why, in that situation, were beauty and death associated? People might disagree with me that the paintings are beautiful, but they are inescapably beautiful for me, and that leads to such questions.

Diarmuid Costello: I generally find the idea of beauty unhelpful in discussions about art, because when one says "*x* is beautiful"—which one rarely does in engaging with actual works of art—it is essentially a way of expressing an honorific judgment; it functions as a kind of placeholder, or short-hand way of saying "That work is good." As such, it has about as much content or substance as a judgment as Andy Warhol's "Wow!" It just isn't informative. It begs the questions "*Why* is that beautiful?"; "What *makes* it so?", etc., and it is the answers to those questions that contain the weight and interest of critical judgments. At best, claiming that a work is beautiful may serve to initiate a conversation or critical exchange; but claiming that a given work is beautiful does not, in my view, constitute what is interesting or informative about such exchanges. I find it is instructive that in the past few days I have swapped many judgments about specific artists and artworks with Arthur, and though we have often been in agreement, I don't think either of us has used the word *beauty* once. It just isn't helpful.

AD: Well, that's a problem, because it is such a canonical predicate.

DC: Yes…

AD: There is this wonderful statement J. L. Austin makes in "A Plea for Excuses": he says we won't make progress in aesthetics until we give over talking about the beautiful and the sublime, and start talking about the dainty and the dumpy. So start with dumpy, if you like, and pick a work where *dumpy* is not a criticism, but goes instead to make a certain kind of point. Or take the *delicate;* we do use that term … or take *clunky*. Diarmuid, we talked about your favorite painter Philip Guston: his paintings are—

DC: He is not my favorite painter!

AD: —are pretty clunky. And what does the clunkiness *do* that beauty, daintiness, or delicacy couldn't?

DC: That's true, they *are* clunky; and "clunky" captures something about what makes his work poignant in a way that "beautiful" doesn't—in the way that one might describe Gober's sinks as "silent" or Whiteread's plaster casts as "unyielding" or Twombly's sculptures as "light." In each case, these would be ways of fleshing out what we would have been gesturing toward, rather vaguely, by saying their work is "good"—which, I take it, is all that would be being said *were* we to call it "beautiful." Though perhaps that isn't quite right. Given that, these days, beauty is often used as a way of deprecating a work, as when one calls it "*merely* beautiful," which would amount to calling it empty. Beauty, when predicated of works of art, needs to be invested with meaning by further explanations and elaborations. On its own it's empty as a judgment about the work.

But perhaps this is just a certain on my part manifesting itself, albeit in a rather perverse way, given that when one calls a work of art beautiful one isn't really predicating a determinate quality of the work at all, at least not for Kant, so much as saying something about the feeling it elicits in the viewer (and, of course, raising a normative claim off the back of that feeling). Perhaps this is why I find the idea of beauty unhelpful as a *critical* term; because it tells you more about how a work disposes a viewer than about the work itself. Predicates such as "delicate" or "dainty," to take Austin's examples, may tell you something about *why* a work elicits such an affect in a subject. And that makes them more useful as critical terms.

AD: I think that once people begin to recognize how rich our aesthetic vocabulary is, the link between aesthetics and art history might be strengthened.

JE: Let's come back for a moment to the initial question, about using art history as a *means*. How does this critique impinge on that?

DC: I'm not sure I know exactly what you are getting at but, but certainly in terms of my own work, I have found art history particularly helpful in understanding the genealogy of certain contemporary attitudes toward the aesthetic in art theory and cultural studies more generally. Recent work on the legacy of modernism—such as Thierry's for example—reveals the extent to which a narrow modernist conception of the aesthetic has overdetermined the anti-aesthetic bias of postmodernism.[3] But this may not be quite what you have in mind, since, on the one hand, I would want to use philosophy to defuse various misrepresentations of the nature of aesthetics in art theory, and, on the other, use art history and theory to show why the aesthetic has become such a contested cultural marker—a fact to which many aestheticians remain blind. This is one of the reasons why philosophy may seem historically insensitive or culturally conservative to many art theorists, and art theory's use of philosophical terms may appear confused or tendentious to many philosophers.[4]

Thierry de Duve: Let me answer by shifting the ground of the discussion. For me, using art history as a *means* would involve asking what is the social function of art history. Are we content to say that art history is an academic discipline that fosters the accumulation of knowledge for the sake of knowledge, in a humanistic and disinterested fashion? I think that's all fine and dandy, but it's irresponsible.

When art historians think of their own practice as having some reason to exist within society at large, that is where aesthetics comes in. My view of the *raison d'être* of art historians is that they are the guardians of tradition. [*Slight laughter from the audience.*] Yes, a dirty word. I mean that tradition is no longer transmitted from one generation of artists to the next without the art historian's help. If you go back to, say, the Middle Ages—times when the discipline of art history did not exist and when some would say that therefore "art" did not exist, though I would never say such a thing—well, in those days, how was tradition transmitted? It was not possible to be an artist in today's sense, an artist *in general*, at that time.[5] As an artist, you had to have a *métier*: you were either a painter or a sculptor, and so on. You were a craftsman. Let's say you were a painter, and you began as an apprentice to another painter; tradition was transmitted in the workshop from one painter to the next. Along with craftsmanship, lots of other things were transmitted, values, mostly: human, cultural, ideological, religious, political, aesthetic values. Or perhaps I should not say aesthetic values. I should say that all these other values were transmitted to you via the exercise of your aesthetic judgment. Brush in hand. That's what made you an artist, capable of embodying aesthetic judgments in your own work. Your tradition preserved a certain taste—not a universal taste, but a certain taste. You belonged to the Sienese school, or the Florentine school, or the Venetian school, and so on. The tradition was built and sustained in the studio.

Now, to jump to the present: we've had the ruptures of the avant-garde; we've had the "tradition of the new"; we've had antitradition as if this were a value in itself. What this all means is that tradition is no longer transmitted in the old way. How and where is it transmitted? In academic institutions such as universities and art schools, where, however, art education is no longer conceived as the transmission of tradition, but rather, as the fostering of creativity, the exploration, criticism, or deconstruction of the medium, and what have you. And that makes tradition *as* transmission problematic. The baton is no longer passed on from one generation of artists to the next in the studio. Or when it is, the link with the past doesn't climb further back than the generation of the students' instructors. So, the responsibility of the transmission of tradition is in the hands of the art history teachers. Unfortunately, they have not been educated to think this way. They think they communicate factual knowledge—interpreted knowledge, at best. Whereas the slides they show are actually the result of aesthetic choices. Whose choices? I find it strange that art history teachers don't see it more clearly that it is their responsibility to pass on aesthetic judgments. They have received their education in art history departments, where they learn to enter into a dialogue with colleagues in art history. Nobody told them that artists were in fact their "natural" constituency.

So much for tradition, the social function of art history, and the role of aesthetic judgments in the context of art schools. Now, what about museums? Museums exist because that is where objects deemed worthy of being preserved for future generations are kept. Museums are run by curators and conservators—people who usually have degrees in art history. Not only are they the guardians of objects, but they wrap them in texts: interpretive texts, texts that attribute and identify, historical and critical interpretations, social histories. … Each of these discourses adds flesh to the mere fact of the preservation of cultural objects.

Now note that we don't keep all human artifacts. When it comes to the *Victory of Samothrace,* there is no argument that it's fine art: it is skillfully done, it represents something recognizable, it's Greek, it's marble, and so on. But when it comes to Duchamp's urinal? There is no difference, as Arthur knows very well, between it and the urinal in the men's room. Are we going to keep this thing? And how long? Is Duchamp's urinal going to be in the Louvre five hundred years from now? If not, why? And if not, what else will we throw away? According to present-day discourse on modernism in art, if we throw away Duchamp's urinal we should also throw away Malevich's *Black Square,* Russian Constructivism, Surrealism, and any number of other things. Some conservative art historians such as Jean Clair would be happy to throw away Russian Constructivism and go back to traditional painting in the nineteenth-century fashion.

So, when I say that art historians are the guardians of tradition, I mean that they are also the guardians of the avant-garde tradition. That's where aesthetics comes in. What, if not those guardians' aesthetic judgments, is going to decide what we shall keep and what we shall throw away, what will be called art and preserved under that name, and what will disappear from the record?

JE: Does that mean art history is inseparable from aesthetics, or is there an art history that is merely diminished by excluding aesthetics?

TdD: Art history without aesthetics is inconceivable to me, because art history is first of all constituted by the evidential record of previous aesthetic judgments. In other words, by their jurisprudence: at once the inventory of what is on the record as art, and the *prudence* that helps aesthetic judges take account of the judgments of their predecessors. We cannot judge out of our personal judgments alone. We have to take into account the history of other people's judgments—which is another word for tradition.

Nicholas Davey: I'd like to widen the meaning of some of the terms we are using, and specifically, the meaning of aesthetics. Philosophers (and I include myself) sometimes become too preoccupied within obtaining a clear definition of a term. We need to be reminded of Stenzel's remark that it is "only because the words of a language are *incompletely* defined that propositions can be formulated precisely." Liebrucks speaks of the "undefined range of possibility" which surrounds the individual word … which provides scope for the progress of thought.[6] Both comments suggest that precision in language is only possible because of the *variety* of meanings that are attached to a term. I am in consequence a little worried about how we seem to be talking about aesthetics in a rather monolithic way.

In my mind, there are at least three meanings attached to the word *aesthetic*. To the Greeks, aesthetics or rather *aisthesis* was a term for the *activity* of seeing well, not just in terms of sensory perception but also in terms of grasping what sensory perception led one to see. For Aristotle seeing (*aisthesis*) "tends" toward an idea or a universal.[7] Second, there is the meaning of aesthetics which has been prevalent in our conference discussions and which derives from Baumgarten and Kant. Within this framework of thought, the meaning of aesthetics becomes attached to discourses about sensibility and taste as well as to debates about how the beautiful might be judged. And then, third, there is a twentieth-century usage of the word which speaks of a

Marxist, a feminist, or a phenomenological *aesthetic*. This usage is linked to the notion of "a way of seeing," that is, to that ideological norms, phenomenological expectancies or evaluative perspectives that literally shape or construct the content of the "seen" world. It is a usage which of course draws on earlier related notions of a *Lebenswelt* or of a *Weltanschauung* and has a great bearing upon how specific themes or subject matters are represented by the art practices they sustain.[8]

This last usage is connected with Heidegger's and Gadamer's attempt to reinterpret the nature of art's aesthetical powers. For these philosophers the power of the artwork lies in its ability to make visible to the viewer what the viewer does not normally see, namely, the horizons of meaning or *Weltanschauung* out of which the work had initially sprung. This, according to this meaning of the term, we can clearly distinguish between, for example's sake, Nietzsche's aesthetics (his account of our experience of art) and a Nietzschean aesthetic (how the world appears within a Nietzschean perspective).

Now, given these three possible meanings for the term aesthetics, what is it that we are wanting to consider in relation to art history? It is obvious to me that any art historian is going to have to be disciplined in the first sense of the word *aesthetics* (the practice of seeing well and attentively). Some might say that the second sense of the word is less important for the art historian. Clearly, an art historian's personal aesthetic preferences, what he or she regards as beautiful, may influence the selection of artworks to be presented or discussed. However, it is often argued that what matters for the art historian are not his or her personal aesthetic preferences. What is important for the art historian is not the artwork as an aesthetic object for personal contemplation but what the work points to, that is, how it represents its subject matter and what the work can be taken to be indicative of or serve as evidence for. The Kantian aesthetician is invariably interested in the artwork *in and for its own sake*. It is not attributed any extra-aesthetic purpose. The art historian is, arguably, interested in the artwork for what it points to beyond itself. It is for this reason that an art historian will clearly be interested in the third sense of the term *aesthetic* (what an artwork brings us to see of its world).

In summary, what am I suggesting? There are at least three ways of thinking about aesthetics. None of them are mutually exclusive but they have different outcomes. The art historian clearly must be attentive, have a trained sensibility, and be able to read the cultural horizons within a picture. However, what is to be emphasized?

So my question to the art historians here is: Why do you seem to want to return to what is primarily the second Kantian usage of aesthetics? Is all the present talk about going back to the concept of the beautiful an attempt to discover a neutral intersubjective starting point for art-historical investigations? My worries about this are twofold. First: to be a Kantian you must treat the art object as something in and for itself independent of all historical narrative. Can the art historian actually do this without a supreme act of self-denial? Second—and I know that Thierry will disagree with this—to go back to Kant is to return to a model of aesthetic judgment which supposes that discourse about art is possible (though difficult) because it is based upon a shared intersubjective *a priori* framework of aesthetic judgments which are unaffected by tradition, history or social circumstance. Against this, however, it is surely the fact that we view an artwork from different historical and social perspectives that gives to art its richness of content, that enables us to learn from the artwork, and that allows us to view both the artwork, ourselves, and others *differently*. Agreeing (or not as the case may be) that we may share the same form of aesthetic judgment may strengthen a hypothetical sense of communal well being, but it in fact teaches us very little about the communicative content of art, and hence offers little insight into ourselves.

TdD: Why go back to Kant? I think because he's got it right. Why would you want a new theory if you have a satisfactory one? That doesn't happen in science. The work that remains to be done would be to generalize Kant, in the way Einstein, for example, generalized Newton, so that the validity of what Kant had to say about aesthetic judgment could be expanded to include later developments in the arts. Aside from that, I am convinced he got it right: no one else made room for such a refreshing astonishment at the fact that people do use sentences such as "This is beautiful" or "This is art" to express no more than what amounts to feelings. Facing the fact that people disagree in their aesthetic judgments, Kant ought to have said such judgments were wrong, but his genius was to say they were right. And why did he say that? In claiming universal validity for personal judgments and feelings, people attribute those capacities to others, and so on, universally. There is room for disagreement, but in making aesthetic judgments we postulate a universal human faculty: that of agreement, *sensus communis.* You are right in supposing that I would refute your assumption according to which returning to a Kantian model of aesthetic judgment bases the discourse about art on a shared intersubjective *a priori* framework. *Sensus communis* may indeed offer such a base, but then nothing guarantees that it exists. In making aesthetic judgments, we merely suppose that *sensus communis* exists, as a universally shared capacity for sharing feelings, i.e., for agreeing by dint of feeling. For Kant this supposition is both theoretically necessary and ethically mandatory—all the more so that reality denies every day that human beings are equipped with the faculty of agreeing universally. I'd say with a leap that Kant's *Critique of Judgment* formulates a transcendental—I say transcendental, not utopian or anything like that—foundation for democracy and peace on earth. [*Good-natured laughter.*]

AD: That's exceedingly noble. But I don't see why the issue of Kant even has to arise in this conversation. If you ask a person who decorates a room why he does it, he might say it makes people feel better. Why would art historians pay attention to the aesthetic qualities of works of art? That's the question, not, "Shall we read Kant?" —or, "Shall we burn Kant?" Kant is something that doesn't belong in this conversation. Beauty belongs in this conversation, but Kant belongs in the library.

John Hyman: We began by speaking of a confluence or intersection of aesthetics and art history; those are things I think we really don't want. A confluence is when two streams join, mix, and continue as some bigger stream; an intersection is when they partly occupy the same ground. My sense is that whatever we can offer one another we can do only by remaining firmly on our own patch. One thing philosophers can offer art historians is a clear exposition of ideas that have had an influence on the history of art, and Kantian ideas are a case in point. But to say that Kant's aesthetic theory is relevant today because it is right seems terribly irresponsible.

TdD: Then I am not a philosopher—

JH: In that case let *me* speak as a philosopher and say that simply can't be right. Kant is a very systematic thinker, and his philosophy as a whole is founded on the idea that geometry and arithmetic are *a priori* bodies of knowledge about space and time, and if you want to understand his thought rather than picking out attractive quotations that have resonance in new contexts, then your first responsibility is to say what significance the idea has in Kant's philosophy.

As a philosopher, I've learned from art historians how to look at examples in their particularity, and not to treat them as tokens in philosophical arguments. I've also learned not to focus on just a few jejune examples, as philosophers are apt to do. (That's an accusation J.L. Austin made against philosophers, quite rightly I think.) And I have learned not to try to publish books with large numbers of illustrations in them, because that, I've discovered, is a nightmare. [*Everyone laughs.*]

Anna Dezeuze: One of the problems that art historians have with aesthetics is that it seems to be obsessed with defining what is art and what is not art. The moment where aesthetics becomes useful for art historians, for me personally, is when it tries expanding its categories in the way that Arthur suggests, asking about the dainty, the dumpy, and other qualities artists *have* explored. I'm curious to know: is there an aesthetics of the dumpy and the dainty?

JE: There are, for example, books like Susan Stewart's *On Longing* which offer an aesthetics of the miniature, and in general a Foucauldian-inspired literature on unrecognized aesthetic categories—for instance the work of Pete De Bolla's "Unconventional Knowledge" group at Cambridge in the 1990s.[9] But I wonder for whom that literature is aesthetics, as opposed to literary studies or history…

Anna Dezeuze: I think that Stewart's *On Longing* is an excellent model for a possible intersection between aesthetics and art history. It mobilizes different disciplines, from psychoanalysis and semiotics to literature and history, in order to describe and analyze the characteristics of a field which cuts across art, literature, and material culture.

Arthur Danto: I don't know why we keep wandering off the path that James has set. The basic issue is: Why is it important for an art historian to discuss questions such as, "Why is the Grünewald altarpiece repulsive?" *Repulsive* is an aesthetic term. We're meant to recoil when we look at his altarpiece. What was Grünewald getting at when he painted Christ in such a repulsive way? That is an historical and an aesthetic question. I don't know that Kant has a single illuminating thing to say on a question like that, and if he does, then OK, read him. We are concerned with how people respond to works that have qualities, including qualities such as *ugly, revolting,* and *disgusting.* Take Paul McCarthy, for example. He is systematically disgusting. The question is: Why? What does that contribute to what he is doing? We don't have to worry about the meaning of disgust because it is part of our discourse—everyone agrees on that. But why does McCarthy make a point, let's say in his masterpiece *Bossy Burger,* of creating an experience so disgusting that it is hard just to stand and look? The parallels between Grünewald and the video *Bossy Burger* are intriguing, and that is where aesthetics and art history can come together.

JE: Let me interject here, because I think it might be possible at this point to begin totting up models of the continuity or discontinuity of art history and aesthetics. Already we have positions at either end of the spectrum:

First, there is Arthur's proposal that aesthetics might be rediscovered by current art history as a source of judgments that then need to be interrogated historically. (I still have my doubts about how aesthetic terms might survive within historical contexts—like those little cyanide capsules spies supposedly keep in their mouths—but that's another matter.)

And second, that idea can be distinguished, I think, from another one that both Anna Dezeuze and Arthur Danto have raised: that aesthetics might be of interest when it investigates words other than beauty. So far we've had dainty, dumpy, disgusting, ugly, silent, unyielding, light, and revolting. (And again I wonder whether those are philosophemes or terms taken within historical contexts, in which case I continue to wonder whether they take their meaning from philosophic or historical traditions.)

And third, we've had John Hyman's proposal that art history deals with the particular and philosophy with universals—an idea that we could perhaps develop further.

Let me complete this totting-up by adding two more models, which I will exemplify—I hope not too inaccurately—with the work of two other panelists who haven't spoken yet.

Fourth, then: it is also possible to imagine that aesthetics might *melt* into art history. Yesterday Dominic Willsdon was saying some things along these lines when he was talking about current artists who put private life on display, but in a carefree, uncathected manner. You [Dominic] noted that among some contemporary artists, aesthetics is seen as "pacifying and regressive" but openness about aesthetic qualities is taken to be "camp, sweet, knowing"—"these are qualities we savor," you said. At least for me, you were mixing and melting art history into what might be called art criticism. It would then be a kind of liquefied aesthetics, evanescent and unrigorous wherever it surfaces in art practice.

Fifth, and last, to take David Raskin as an opposite figure to Dominic, just for conversation's sake. I've known you, David, for a number of years, and a couple of years ago I would have said that your project in regard to minimalism was to leave art history behind in order to think seriously about the philosophy of realism and idealism. Now, I think, you've moved a bit back, and if a philosophy of realism is still worth pursuing, it would be for heuristic reasons, in order to illuminate the aesthetic and the anti-aesthetic from a new vantage point. I feel that in your work, aesthetics or philosophy really is a solid discipline, outside of art history as John Hyman says, and I think that in Dominic Willsdon's work there really is a confluence—to take another metaphor John used.

Dominic Willsdon: I think you're right, that I work with a particular sense of the aesthetic; it comes up strongly in museum work, where art has a kind of pragmatics that feels different from what's been said here. The difficult thing when it comes to thinking about art in museums—and this links with what Thierry was saying about traditions—is what gets into the museum. That is a question of art and the wider visual culture. It's strange to me that over the last decade or two, there was a point at which people were very anxious about the canon of art. I was a student in Edinburgh at the time when, controversially, the National Gallery of Scotland started including applied art, decorative art, to create around the paintings something like the "scene" of an eighteenth-century Salon. If nothing else, it was thought-provoking about the status and quality of the objects. This kind of anxiety seems to have disappeared. Curators seem surprisingly, and unjustifiably, secure about the category of art. Without any workable principle for doing so, they exclude whole genres of images and works that would participate in a kind of aesthetics-at-large … .

JE: What is an aesthetics-at-large?

DW: There's a growing idea that once we take away the really big claims that were made about beauty, and begin to explore the many kinds of qualities that I was talking about yesterday [art that is "sweet, candid, camp, and knowing"] and that Arthur was mentioning, then people find the new aesthetic qualities in new areas.

Aesthetics-at-large is just a heading under which we could talk about the affective traits of any number of images and objects, inside or outside art museums or art history. It would give us a license to explore, for example, certain works by Félix Gonzalez-Torres (who is a wonderful artist) alongside the memorials to the victims of traffic accidents or fatal crimes that we see so often in the streets of big cities. Even if we were to judge a particular example of the latter to be somehow more valuable than a particular Gonzales-Torres, the Gonzales-Torres is acceptable to the curator, in his or her professional judgment, and the street memorial is not. We can distinguish between art happenings and raves, but not aesthetically. There's no difference between the kind of aesthetics assumed by curators and the aesthetics-at-large that includes street memorials and raves.

And there is more, because it is less and less the case that curators have backgrounds in art history, and historical knowledge is less often important. Artists have a larger and more capacious sense of what they are doing even than curators, who in turn have a more generous sense of things than art historians who try to encapsulate what artists have done.

Arthur Danto: What really got me started in aesthetics at all—not as an academic discipline, but as a living thing—were the shrines that were set up all over New York City the day after 9/11. They were put together spontaneously out of balloons, cards, and flowers. No one taught anyone how to do that, or gave anyone instructions for how to put them on the sidewalk, in foyers, in stairways. I wondered why people responded not with anger but with beauty. No artist could have done better. That phenomenon does raise the question of where beauty fits in the normal, or abnormal, course of human life.

Anna Dezeuze: Artists have been exploring the relation between art and everyday life, and aesthetics has lagged far behind: not because of problems defining art, but because of problems defining the everyday. Art history can turn here to theories from sociology and psychoanalysis that have been crucial for cultural studies; but especially in the Anglo-American world aesthetics still seems to have a restricted idea of how art relates to the everyday.[10]

David Raskin: It might be interesting to distinguish between a strong and a weak sense of aesthetics, and between the *directions* in which aestheticians and art historians go after their initial encounter with a work. Most art historians, I find, are guided by a weak sense of aesthetics: we make our decisions based on what is worth our time, what seems most compelling. I might find a Donald Judd more compelling than a Robert Morris, and at that point I will take a strong sense in my engagement: I will ask what the work means and why. On the other hand, an aesthetician might take a strong sense of aesthetics and a weak sense of art. From the initial decision to consider a work, they will go backward, questioning the premises of their engagement, and asking where it comes from.

Nothing illustrates this better for me than the contrast between my concerns and Diarmuid Costello's: we begin with the same works, but we flip-flop the relationship between the art and the philosophy.

DC: I suppose that in this respect I find myself in the place that John Hyman thinks is the worst place to be, because I would have to define myself, reluctantly, and largely negatively, as an art theorist rather than either an art historian or an aesthetician, strictly speaking. Though I have a foot in both worlds, I don't subscribe to the self-understanding of either discipline, in so far as it manifests itself in the image each typically holds of the other.[11]

So, when Arthur says Kant belongs in the library and beauty in the conversation, I think that's getting things back-to-front. To my mind beauty generally doesn't help in discussions about works of art, but Kant does, if only because Kant has massively overdetermined the way in which ideas such as beauty or *aesthetic* value more generally are discussed today, certainly in art theory, and possibly also in art history.

To respond to Nicholas's and Arthur's earlier remarks: one reason you might want to go back to Kant, in the light of this, would be to dissolve certain presuppositions about what we *mean* when we talk about aesthetics. Returning to

Kant need not mean a simple regression or recapitulation, as Nicholas seemed to be suggesting, but an opportunity to diagnose certain problems in the reception of aesthetics, notably what we mean when we speak of something having "aesthetic value," that have arisen as a result of the way in the third *Critique* has overdetermined subsequent debates. Some of these problems may be a result of trying to apply what is for the most part an aesthetics of natural beauty—to apply it anachronistically to recent art, but some of them are also the result of prejudicial, tendentious, or historically overdetermined readings of what Kant had to say, taken on his own terms.

One of the problems of the dominant formalist reception and interpretation of Kant, for example, is that it has led to the idea of beauty being taken as synonymous, for all the wrong reasons, with the notion of the aesthetic in general. This is a point on which Arthur and I agree.[12] But when Arthur talks about how the 9/11 shrines led him to reconsider the role of beauty in everyday life, what that illustrates, to my mind, is the fact that the category of the aesthetic is far broader than the category of the artistic—a fact often glossed over in art-historical and theoretical debates. So you can talk in many ways about what people were doing when they put up shrines for those who died in 9/11, or to victims of rape or murder, as frequently happens in the area of London where I live, but it strikes me as highly questionable to run that together with what artists, such as Félix Gonzalez-Torres, are doing. That's so in part because of the intentions and self-understanding with which their respective objects are made, but for all sorts of other moral, historical, and cultural reasons as well.

Martin Donougho: David Simpson has a wonderful book called *Situatedness*, which has a meditation on "as a …"

sentences.[13] I think we all have such sentences, which help articulate what we are, but also give voice to our fears—the other discipline, the one that isn't really mine.

JE: What implications would *Situatedness* have for the positions and disciplines that articulate this discussion?

MD: Briefly, I think Simpson touches a contemporary nerve, in that situatedness constitutes our shared situation—all too insistently. Declaring "where I'm coming from" can be used to legitimize my position and equally to excuse it, whether as local knowledge or as universal avowal. It's both very annoying and unavoidable: there is no unsituated position from which to survey the field and proceed in a fully informed manner. Simpson is right, I'd add, to claim that this should not tempt us into an ethical (let alone religious) acceptance of mutual ignorance, which serves only to advance one's unearned condescension. He recommends that we resort instead to what the sociologist Niklas Luhmann calls an "ecology of ignorance"—a sustained communication of what we don't know. (As Luhmann remarks, there's plenty of ignorance to go around.[14]) Perhaps we are already engaged here in such communication, even as some of the talks I heard [in the conference preceding this roundtable] resolutely talked past one another while others showed themselves uncomfortably self-aware of the unfamiliar other (art history, philosophy, in their many and various guises and commitments). So I'd disagree with John Hyman: I think interaction is good, and that it happens anyway. Can I add that I especially welcome Jim's brave attempt at sorting the different (sometimes incompatible) models at work in our discussions. It might not resolve matters, but it does help channel our (mis)communications!

That is by way of general comment. I would also second the idea of historicizing Kant, putting him in his place. Philosophers have looked at the language of affect in the last four or five hundred years, and have not relativized it, but given it a much freer play. Not just philosophers: I think of Philip Fisher's recent book on the "vehement passions," arguing for a closer look at how passions are volunteered rather than just elicited, a look too at how art activates rather than (as with Kantian aesthetics) domesticates these forces.[15] If we adopt a broader approach to the passions, we wouldn't be stuck with just the language of beauty and the sublime—and philosophers haven't done much with ideas of the sublime, either—and we could look at other ways in which music, literature, and painting have been received in the past. As for the sublime, this strikes me as a phenomenon or category that is a good deal more fascinating than its canonical status would lead us to expect. What was the sublime before the seventeenth-century rediscovery of Longinus? Why has it been invoked—and in very different religious and political modes—through the eighteenth century, and again in the Romantics? What is the "subjectivity effect" it elicits or invokes? And why did it suddenly become interesting once more to some poststructuralist thinkers? These are questions for both aestheticians and art historians.[16]

One art historian whom philosophers *do* read (and who shows himself to have read philosophers) is Michael Baxandall. He is wonderful at showing the dialectics of concepts such as *commensurazione,* as well as the history of ideas such as *affect.*[17] One realizes the world was different then, so that maybe we should think about the present differently as well.

JE: Would an historicized aesthetics operate along the lines Arthur has suggested, with nonhistorical concepts taken from experience and embedded in, or used for, art-historical writing? Or do you have a different model of that interaction?

MD: I fully agree with Arthur's distinction between philosophy of art and aesthetics, especially if the latter has to do with things like judgments of taste. I'm intrigued by his recommended separation (on grounds of disciplinary health) of the theory of art from an aesthetics that treats of the rhetorical effects obtained (though not exclusively) by artworks. I do wonder whether such aesthetic experience—of the beautiful, gory, erotic, even the dainty or the dumpy—is entirely nonhistorical. Rather, I think that we might locate a salient property in a certain period before moving to the rational redescription Arthur proposes. In fact his book on how modernist artists were committed to shunning beauty seems historical in just that way. I've already suggested how we might begin to do such redescription with the sublime. The sublime was attractive first because of its assault on neoclassical rules, then also because it responded to the fear of a loss of authority once that was no longer observable (as God or sovereignty, for example) whereas the subject's own observing activity became all too evident—to speak again in a Luhmannian mode. Perhaps the dainty and dumpy could be historicized too, and as more than Oxford common-room dialect (though the only direct application of the terms I've come across, by the way, is to varieties of tree frogs).

RW: I think we can distinguish the aesthetic and aesthetics as a discipline. And we can recognize that across the world, there are people who call themselves aestheticians, and who are interested in attending aesthetics conferences, who aren't actually philosophers. Are philosophers the best people to discuss the aesthetic? Jim, your paper strikes a chord with people who turn up at aesthetics conferences but who aren't philosophers. I agree that the aesthetic is related to the particular, while philosophy is related to the general. Where I find Arthur's activities most valuable, speaking as a philosopher, is in his criticism. His criticism is shaped by a philosophic mentality, but he is delivering criticism.

AD: As a critic, let's say—putting on another hat here—I don't think I would get very far if I said, "See this exhibition because it's beautiful," or "Modigliani is to be preferred to Picasso because he is prettier." Those are not interesting critical judgments. What's interesting is the role beauty plays in their paintings, or for example the role played by melancholy. Modigliani probably read Kant somewhere along the line, but I don't think any of that enters into why he is popular, or why he painted as he did. In explaining Modigliani, a critic is obliged to explain how the aesthetic qualities are transmitted into the work.

TdD: Arthur, you force me to drive a wedge into the space that separates us. You said that what really got you started in aesthetics were the shrines set up all over New York City the day after 9/11. That's interesting. Must we understand that until then, you were involved with art theory *as opposed* to aesthetics? It is my feeling indeed that you have always opposed art theory to aesthetics, whereas I let both fields overlap to the point of perfect congruence. We might frame our debate within David's "strong" and "weak" senses of aesthetics, or, as I would prefer, within the alternative set by Dominic when he spoke of aesthetics-at-large, as opposed to what I would call art-at-large. It could be argued that you use aesthetics in the broader sense, whereas I use it in the narrow sense. I confine aesthetics to the domain of art, whereas you take aesthetic qualities, predicates, attributes, and feelings out of art and into the domain of everyday life. Coming from someone who has made the question of indiscernibles the cornerstone of his theory of art, it makes me wonder where you draw the line. It struck me how, all of a sudden, by a strategic move in this conversation, you widened the field of aesthetics in everyday life to include the 9/11 shrines—hardly just a day like any other. And now it strikes me how you make aesthetic judgments about art look ridiculous by saying that "Modigliani is to be preferred to Picasso because he is prettier." Is this your way of preventing that the 9/11 shrines could be seen as art? You allow yourself, as a human being, to be moved by the shrines, whereas Warhol's *Brillo Boxes* merely titillate the theorist in you and Modigliani prompts you to make fun of aesthetics when applied to art. I wish someone, some day, will present a 9/11 shrine in an art gallery. Then you will be faced with the question of indiscernibles in such a way that it will force you to let your own emotional responses intervene in your notion of art—or else, surrender to the institutional theory of art, which many people ascribe to you and which you have refuted so far. Now I am going to argue that you are in fact narrowing aesthetics, while I am broadening it, because the field of art includes anything and everything today. Once a urinal or a Brillo box can be art, anything can be art. At stake in your Hegelian, "post-historical" approach to art, on the one hand, and in your rehabilitation of aesthetics provided it is kept separate from art, on the other hand, is the question of how we should conceive the autonomy of art. In evoking the 9/11 shrines, you reminded me of the oddity of modernity. It could be said that art, as an aesthetic practice, has been embedded in religion for thousands and thousands of years, back to the point where we can locate the origins of both art and religion in funeral rituals. The so-called autonomy of art is autonomy *from religion*, and it is at the most two hundred years old; it is congruent with modernity. Are you in a way saying, "Close the parenthesis of modernism, terminate the autonomy of art from religion"? I'm pretty sure you're not saying that, because you don't see the shrines as art. But consider the indiscernibles. The minute such a shrine will be seen in an art gallery, your brand of rehabilitation of aesthetic qualities and feelings will be tantamount to allowing the confusion of art with religion to take over. I think this is very dangerous. There are signs everywhere that postmodernism might very well be the closing of the parenthesis of art's autonomy. And everywhere, religiosity is around the corner. My political philosophy is to keep the realms of the artistic and the religious separate. It is the achievement of the Enlightenment to keep *thinking*—cultural thinking, artistic thinking—from the domination of religious thinking. This is why Kant is the most enlightening philosopher in the Enlightenment, and why he is so useful and timely now, politically as well as intellectually.

One last thing, please, to make the opposition between us clear. The issue is not, Why is Paul McCarthy disgusting?, or, What kind of point does McCarthy's *Bossy Burger* make that parallels Grünewald's *Isenheim Altarpiece?*, but rather, Is Paul McCarthy on the level of Grünewald? I agree with you that this is where aesthetics and art history can come together. Assuming that McCarthy's work is disgusting (to me it's not: it's much too funny for that; it stages disgust at a remove, so to speak), the issue, however, does not revolve around our analysis of the words *disgusting* or *repulsive* as aesthetic terms. It revolves around whether *you* are ready to admit disgust among the feelings that make *you* say that something is art. That's the aesthetic issue. And it revolves around what makes McCarthy comparable to Grünewald. That's the art-historical issue. I happen to like the work of Paul McCarthy enormously; I think he's a major artist. I also think his link to the past goes via Bruce Nauman—that's the genealogy I would construct for Paul McCarthy. Once you get to Nauman, you can go back to Dada, and then further back to Courbet, when it was first an issue whether disgust—unredeemed by religion—could be a legitimate quality of art. And from there, the tradition goes back to Grünewald, easily. So for me, aesthetic issues and issues of art history are not separated.

Incidentally, I was almost insulted by Richard Woodfield's insinuation that nonphilosophers had, *per definitionem*, no access to aesthetics, or no legitimate claim to practice aesthetics. What does that mean?

RW: Sorry, you misunderstood me. I said the reverse: internationally, there are people who attend aesthetics conferences who are not philosophers, and their concern is the particularity of artworks. My thought was that one of the problems with philosophy is that to the degree it is concerned with abstract intellectual structures, it does not engage with objects in the way that practical art criticism does. My own preference is to listen to nonphilosophers talk about artworks, rather than listen to philosophers talk about aesthetics.

TdD: All right, sorry about the misunderstanding. Now, what about the kind of philosophers who think along a path of generalization that goes from the singular to the universal and not from the particular to the general?

RW: For example?

TdD: I'm talking about reflective thinking, reflective judgment. You do not have the rule, so you cannot subsume the particular under the heading of the general the way you can in science and philosophy. Instead you work from singular cases and you claim universality for those cases. Kant offers us a way of thinking from the singular to the universal that bypasses the famous particular-general issue.

DR: One of the most important attributes of works of art, I think, is their vagueness or messiness. Philosophy's particularity comes out especially well in what it takes to be its central questions, things like: What precisely did Kant write in paragraph nine? What exactly are the nine qualifications we can make on the idea of play? Art is not like that, even in the most reductive of formalist practices. Even in someone like Morris Louis, it seems that what philosophy does not address very well is art in its generality.

TdD: Personally, I am totally unable to speak of art as a generality, without showing or naming a specimen. I don't know what art is, I have no general, conceptual definition for art. But I know a work of art when I see one.

Anna Dezeuze: Another way to problematize the question we are asking, concerning whether aesthetics can be useful to art history, is this: Why is Kant more useful for understanding Paul McCarthy than, say, psychoanalysis?

TdD: Kant is not at all useful, neither in understanding nor in appreciating Paul McCarthy. Of course not.

Anna Dezeuze: Okay…

TdD: Say you throw yourself out of the window, and you land on the sidewalk. Is Newton useful to you? You have just obeyed the law of universal gravity, that's all. [*Laughter and applause.*]

JE: This may be a good moment to supplement the provisional list of models we have been using. Thierry, yesterday you proposed a five-part schema for understanding the aesthetic encounter, taking as an example a work by Robert Morris that consists of three L-shaped volumes. If you don't mind, I will summarize it very quickly, because it suggests a sixth model that has not yet appeared in this conversation.

You proposed that the initial moment of encounter is a matter of perception, using, as Kant would say, the faculty of the imagination. It would result, you said, in a simple description of the work—in that case, a statement like "The three volumes look different."

The second moment, sensation, would be enabled by the faculty of understanding, and it would produce a conclusion: "The three volumes are actually identical."

The third moment is made possible by the free (or constrained, in the case of Morris's work) play of imagination and understanding; the fourth moment, judgment, is enabled by the faculty of taste and results in an aesthetic such as "The work is bad" or "The work is good." And the final moment, interpretation, is a function of the faculty of understanding, and permits a synthetic look back at the judgment and its precursors.

Now I don't mean to do justice to your exposition with that truncated exposition, but I would like to propose that it might collapse in an interesting way, leading to a new model of the relation of aesthetics and art history. You said that in the anti-aesthetic position, the fourth moment, aesthetic judgment, is occluded—it isn't acknowledged in anti-aesthetic writing. And you also suggested that the third and fifth moments might fold into one another, in part because a work like Morris's constrains the "free play" of imagination and understanding. It occurred to me that in some contemporary art-historical writing that is dependent on versions of phenomenology, the collapse could continue because the second moment would be understood as wholly determined by the first: that is, cognition would be taken to be epiphenomenal on perception, an effect of perception. And in that way the entire five-part schema might fold into one or two moments.

This implies, I think, a different way in which aesthetics might speak to art history: it might provide *flexible* schemata, which could be adapted for specific historical contexts. In this case a Kantian reading of an encounter with Morris's work yields the five-part schema, which is truncated to three parts in anti-aesthetic position, and into two in a phenomenological account. Could the flexibility of aesthetics be another way in which it could become recognizable, and then useful, to art history?

It is interesting to me that we have hardly mentioned the anti-aesthetic—meaning not the shift in art beginning in the 1960s, but the academic moment crystallized by the book *The Anti-Aesthetic.*[18] I imagine that for some readers it may seem surprising that we did not begin with the anti-aesthetic, or at least with its continuation and dispersal in subsequent art practices. It may seem we have refused to acknowledge that our discussion could only begin from the anti-aesthetic or its construction of modernism. It might even seem our freedom is more careless than carefree, to adopt a trope of Dominic's.

This suggests a seventh model: in it, a rediscovery of aesthetics by art historians would be a nostalgic attempt to return to elements of a modernist or even premodernist aesthetic. A certain support for this reading could be found in the recent spate of work on beauty by Dave Hickey, Elaine Scarry, Wendy Steiner, and Alexander Nehamas.[19]

DC: Well, it can be but it need not be. I think the problem is that the "return" to aesthetics, signaled by slogans such as "a return to beauty," often boils down to a retrieval of what postmodern anti-aestheticism rejected. To the degree that postmodernism cashes out as a negation of the privileged terms of modernism, this would simply be a negation of postmodernism that returns us to the previous moment. But taking issue with the characteristic expressions of postmodern anti-aestheticism need not issue in a nostalgic return to a modernist aesthetic, unless it is driven by an implicit or unwitting assumption that modernism got the aesthetic dimension of art more or less right. That, for example, the privileging of form over content, of feeling over cognition, the strict separation of the media, or of the high art from popular culture, and so on, are intrinsic to the idea of an aesthetic response to art. But even when such specific modernist assumptions are not at work, what is too often meant by "a return to beauty" is, implicitly, returning to a broadly *formalist* conception of the aesthetic: one that focuses, crudely speaking, on how things look, and the feelings this induces, *at the expense* of the kind of cognitive engagement works elicit in their viewers. This opposition is itself questionable, and one which I would want to resist.

JE: Certainly it could be argued, against this seventh model, that the anti-aesthetic is already almost a quarter-century old, and the space "beyond" its dichotomy of modernism and postmodernism is no longer an unoccupied space. But the strength of that assertion depends on what we take to be in that space. There have actually been very few attempts to think about what happens beyond the opposition of the aesthetic and the anti-aesthetic: several essays by Steve Melville, and a group of papers in the most recent *Art Journal.*[20] It is fascinating how hard it continues to be to think outside that opposition, and how seldom it seems important to put the problem of the present in those terms.

DC: Again, yes and no. I think Melville is a good example of someone who has been trying, against the orthodoxy that one is either a postmodern anti-aesthete or a modernist aesthete, to *displace* this opposition, particularly in his writings on Smithson.[21] This is also true of Thierry's work. I mean, what could have looked stranger, given the usual lines along which such debates tend to break down, both philosophically and art historically, than to try to do justice to *both* Duchamp and Greenberg? What is refreshing about the work of both, to my mind, is that it cannot be located in terms of the divide you are referring to. What is surprising though, as you say, is that this seems to *remain* such a marginal position—despite the fact that the high point of postmodern anti-aestheticism crystallized in early 1980s. As someone who started out as an art student in the late 1980s (which Arthur once referred to as "the *October* decade"), and felt its prescriptive force on intellectually ambitious young artists firsthand, I would align myself today with what I take to be the *aspirations* behind Thierry's and Stephen's work—even if I do not always find myself in agreement with the specific arguments in support of those aspirations.[22]

JE: A strong realist position, such as the one David's work is exploring, might be able to push against both Fried's modernist position and the anti-aesthetic position exemplified by Krauss. I wonder whether an eighth model for the encounter of art history and aesthetics might be a run *around* aesthetics and into something wholly different.

DR: As you know, Jim, for a while it's seemed to me that art history has been trapped within a relatively unexamined dialectic of aesthetics vs. anti-aesthetics, which is basically a Fried-against-Krauss kind of argument. These positions basically date to the 1960s, and have dominated ever since. We've got to get rid of these boundaries if we're going to get anywhere instead of just rehashing old debates over and over again. What I think we need to do is to step back and ask what are the basic assumptions of each position, and then argue about whether or not those are valid. Can they stand up to scrutiny? I think that when we look more closely, we'll find that each option has an implicit antirealist economy of belief, a conviction that what the world's like is how it appears to us, and that art has a role in picturing our reality. This is a pretty shaky claim on which to anchor the range of possibilities for what art is and does, since it's an idealist position that stands in contrast to the realist claim that reality is mind-independent. For me, it's the realist who's going to win this debate. Art historians need to think about our baseline commitments and uncouple art history and aesthetics. One possible way of breaking out of this confining structure is, I think, and we've talked about this, to evaluate the ability of our beliefs to get at truth and reality, which should be our goal and art's project.

MD: I don't know whether art historians have been at all influenced by systems theory, as some literary theorists have—I'm thinking here of the sociologist Niklas Luhmann in particular.[23] I for one would be interested in the results! It seems to me that Luhmann's notion of "autopoiesis"—here, an art system defining itself as and by self-reflection, "second-order" observation—would change the way we think about production and reception of artworks. Speaking about art as communication (in a very general sense), via codes that can be operationally specified in an available medium, allows a flexible approach to historical circumstance. Formalism and historicism come together, get engaged, so to say.

In philosophy (at least, in the sort of thing *I* do) such an approach historicizes the vocabulary of "autonomy," "judgment," and so on, while pointing to a syntax and indeed a "pragmatics" by which such autonomy came to be asserted, namely, as self-distinction. It helps make sense of how the Romantics mixed the code of art with that of beauty, as a way of seemingly closing the circle of self-reflection. Moreover, though it doesn't pretend to draw a bottom line under our various disciplinary accounts, it makes a virtue of the theoretician's necessary blind spot. (I'll also confess to being attracted to what sometimes seems like Hegel minus the metaphysics.)

JE: Aesthetics has almost been a material substance in this conversation: it has hardness or softness, broadness or narrowness, it flows (there are "confluences" of aesthetics and other disciplines), it melts, it is flexible and can be folded and even placed inside something else, like art history. I will add one more metaphor, which also produces a ninth model: it can be opened. It can be opened, and Kant can be taken out: not wholly, of course, but in pieces. The possibility of an operation in which parts of Kant are removed from the body of aesthetics might be the not-so-hidden theme of this conversation. So let me propose, in ending, a ninth model and a metaphor to go with it: art history might be the acid that corrodes aesthetics. Has it ever happened the other way around?

Notes

1. See Alex Potts, *Flesh and the Ideal: Winckelmann and the Origins of Art History* (New Haven, CT: Yale University Press, 1994); and Abigail Solomon-Godeau, *Male Trouble: A Crisis in Representation* (London: Thames and Hudson, 1997).
2. Danto, *The Abuse of Beauty: Aesthetics and the Concept of Art* (Chicago: Open Court, 2003). See further Diarmuid Costello, "On Late Style: Arthur Danto's '*The Abuse of Beauty,*'" *British Journal of Aesthetics* 44 no. 4 (October 2004): 424–39.
3. Thierry de Duve, "The Monochrome and the Blank Canvas," in *Kant after Duchamp* (Cambridge, MA: MIT Press, 1996); de Duve, *Clement Greenberg Between the Lines* (Paris: Dis Voir, 1996). See also Stephen Melville, "On Modernism" in *Philosophy Beside Itself: On Deconstruction and Modernism* (Minneapolis: University of Minnesota Press, 1986) and *Seams: Art as a Philosophical Context* (London: G+B Arts, 1996).
4. See Jim Elkins's discussion of this comedy of mutual misrecognition in "Why Don't Art Historians Attend Aesthetics Conferences?" in this volume.
5. Compare this assessment with, for example, Hans Belting, *Likeness and Presence: A History of the Image Before the Era of Art*, trans. Edmund Jephcott (Chicago: University of Chicago Press: 1994).
6. Both Stenzel's and Liebrucks's arguments are lucidly discussed in Wolfhart Pannenberg's *Theology and the Philosophy of Science* (London: Darton Longman & Todd, 1976), 217.
7. Aristotle, *De anima*, 425 a 25.
8. For the terms *Lebenswelt* and *Weltanschauung* see Wilhelm Dilthey, *Selected Writings*, ed. H.P. Rickman (Cambridge: Cambridge University Press, 1976), 123–4 and 133–54; also Edmund Husserl, *The Crisis of European Sciences,* (Evanston, IL: Northwestern University Press, 1970), 139–41.
9. Stewart, *On Longing: Narratives of the Miniature, the Gigantic, the Souvenir, the Collection* (Baltimore, MD: Johns Hopkins University Press, 1984).
10. Anna Dezeuze, "Everyday Life, Relational Aesthetics, and the Transfiguration of the Commonplace," *Variant* 2 no. 22 (Winter 2005): 17-19.
11. See Elkins, "Why Don't Art Historians Attend Aesthetics Conferences?" in this volume.
12. Costello, "On Late Style: Arthur Danto's 'The Abuse of Beauty,'" *British Journal of Aesthetics* 44 no. 4 (October 2004): 424-39.
13. David Simpson, *Situatedness*, or *Why We Keep Saying Where We're Coming From* (Durham, NC: Duke University Press, 2002).
14. Luhmann, *Observations on Modernity* (Stanford, CA: Stanford University Press, 1998), chap. 4.
15. Fisher, *The Vehement Passions* (Princeton, NJ: Princeton University Press, 2002).
16. Much more needs to be done on the sublime, following up the work of Weiskel and de Bolla. See my own "Stages of the Sublime in North America," *MLN* 115 (2000).

17. Baxandall, *Painting and Experience in Fifteenth-Century Italy: A Primer in the Social History of Pictorial Style* (Oxford: Oxford University Press, 1988); and *Patterns of Intention: On the Historical Explanation of Pictures* (New Haven, CT: Yale University Press, 1985).
18. *The Anti-Aesthetic: Essays on Postmodern Culture*, ed. Hal Foster (New York: New Press, 2002); the other candidate for a crucial text in this regard would be *Art after Modernism: Rethinking Representation*, ed. Brian Wallis (New York: New Museum of Contemporary Art/David Godine, 1984). [I thank Diarmuid Costello for suggesting I add this—J.E.]
19. For example, Scarry, *On Beauty and Being Just* (Princeton, NJ: Princeton University Press, 1999); Hickey, *The Invisible Dragon: Four Essays on Beauty* (Los Angeles: Art Issues Press, 1993); Steiner, *Venus in Exile: The Rejection of Beauty in Twentieth-Century Art* (New York: Free Press, 2001); Nehamas, "The Place of Beauty and the Role of Value in the World of Art," Critical Quarterly 42 no. 3 (2000): 1–14. Interesting in this regard is M. Yablonski, "The Beauty Fallacy: Dave Hickey's Aesthetic Revisionism," *Art Criticism* 16 no. 1 (2001): 7–11.
20. Melville, "What was Postminimalism?" in *Art Theory,* ed. Dana Arnold (London: Blackwell, 2003); James Meyer, "Aesthetic/Anti-Aesthetic: An Introduction," *Art Journal* 63 no. 2 (2004): 10.
21. See also Melville, "Robert Smithson: 'A Literalist of the Imagination'" and "Notes on the Re-Emergence of Allegory, the Forgetting of Modernism, the Necessity of Rhetoric, and the Conditions of Publicity in Art and Criticism ," in *Seams: Art as Philosophical Context* (New York: Gordon and Breach, 1996).
22. The possibility of thinking "beyond" the aesthetic/anti-aesthetic duality is one of my principal interests: for example, Costello, "Lyotard's *Modernism*" in *To Jean-François Lyotard*, special issue of *Parallax* 17 (October 2000); "Aura, Face, Photography: Re-Reading Benjamin Today," *Walter Benjamin and Art*, ed. Andrew Benjamin (London and New York: Continuum, 2004); "Towards an Aesthetics of Conceptual Art: in *Philosophy and Conceptual Art*, eds. Peter Goldie and Elisabeth Schellekens (Oxford: Oxford University Press, 2005); and "Retrieving Kant's Aesthetics for Art Theory after Modernism," in *Re-Discovering Aesthetics*, eds. Francis Halsall, Julia Jansen, and Tony O'Connor (New York: Columbia University Press, 2006).
23. Luhmann, *Art as a Social System* (Stanford, CA: Stanford University Press, 2000).

4
Assessments

Diarmuid Costello

Overcoming Postmodernism

In terms of the possible ways of conceiving the relation between art history and aesthetics that Jim Elkins suggested during the roundtable, my own view is that one can run this relation both ways: appealing to philosophy to defuse some of the more prejudicial presentations of the aesthetic tradition that have gained currency in art theory, while also appealing to art theory to culturally and historically contextualize the significance of the aesthetic in terms of recent debates. In doing so, the goal would be to outflank some of the tired, yet still ingrained, oppositions that are the afterlife of debates around "modernism" and "postmodernism" in art theory, on the one hand, and to illuminate why the aesthetic has become such a culturally contested term, on the other.

In my own work I try to do this by tracing the genealogy of these debates, and interrogating how they tend to set up certain terms (aesthetic versus anti-aesthetic, form versus content, feeling versus meaning) in particular ways, often tendentiously, thereby overdetermining how those terms have come to be perceived, and the values (typically conservative) that are associated with the aesthetic in art theory as a result. If this can be achieved, then canonical aesthetic ideas, such as that of something having a distinctly aesthetic value, might be retrieved from the uses to which they have been put, and the abuses they have suffered in the process, thereby becoming available for art theory once more. Liberated from the historical baggage that has accrued to them, such ideas could then be reformulated in the light of their contemporary objects. Doing so would free aesthetic theory, viewed from an art-historical and theoretical point of view, from the yoke of always having to be seen through the distorting optic of a partisan reception history. Or, at least it would make it apparent that aesthetic theory *is* routinely seen through such an optic. While, conversely, tracing the genealogy of recent debates such as those around aesthetics/anti-aesthetics back to their art-historical antecedents ought to alert philosophers to some of the wider cultural ramifications and sociological significance that have accrued to certain aesthetic terms as a result of the uses to which they have been put over the last century.

In concert with art historians and theorists such as Thierry de Duve and Stephen Melville, and philosophers well versed in recent art history and theory, such as Arthur Danto, I see such debates as one of the main legacies of modernist theory (whether Greenberg's or Fried's) for recent art theory and practice. Though it has by now become a commonplace, it nonetheless remains telling to observe the extent to which the generation of artists that came to prominence in the latter half of the sixties—that is, right on the cusp of modernism's influence transforming from critical orthodoxy to orthodox target of critical censure—felt the need to do theoretical battle with the work of Greenberg and Fried (Judd, Kosuth, and Smithson being notable examples). To the extent that their antipathy for *modernist* aesthetics was widely understood (and frequently presented) as a critique of aesthetics per se, the theoretical antipathy toward aesthetics (notably, formalist aesthetics) that subsequently crystallized in the guise of the anti-aesthetic, tends to cash out as a hostility toward *modernism's co-option* of the discourse of aesthetics, rather than of aesthetic theory per se—despite the fact that formalist aesthetics generally neither recognizes nor, therefore, presents itself as such. One need only look at the highly influential work of many of the theorists associated with the journal *October* in the early 1980s to see as much.

Against this widespread censure of, or at best indifference to, aesthetic theory, I would like to see the relevance of aesthetic theory retrieved for recent art. But taking the absence of aesthetics from recent theories of art as one's starting point immediately raises a question as to whether the historical or conceptual limits of aesthetic theory may not have been breached by the internal development of art after modernism. Art-world debate on this topic, to the extent that there has been any, generally divides along predictable lines: cultural conservatives censure recent art for its alleged insensitivity to art's aesthetic "vocation"; avant-garde theorist-critics reject aesthetics in the name of recent art and theory. It is notable that both sides *agree* about what I would want to contest, namely, that recent art and aesthetics have indeed parted company. Against this underlying (if largely unremarked) consensus, the challenge is to reformulate aesthetic theory in such a way that its purchase on recent art is re-established. In doing so, the objective would be to get beyond the tendency to reject aesthetic theory *in general* on the basis of its modernist formulation. It should be apparent that rejecting aesthetics on that basis amounts to relinquishing the terrain of aesthetics to modernist theory, when what recent art actually shows is that modernism had an unacceptably restrictive conception of aesthetic value. To redress this situation requires retrieving aesthetic theory from its modernist appropriation and its postmodern rejection alike, thereby affording new ways of thinking about art and aesthetics precluded by present orthodoxies.

Like de Duve, I hold Greenberg's modernist aesthetic—his account of modernist medium-specificity as "a tropism toward aesthetic value"—largely responsible for the subsequent rejection of aesthetics in the light of art's later, *non*-medium-specific, development. Unpacking the equation of modernist medium-specificity with aesthetic quality at the heart of Greenbergian theory involves interrogating both his modernism and his formalism. Greenberg's formalism is vitiated by his attempt to apply Kant's analysis of *pure* aesthetic judgment—paradigmatic judgments concerning natural or, better, "free" (conceptually unconstrained) beauty for Kant—to artifacts as culturally and historically complex as works of art; and by his tendency to psychologize and empiricize Kantian theory in line with his own, essentially Humean, conception of taste and criticism. Greenberg's modernism, on the other hand, is compromised by his attempt to align specific arts with individual senses under the influence of music: this is at odds with both his alleged Kantianism, in so far as Kant held all perception to be grounded in an underlying *unity* of sensibility, and Greenberg's own stress on the "opticality" of *both* painting and sculpture. If correct, taken together these arguments show that rejecting aesthetics, and especially Kant's aesthetics, on the basis of Greenberg's claims about either is unwarranted.

Some of the most philosophically acute internal criticisms of Greenbergian modernism were mounted early on by Michael Fried. Despite this, Fried's reworkings of Greenbergian theory failed to redeem modernist aesthetics. Hence, although he took issue with Greenberg's essentialism (the idea of modernism as a reduction of each art to its essential *timeless* core), Fried only succeeded in further entrenching the cornerstone of modernist theory—the idea of medium-specificity itself. Despite taking issue with Greenberg's *conception* of it, Fried nonetheless concurred, at a deeper level, with Greenberg that notions such as aesthetic value are only meaningful *within* specific arts. Given the development of art after minimalism, this had predictable results for Fried's critical standing. This much is common knowledge. But what has passed entirely unremarked is that Fried's *own* critique of Greenberg's essentialism renders his simultaneous censure of minimalism for blurring artistic media incoherent. That, in effect, Fried's critique of minimalism can be defused, internally, on *Friedian* grounds. For, if the essence of each art is conventional—and thus open to revision over time—as Fried himself maintains in differentiating himself from Greenberg—then there is no space "between" the arts that may be safely rejected *a priori* as inimical to aesthetic quality. What lies between artistic media today need no longer do so tomorrow. Hence, while Fried may be said to have philosophically forfeited modernist theory's understanding of essence and convention, he failed to displace it, more fundamentally, from its Greenbergian origins.

Assuming it is right to say that it was above all Greenberg's appeal to Kant's formalist account of judgments of natural beauty that overdetermined later art-world reference to aesthetics, the obvious way to redress this would be to return to what Kant himself had to say about fine art in the third *Critique*. This move has also been central to Paul Crowther's project to retrieve Kant's aesthetics for contemporary debate, although he pushes it in a rather different direction. Kant's theory of *artistic* (as opposed to natural) beauty centers on how meaning is embodied in the material form of the work; as such, it focuses on the *relation between* form and content. The error of taking Greenberg's Kant as the last word on what Kant has to offer art theory today is that artistic meaning all but drops out of Greenberg's account of artistic value. By contrast, Kant views works of art as vehicles for expressing "aesthetic ideas," ideas the distinctive nature of which prompt the imagination to spread over more associations than can be captured in words. As such, works of art have a complex cognitive function in Kant's own account. Kant attributes the ability to generate such ideas to "genius," specifically, to the genius's "ability to apprehend the imagination's rapidly passing play" and embody it in such a way as to communicate it to the work's recipient (*Critique of Judgment*, §49). As genius can neither be taught nor, as a consequence, explain its own productive process, Kant is forced to credit this ability, obscurely, to "nature in the subject" (*Critique of Judgment*, §46). Suggestive though this is, it raises more questions than it answers. What does it *mean* to say that "nature in the subject" is responsible for art? What is it about the mind that *enables* it to embody an imaginative play in a work of art, or grasp its meaning once it has been so-embodied?

One way to address such questions is to point up some of the notable structural parallels that pertain between the creation and reception of art on the one hand, and wit (in the broadest sense of an acute mind, gifted in seeing connections) on the other. Construing wit as an aesthetic capacity sheds light on what is involved in grasping formal and semantic relations *intuitively*, as when we immediately *see* the point of the connections made by a joke, or the novel conjunctions made in a work. One obvious limit of this analogy is that, *unlike* jokes, works of art do not exhaust themselves in the telling. And this is where Kant's idea of "nature in the subject" becomes important. Building on Kant's skeletal account, one might try to flesh it out as a primitive, unstructured element of cognition manifest in working an artistic medium, despite remaining irretrievable to rational reflection. If this can be done it would account for both the opacity that differentiates works of art from more transparent forms of utterance, and go some way to explaining why genius cannot explain its own productivity. By such an account, aesthetic ideas and genius would serve as one way of tracing back the "two faces" of the work of art to their grounding in aesthetic subjectivity. By this I have in mind the frequently observed fact that works of art are, paradoxically, both "intelligible" and "opaque" simultaneously. That is, the fact that they are both amenable to being understood, and even seem to encourage us interpret them, while evading exhaustive or definitive analysis. Any adequate theory of art has to address this distinctive feature of works of art, and have something to say about what it is about human beings, as producers and receivers of art, that makes this possible. I think this would be internally connected to the fact that works of art are products of intention, that is, made for reasons, and imbued with meaning in the service of those reasons, while nonetheless routinely exceeding or transcending the intentions motivating their creation. That this is so must be at least partly due to the fact that the meaning of works of art is invested in materials that have been worked in such a way as to elicit affective as well as cognitive responses, which is to say that it is embedded in an artistic medium.

Of course, to show that such a theory is adequate to its contemporary object it must at some point come to examples. The most direct procedure here would be to hold it up to as broad a range of recent works as possible, but especially to works construed as anti-aesthetic (in the modernist terms that I maintain continue to overdetermine art-world aesthetics) while pitting it against the competing views of those art theorists and critics who do perceive such works, implicitly or explicitly, in anti- or nonaesthetic terms. What is required is not that such readings be contested head-on in their entirety but rather to show that they routinely fail to account for the aesthetic *dimension* of the works under discussion, for all their—often ingenious—attention to other aspects of their meaning or significance. Further, such readings need to be supplemented by some account of the distinctive nature of our cognitive engagement with the works under discussion that serves to distinguish the nature of *that* interaction from our cognitive interest in other kinds of artifact or occurrence, or from other kinds of interest we might have in works of art and, in virtue of which, we call this kind of response a response to something *as a work*, rather than as something else (document, symptom, etc.). This, I take it, would be one way of bringing recent art history, theory, and practice into contact with the post-Kantian aesthetic tradition, while transcending the increasingly stale legacy of the aesthetic/anti-aesthetic divide in the process.

Anna Dezeuze

Art History, Aesthetics, and the "Spheres of Experience"

I am certain that many an art historian would be baffled, as I was, by Jane Forsey's rigorous account of "The Disenfranchisement of Philosophical Aesthetics" a few years ago.[1] Her demonstration of analytical aesthetics' grounding in turn-of-the-century "art for art's sake" theories and formalist models of inquiry is surprising for those who know how extensively these discourses have been challenged by artists and historians alike; her call for philosophers of aesthetics to "pay more attention to what artists have to say about their art" and to the relations between art and life may sound faintly comical to art historians for whom these two statements have been long-established concerns (if not clichés) to be handled with care.

Forsey's text would also startle most philosophers rooted in a continental tradition. After all, an emphasis on the artist's perspective and the overcoming of the boundary between art and life was a recurrent trope in German aesthetics as much as in Nietzsche's writings. Similarly, Merleau-Ponty's phenomenological aesthetics, and Derrida's and Deleuze's oppositions between aesthetics and the rigidity of language, all sought to dismantle *a priori* reductions through an openness to the world of experience and an emphasis on sensation which analytic philosophy has done much to exclude. In France, the Kantian aesthetics at the core of much analytic philosophy has been radically questioned by authors as different as Bourdieu and Lyotard.

In addition to this wider range of references, continental aesthetics seems to offer a broader definition of its field of interest. Jacques Rancière defines aesthetics as the intersection between artworks and the other "spheres of experience" to which they are linked, whether "ceremonies, entertainment, education, commerce, or utopias."[2] As such, all writings about art that explore these relations could be seen as engaging with aesthetics. Anne Moeglin-Delacroix's *Esthétique du livre d'artiste*, for example, is an impressive analysis of artists' books as specific objects with their own history, ontology, and relations to "spheres of experience" as varied as play, politics, and everyday life. Even Nicolas Bourriaud's *Relational Aesthetics*, which obviously lacks the rigor and coherence of an academic inquiry (would any Anglo-American critic dare use the term "aesthetics" in the title of a loose grouping of journalistic articles?), aims at defining the qualities and sociopolitical implications of certain types of 1990s artistic practices.

If art history is to engage in a dialogue with aesthetics, it can only do so in the context of these broad definitions and wide range of models, which would allow it to become more self-critical and more receptive to the specificities that each artwork has to offer. The qualities deemed important by art historians—whether they are perceptual, material, conceptual, expressive, or sociopolitical—can all be subjected to an in-depth aesthetic analysis that can shed light on general trends, categories of objects, moments in the history of art and ideas. To achieve this, aesthetics must open itself to an interdisciplinarity, now current in much art history, which allows specific areas of experience with which art engages to be analyzed through as varied fields as psychoanalysis, feminism, the history of ideas and science, anthropology, and sociology. As Georges Didi-Huberman put it, philosophers of art should ask questions rather than try and resolve them, and "aesthetics should allow a reciprocal questioning between thought inherent to the organs of speech, writing and concept, and thought which is inherent to other organs and materials," whether ink, gesture, or sound.[3] For example, according to Didi-Huberman, a discussion of the relations between the Three Graces in Botticelli's *Primavera* and Seneca's account of their attributes remains incomplete if not complemented with an anthropological description of the dance which young ladies would engage in for the spring festivities in Renaissance Florence. Closer to us, Fluxus artist Alison Knowles's 1962 *Proposition*—a printed text which simply reads "Make a salad"—can tell us as much about art (through its relation to the musical score and the Duchampian readymade) as about everyday life (What is a recipe? Is cooking an aesthetic activity?).

If aesthetics concludes, as Arthur Danto does, that Knowles's *Proposition* questions solely the difference between art and "the commonplace," it can only offer answers about art. To answer questions about the "commonplace" we must first define it by referring, for example, to Michel de Certeau's socioanthropological study, *Practice of Everyday Life*. The dynamic movement between general aesthetics and the specific areas of human experience to which each artwork refers can offer fresh insights for art history. After all, as Robert Filliou (another artist associated with Fluxus) put it: "art is what makes life more interesting than art."[4]

Dominic Willsdon

The Aesthetics of the Small Deal

Doubtless my sense of the aesthetic comes from the experience of working in a museum of modern art and that of teaching contemporary art to curatorial studies students. Curators—that is to say, people who make professional judgments about works of art with a view to making them public—seem to speak very easily about the aesthetic traits of those works, more easily than art historians do. It is art historians (some, anyway) who have a negative view of the aesthetic, not curators or artists. But if there is an openness about aesthetics among curators, it is very much more about a feeling for the kind of everyday qualities mentioned by Arthur and Anna (I find Aleksandra Mir's *First Woman on the Moon* (1999) sweet in the way that Arthur finds Guston clunky) and very little, if at all, to do with the aesthetic as we find it in Kant and in what Thierry and many of the philosophers here have been saying.

It is an aesthetics of the small deal. Curators do not seem to work with a sense of the aesthetic that includes any claim at all about art per se let alone with any idea of a connection between aesthetic judgment and universal humanity such as that for which Thierry argues. I am not even sure that many people really do evaluate the works they value by making the judgment "this is art."

The problem with the curator's aesthetics, however, is that although it makes no claim about what is and isn't art, the business of the art museum carries on as if it does. Nobody doubts the integrity of the category of art, but nobody's assuming any principle for deciding what gets into the art museum other than that it was made by an artist as art—and that's not a principle that works. When we start to think about who's an artist and what do they do, there are, in the modern period, so many undecidable cases that decisions about art and nonart have no basis. (In fact the undecidable cases are often the exemplary ones; take the Independent Group, for example.) Art remains an administrative rather than an aesthetic category: it has to do with the professionalization of both art and curating.

David Raskin

Dead and Deader

Now that I've spent a most enjoyable weekend listening to aestheticians speak on the relationship between art history and aesthetics, I can safely venture that aesthetics is a problem. It's a problem because it seeks to quantify something as messy as experience, to divide one type of experience from others, and to set up some kind of timeline hard-wired into our psyches—where, in looking at art, we pass from "aesthetic" experience, to intellectual experience, to political experience, to who knows what. I can't tell these apart, and no one else can either, except when drinking too deeply from the cup of abstraction, but none of us lives like that. Experience comes in full, and there's something that strikes me as misguided in any attempt to try to carve out a narrow slice, analyze it, explain it, justify it, and tie it back to the particulars of a work of art. Art's too messy for this.

This being said, there's no reason aesthetics shouldn't continue to thrive as an academic discipline; it seems to have a great deal to say about writings on aesthetics, and I see this as very useful, but solely as a kind of private practice for the scholar. Let's just not pretend it has much to do with anything beyond that.

And I must admit that there's something ironic about an art historian writing this assessment. For as aestheticians seem to have won little respect within the philosophy community at large, art historians also seem to have a similar standing with artists and historians. Neither discipline, the others think, gets their interests right or even gets the right interests. Blame it on compartmentalization; the very feature required for expertise is exactly why our fields fail at a practical level. Abstraction, a good formalist would say, takes itself as its own subject. If we have any true intentions of talking across disciplines, and of even being relevant, the disciplinary specificity that drives our own disciplines needs to go.

Let's let aesthetics and art history be for the birds.

John Hyman

Art History and Aesthetics

Few art historians attend conferences in aesthetics or read *The Journal of Aesthetics and Art Criticism* or *The British Journal of Aesthetics*—or at least few of them do one of these things for a second time. But I don't think we should be either puzzled or dismayed. In the first place, art history and aesthetics do overlap, but not much. And secondly, as Quine observed, quality control in philosophy is spotty. This is especially true of conferences, since papers are generally accepted on the basis of an abstract.

I shall elaborate on the first of these two points. There are two main reasons why art history and aesthetics—by which I shall mean English-language aesthetics—do not overlap much. In the first place, a substantial part of aesthetics is concerned with very abstract questions about art, or with questions that are not about art at all. Here are a few examples of the first kind: How, if at all, should we define the concept of a work of art? Is a work of art an abstract object or a concrete object? Is there a distinctive kind of value that all and only works of art aspire to or possess? What kinds of properties can contribute to the value of a work of art? Can the evaluation of works of art be guided by rules or principles? Is artistic value absolute or relative?

Art historians may find these questions interesting. Other things being equal, they are more likely to find them interesting if they encounter the best writing about them. But they are not *bound* to find them interesting; any more than literary critics are bound to find philosophical questions about linguistic meaning interesting, or historians in general are bound be interested in the metaphysical status of events.

Where the art historians who are really cultural critics or art theorists are concerned, another consideration matters more. It should be obvious that the questions academics raise about art are never simply the result of encountering works of art and thinking about them. They are usually the result of combining a literary education, by which I mean studying texts, with studying works of art; although admittedly a few philosophers—inspired perhaps by the notorious example of Kant—continue to imagine that studying works of art is an optional part of the process.

So the second main reason why aesthetics and art history do not overlap much is that for the most part philosophers and academics in visual studies or art theory study, are influenced by, and refer to different texts. For example, Plato's *Republic* and Kant's *Critique of Judgment* are canonical texts for philosophers working in aesthetics, whereas Marx's *Grundrisse* and Freud's *Beyond the Pleasure Principle* are not. For academics in visual studies, it may be the other way around. As a result, the questions raised about works of art in these disciplines only partly resemble each other, even when the broad topic-headings are the same.

These are the main reasons why art history and aesthetics do not overlap much. Personally, I don't find this troubling in the least.

If a hundred flowers bloomed for a year or so in Maoist China, we should be able to tolerate some intellectual diversity as well.

Perhaps the more interesting question is why philosophers working in aesthetics and art historians can assist or influence each other at all. I suspect that the main reason why philosophers can benefit from art history is this: "Over-simplification, schematization, and constant obsessive repetition of the same small range of jejune 'examples' are ... far too common to be dismissed as an occasional weakness of philosophers."[5] This remark was made by J. L. Austin in the 1950s; but it remains true. For example, Duchamp's urinal occupies almost as preeminent a position in the philosophy of art today as Plato's example of a straight stick that looks crooked in the water did in the philosophy of perception fifty years ago.

Art history can help philosophers to combat this weakness, which can make what they write numbingly crude and banal. To make the same point more politely, studying the history of art can encourage philosophers to be skeptical about the generalizations they have inherited; and it can teach them that some of the concepts they find useful have a far more local and contingent value than they tend to assume. Just seeing the latest exhibitions is not likely to do the trick.

As for the reciprocal benefit art historians can gain from philosophy, I think it is mainly due to the influence that philosophical ideas—many of them myths—have had on art history, either directly or mediated by science. Here, for example, are three myths which have captured the imagination of many historians of art: first, the idea that colors exist only in the mind, and not in the physical objects we perceive; secondly, the twin ideas that a painting is a kind of text and that "realism" is an honorific term, which we bestow on art in a congenial style; and thirdly, the idea that perspective is a successful technique for depicting space because it reproduces the geometrical structure of the retinal image—the picture from which our perception of space is naturally derived.

These ideas will be familiar to most readers. They stem, respectively, from Galileo and Descartes, from Peirce and from Helmholtz; and one or another of them exerted a powerful influence on the most important twentieth-century historians of art. Philosophy can enable us to criticize them effectively; and it can also enable us to replace them with a clearer picture of the fundamental concepts they involve. (Here I simply assert these things. I have tried to prove them in a forthcoming book.[6])

Of course, many historians of art escape the pernicious influence of philosophical myths; and many philosophers avoid the intellectual sin Austin describes. But the sad conclusion—sad for a philosopher, that is—is that art history can enable philosophers to resist the tendencies a training in philosophy can instill or reinforce, and philosophy can enable art historians to resist the allure of philosophical myths.

The more positive conclusion is that philosophy and art history—I mean philosophy in general, not just aesthetics—can benefit each other most by remaining what they are. To use the current jargon, multi-disciplinarity is a better model for dialogue between art historians and philosophers than interdisciplinarity. We should not attempt to find a common ground, but communicate with each other from within our separate fields, using the skills our different intellectual training can provide.

Francis Halsall

Art History versus Aesthetics

I find the sense of theatrical antagonism implied by the title *Art History Versus Aesthetics* both convincing and misplaced at the same time.[7] It seems convincing because art history has relied upon its distance from aesthetic reflection as a means of ensuring its autonomy and validity since its inception as an essentially modernist discipline in the nineteenth century. This has set the conditions for the subsequent uneasy relationship between the systems of art history and aesthetics. It's easy to see how both may share a suspicion of one another's modes and methods. Art historians often distrust what they assume to be the philosophical impulse to subsume material and historical particularities under conceptual or ideal universals. And likewise, the philosopher might be skeptical of the epistemological benefit in the historian's attention to taxonomic detail.

Traditionally, art history is seen as actually requiring a certain distrust of aesthetic judgments. From the perspective of the art historian, aesthetics is the source of an internal and potentially destructive tension which emerges within systems of art-writing. This tension emerges from the dichotomy between, on the one hand, a mode of art-historical writing which is (at least nominally) concerned with ensuring objectivity in historical statements. (This is the rigorous, or scientific, study of art in the Germanic tradition of *Kunstwissenschaft*, the history of which has been extensively rediscovered over the last two decades.) On the other hand, there is a mode of connoisseurship or criticism which is concerned with making, and responding to, value judgments about art. Aesthetic judgments are, then, seen as not necessarily recognizing the social and historical particularities of art. They inform qualitative statements about how good or even how valuable (in all senses of the word) artworks may be. More dramatically still, aesthetics need not even be concerned with art as a separate category of objects or experience; for example, we can have an aesthetic experience of a landscape but we can't analyze it art historically. In short, at the heart of the aforementioned tension is the belief that in applying aesthetic judgments, personal taste, or lack of attention to a specific object would obscure or short-circuit historical reconstruction. This is to say that anthropological, historical, sociological, psychological, or even scientific analysis of the work of art precludes aesthetic reflection, and aesthetic judgment could compromise such activities.

Yet, despite this tradition of skepticism toward the aesthetic in the history of art history, it is precisely the grounds of implicit taste and aesthetic judgment upon which a critique of its ideological systems has been mounted. The recent well-documented revaluation and restructuring of institutional art history (through the observations made from the "other" systems of Marxism, psychoanalysis, semiotics, and so forth) gain their rhetorical purchase through their analysis of the matrices of taste and subjectivity which underpin institutional art history; that is, a critique of the ideology of their aesthetic presumptions. If, then, there is a continuity to be theorized between the new art history (whatever this may be) and its institutional ancestor, then it might be that both share an interest in the possibility or impossibility of an objective, historical, or universal status for subjective judgments. This continuity is explained by the dominant presence of Kant in different historical articulations of subjectivity from the Enlightenment to the present. For while the Kantian claims to the universality of judgments of taste have been extensively critiqued, the attractiveness of the overall Kantian project, that is, of a coherent and subject-centered epistemological system, to discourse on art means that it has been continually and consistently revisited; we need only look to Diarmuid Costello and Thierry de Duve's work as exemplary instances of this sustained interest in Kant.

However, I would argue that any apparent rejection of aesthetics by traditional and contemporary art historians is both disingenuous and misplaced.

It is disingenuous because the thread of humanism and the universal man which runs through the search to uncover lost origins or to establish the famous "Archimedean Point" (which Michael Ann Holly has traced through Cassirer, Worringer, and Panofsky) from which to reconstruct the past, has been systematically unraveled. It is the lasting legacy of poststructuralism that the classical distinctions between text and context, signifier and signified, and subject and object have collapsed in the labyrinthine systems of observation and interpretation whose centers are everywhere and whose limits are nowhere. This was undoubtedly a necessary historical moment that we do well not to forget; but debates which do no more than re-emphasize the situatedness, perspective, or ideology of particular rhetorical positions are, by now, quite tired and stale. Now it is time to move on. We may do so by investigating the process of observing the work of art from the perspective of our own, "other," and historical systems. Aesthetics provides the opportunity for this via the conditions I sketch briefly below.

Any wholesale rejection of aesthetics by art historians involves a misunderstanding of its more beneficial implications for their practice. At the heart of this misunderstanding lies an issue of translation. There are different understandings of how aesthetics is defined: the narrow and the broad definitions. One narrow view identifies aesthetics as the concern with beauty and the claims of taste. A second narrow view identifies aesthetics with philosophical accounts of works of art which can quickly lead to esoteric technical discussions about specific ontologies or definitions of art. Both narrow definitions of aesthetics describe activities somewhat removed from the day-to-day business of art history.

While art historians are right to be suspicious of these narrow views of aesthetics, in being so they deny themselves access to the potentially transformative interpretive method that the broad definition of aesthetics provides. A broad definition of aesthetics is firmly rooted in the Kantian conception of aesthetics as related to sensibility and to particular experiences of objects in time and space. In short, aesthetics is about more general questions of perception and experience rather than particular problems of beauty and definitions of art. Thus, because art history is the record of encounters with objects in specific times and places, aesthetics is, by necessity, at the very heart of any art-historical account.

I argue that aesthetics—in its broad definition—can be rediscovered as the set of conditions from which to stage a detailed and sustained engagement with works of art. This engagement is framed in terms of both historical and contemporary contexts. Conceived in these terms, aesthetics form part of a reconstruction of the work of art, but in broader terms than its relative beauty or ontology. This reconstruction is a project by which an account might be provided of an object which is sympathetic to its past, present, and future receptions; to its material particularities; and to the conditions of its reception. Reception is here understood as the process by which the individual subject or larger systems of "observation" (to use a term from Luhmann's systems theory) reconstitute the work. These are systems such as those of display (the gallery), discourse (art history), education (the university), and commerce (the art market).

Speaking optimistically, an attention to aesthetic reflection on the work of art provides the conditions by which it may be historically reconstructed in the present. This is to say that it allows the work of art to be grasped, in Panofsky's terms, "with necessity." In doing so, aesthetic reflection provides a bridge between the contexts of the works' reception and the historical and material particularity of their creation. That is, provided we exercise our judgment in its application.

Richard Woodfield

Aesthetics: Field and Discipline

It would be useful to open the question of the possible intersections of aesthetics and art history by clarifying the notion of "aesthetics," as it has a number of meanings including, in Mediterranean countries, the work of beauticians. In our context, aesthetics has two significantly different meanings: it is an academic discipline and a domain of experience.

As an academic discipline, aesthetics has had a checkered history.[8] It was initiated by a circle of intellectuals associated with Joseph Addison and *The Spectator*, to explore the pleasures of the imagination and judgments of taste. It became incorporated into a major philosophical system through the work of Kant, drawing on earlier British and German sources, and focused primarily on beauty and sublimity in nature and on the judgment of taste. Through Hegel, aesthetics became specifically associated with fine art and continues to be so to the present day. There was, however, a critical moment at the turn of the nineteenth century when a number of academics became tired of the increasingly abstract nature of German idealist aesthetics and sought to create "aesthetics from below." That moment became associated with Max Dessoir, his *Zeitschrift für Ästhetik und Allgemeine Kunstwissenschaft* (1906–1943), and his international congresses on aesthetics, which have continued through to the present day. The early congresses attracted a galaxy of stars from a wide variety of different disciplines, including Ernst Cassirer, Georg Simmel, and Erwin Panofsky, who theorized the empirical domain of the aesthetic from their own disciplinary perspectives.[9] Those congresses also resulted in the formation of American, British, and other national societies of aesthetics all over the world. Today the journals of the American and British societies are dominated by analytical aesthetics, but they weren't in their origins.[10]

The domain of the aesthetic was initially the beautiful and the sublime (as attributed properties of nature); later, it expanded to include art; and later, it expanded again to take in the area of experience subjected to judgments of taste. A typical English philosopher of the 1920s, W. T. Stace, following Benedetto Croce, declared that beauty was an all-encompassing concept including "the pathetic, the comic, the sublime, the grotesque, the magnificent, the grand, the whimsical, the romantic, the idyllic, the realistic, the impressionistic, the symbolic, the classical, the sad, the melancholy, the graceful, the humorous, the majestic, the pretty, and so forth." Stace declared Croce's great insight was that "all these supposed divisions and modifications of the beautiful are arbitrary and not based on any scientific or philosophical principle. No special aesthetic theory is needed for them."[11] With the rise of analytical philosophy there has been a considerably more rigorous analysis of aesthetic concepts, particularly in the work of the late Frank Sibley whose collection of essays published posthumously as *Approach to Aesthetics* is probably one of the most sophisticated explorations of their logic. He observed: "The objects to which we apply aesthetic words are of the most diverse kinds and by no means esoteric: people and buildings, flowers and gardens, vases and furniture, as well as poems and music."[12] To this we can add paintings and sculpture, of course. Sibley's list of aesthetic terms includes: beautiful, graceful, delicate, lovely, elegant, dainty (connected with liking, delight, affection, regard, estimation, or choice), ugly (connected with fear or revulsion), garish, splendid, gaudy (what notably catches the eye or attention), nice, pretty, exquisite (what attracts by noticeable rarity, precision, skill, ingenuity, or elaboration), and handsome (suitability to ease of handling).[13] The logic of such terms is that they may not be defined in terms of necessary and sufficient conditions. Reasons can be given for their use, in terms of their objects' features, but these are indicative, and of no logical force except in a potentially negative way: a straight or angular line cannot be graceful but you cannot create a rule for a graceful curve. Aesthetic judgments are judgments of taste and they are not confined to the world of high art.

Interestingly, Sibley argued that an engagement with the aesthetic was universal and deeply rooted in human responses to the natural and artifactual world around them. In his essay "Arts or the Aesthetic: Which Comes First?" he argued that, conceptually, aesthetic experience takes priority over artistic activity.[14] Without going into all the nuances of his argument: it is a feeling for the aesthetic that leads people into the production of artworks. Even the deliberate production of anti-aesthetic artworks is parasitic upon the concept of the aesthetic. If we recognize that Sibley's points are broadly correct, then we also have to allow that he used distinctions drawn from a particular moment of English linguistic usage, just as Stace used English words drawn from Western European artistic traditions. While the phenomenon of a feeling for the aesthetic may be universal, it may well be articulated in different ways by different cultures at different times. (And, just to be clear, this does not mean to say that there is an identifiable feeling that is a feeling for the aesthetic.) This is something best explored by linguists, philologists, and anthropologists, not by philosophers, because it is a matter of empirical facts.

So I now get to the core of my argument. Human beings, across cultures and through history, have responded to the natural and artifactual world around them in a variety of ways articulated through both language and behavior. Some of it has been documented; most of it has not. It is a major logical error to believe that one can infer such responses through works of art alone. It is also an error to believe that one can theorize about artistic activities without recognizing that they have had different functions at different times and places, and were frequently multifunctional. Both the "discipline" of aesthetics and the concept of fine art are modern and European. That does not mean that the feeling for the aesthetic or the creation of works of art had to wait for the emergence of modern Europe.

Art historians have done very little work trying to recapture distinctively aesthetic responses to artworks. One reason for this is the relative lack of documentary evidence, though I would recommend Philip Sohm's ground-breaking book *Style in the Art Theory of Early Modern Italy* and, for very different reasons, the anthropologist David Lewis-Williams's *The Mind in the Cave* on

Paleolithic cave-painting.[15] Another reason is that the discipline of art history is lacking an equivalent to literary criticism: art criticism is widely regarded as journalism and is light-years behind the practices of academic literary critics. One exception is Arthur Danto's writings, which I value for its engagement with practical art criticism. But this is not the sort of thing that typically comes from philosophical aestheticians. It's not part of the job of philosophical aesthetics.

Philosophical aesthetics has its place in the larger domain of philosophy and some very good work has been done but it is fundamentally abstract and ahistorical, and is getting more so.[16] Peter Kivy's *Philosophies of Arts: An Essay in Differences* is an outstanding exception to this generalization (and I note that the book is dedicated to Frank Sibley "who showed me the way").[17]

Arthur hit the nail on the head when he said during the seminar: "The basic issue is: Why is it important for an art historian to discuss such questions as, 'Why is the Grünewald altarpiece repulsive?' Repulsive is an aesthetic term. We're meant to recoil when we look at his altarpiece. What was Grünewald getting at when he painted Christ in such a repulsive way? That is an historical and an aesthetic question." Indeed. But these are not questions that are typically posed to art historians, and they cannot be answered by philosophers.

Ladislav Kesner

On the Diffculty of Remaining "on One's Own Patch"

In my brief comment, I wish to follow a thread offered by Thierry de Duve in his first sentences in this volume, where he insists that we should be asking what comprises the social ground of art history. He suggests that the raison d'être of art historians is that they are the guardians of tradition, which means that tradition is no longer transmitted without their help. But is it really being transmitted? And how so? My feeling is that tradition (that part of it which is embodied by works of art) is transmitted in an increasingly impoverished way. I am concerned about the tremendous gap that obtains between what works of art (or, rather, encounters with them) have to offer in terms of emotional, cognitive, and intellectual responses—and in terms of enrichment for their viewers—and what people are actually obtaining. And I do not think that art historians (as well as art critics and aestheticians) are, by and large, particularly bothered about it. What could loosely be called traditional art history was usually very keen to beat a retreat from a shaky ground of sensory aesthetics (as Otto Pächt nicely put it forty years ago). Similarly, all strands of "new" or "revisionist" art history or "visual studies," for all their critical vocabulary and focus on vision and subjectivity, have been ignoring viewers and their experiences, engulfed as those disciplines are in their narcissistic preoccupation with the subject of the interpreter—that is, with the interpreter who is also a practitioner of "new" art history. (Notwithstanding some remarkable examples which cannot be neatly placed in either camp.) Meanwhile, the concept of experience has been usurped with good intention by people in consumer research, museum marketing, and education, and it has mostly been subjected to simplified and trivialized systematization. In any mainstream museological literature one quickly learns that the duty of the contemporary museum is to "improve," "design," or "deliver" experience—a *better* art experience, much like ads that promise stronger muscles, improved memory, or longer orgasms. In between this kind of rhetoric and tradition of aesthetic discourse, most art historians (perhaps understandably) prefer to stick with the hard facts of their objects and their histories, rather than the soft matter of how they are perceived and responded to.

But if the social ground of art history is at least partly to be seen in transmitting the tradition embodied in works of art, such a task cannot be accomplished by asserting values and qualities, no matter how convincingly and skillfully that is done, but only through sustained attention to the possibilities and constraints of meaningful encounters between works of art and their viewers. (Performed not so much in a spirit of social activism or politics of accountability, but more as an ethical obligation and practical concern—so that we continue having an interested public to write for and talk to.)

However, I doubt that any model of the relationship between art history and aesthetics has much to offer here, unless other parties are invited to the table—including the philosophy of mind, cognitive science, and neuroscience. Perhaps art historians (as well as some aestheticians) are justly reserved in their reaction to some blatant claims of recently fashionable neuroaesthetics, and understandably ignore bad attempts from the neuroscientific camp to construe grand, universal aesthetic theories based on the most brutal and trivial reductionism.[18] Some might even agree that the cultural prestige of art is being recruited to give glamour to brain research, as Thomas Crow dryly observed during a 2002 Getty symposium, *The Brain, Cognition and Art*. At any rate, it seems to me that art history has not yet begun seriously to ponder the consequences and potential of the newly emerging knowledge about the human mind. Agreeing instinctively with John Hyman that holding to disciplinary identities is important, I would nevertheless like to know how one can remain on "one's own patch" in such a situation. Does it make sense for art historians and aestheticians to invoke terms like "feelings" (elicited by works of art), or qualities of art, based on complex psychological reactions (ugly, revolting, disgusting), and others that reverberated through the conversation, without engaging science and the philosophy of the mind? By my count, "Kant" or "Kantian" appears no less than 37 times in the transcript and perhaps one can indeed have a productive discussion on the intersection of aesthetics and art history along these lines. Personally, however, I find the writing of some contemporary cognitive scientists and neuroscientists (those who are not at all explicitly concerned with art), such as Antonio Damasio or Jean-Pierre Changeaux, so much more relevant and interesting than Kant in the context of thinking of why and how people respond to works of art, and how our interpretations and presentations should be tuned in order to facilitate, rather than stand in the way of, deep experience.

So it would seem that instead of the model of the relation *between* art history and aesthetics, a more intriguing possibility would be to consider a more complicated set of players, including also the philosophy of the mind, cognitive science, and neuroscience. If we take works of art to be a material embodiment of the somehow special and exceptional working of the human mind and consciousness, and if we agree that what makes a thing art is precisely its capacity to elicit exceptional states of consciousness in viewers, and finally, if we take it that the study of art has a potential to shed some light on these mental phenomena, than some kind of accommodation among all these fields seems necessary. One gets an impression of the difficulties a more sustained and careful dialogue might present by considering how difficult the dialogue on some aspects of consciousness or mind has proven to be when it takes place between a philosophically oriented discourse (in general terms, the philosophy of the mind) and empirical neuroscience, where both sides are dedicated to conceptual precision and share some common frame of reference. At least art history, unlike aesthetics, might be in the slightly more advantageous position of having an option of retracting such experiments: if such a dialogue turns out to be unproductive or too difficult, it can always redraw its demarcation line, reaffirming its primary identity as an object-centered discipline, focused on tangible objects and images. It is an agenda that has few competitors. In that retrenched position we could then leave all the "soft" issues of how art works in the mind to others.

Joseph Margolis

Toward Rapprochement

Let me offer a lesson that may bear instructively on Elkins's question about his "starting point"—to the effect that neither art history nor aesthetics has successfully explained or overcome the "disconnection" between the two disciplines.

I think of a lesson that can be easily drawn from reflecting on Cézanne's unfinished watercolors. If you look at them in a way that is akin to, but not quite the same as, playing with the gestalt phenomenon of figure and ground, you see that familiar objects begin to emerge, perceptually, from very small, somewhat uniformly scaled, informally but carefully brushed overlapping patches of different shades of green (and the like). By themselves, they have no obvious representational features. Cézanne introduces us here to a marvelous piece of pictorial magic, which, allowing for the great difference between watercolors and oils, invites comparison (at a distance) with his treatment of the oils in the late Mont Ste. Victoire canvasses.

Now, if you view this matter in terms of the details of his innovative way of working his magic, you may reasonably be said to do what belongs centrally to art criticism; and if you view it in terms of the development of Cézanne's distinctive way of treating the representation of nature and the emergence of his originality from the work of earlier figures of influence, you may be said to do what is central to art history. But if you turn instead to explore, in the company of the Cézanne example, the conceptual question of how we should characterize the very act of *perceiving* paintings and, in particular, perceiving pictorial representation, you would have turned to aesthetics or the philosophy of art, no matter how far you veered off from art-critical and art-historical interests narrowly construed. It is that sense of disconnection that makes aesthetics seem so dubious to critics, historians, and appreciative audiences.

I think we all realize that each of the three disciplines is prone to local forms of professional madness. Well, as a "philosopher," I can tell you that aesthetics or the philosophy of art is peculiarly prone to zealous excesses that too often implicate a kind of illiteracy regarding such disciplines as art criticism and art history and *their* data: a kind of analytic bungling as deep as anyone would ever dream of, often driven by philosophical priorities rather than art-critical or art-historical ones.

I myself would insist that philosophy (*a fortiori*, aesthetics) is, at its best, benignly parasitic ("second-order," as the academy says). It has no primary field of investigation of its own, and is normally engaged, as a serious practice, in a close analysis of the key conceptual distinctions of some other, more or less empirically minded inquiries like those of art criticism and art history—for instance, regarding the meaning of "perception" itself, in the context of examining problems like those posed by viewing a Cézanne watercolor in the light of conceptual puzzles collected and refined by knowledgeable philosophers of art (who take the trouble to inform themselves about the pertinent work of critics and historians—and artists). This way of construing matters is not meant to favor any particular philosophical ideology, unless the barest idea of relevance in the service of a unified larger undertaking is already suspect.

I certainly believe that specialists in criticism and art history would be less inclined to shun philosophers of art if something close to the relationship I suggest were respected on all sides. (My remarks are meant only as a specimen of how we might proceed; there are many different congenial ways of viewing the matter.) But behind the scenes, Kant obviously looms as a peculiarly intrusive influence. No doubt his emphasis on the analysis of our "affective" responses to artworks is an important piece of advice bearing on the theory of "aesthetic properties" and the "appreciation" of art itself. But, for my money, what Kant has to say about "the beautiful" and "the sublime" contributes remarkably little to the analysis that is needed: affective predicates are all but vacuous when separated from descriptive or interpretive predicates. "Beauty" may well be the most useless of these. (Kant, as we know, knew almost nothing about the arts.) The reason, finally, is this: the analysis of generic notions like beauty and appreciation are too easily detached from any study of particular artworks; they lend themselves to the philosopher's perverse inclination to study the supposed logic of abstract predicates in contextless ways. That surely courts disaster.

Kant's influence, I'm afraid, has entrenched some of the worst habits of philosophers to veer off from their primary responsibility to other disciplines and other well-defined runs of experience. There's nothing wrong with the study of the concepts of beauty and art and appreciation and interpretation unless, as the record confirms, it tends to be vacuous and contrived — literally, uninformed about what it needs to know. In fact, as things now stand, the concept of "aesthetic properties" has almost nothing to do with defining the discipline known as "aesthetics," where "aesthetics" includes what we also now call "the philosophy of art." The analysis of the concept of affective responses to artworks is never more than marginal to the analysis of the concept of artworks themselves, even though our responses are hardly marginal to what we count as art. There's the source of one important misunderstanding. Perhaps we had better disallow the discussion of these matters until after one's ninetieth birthday.

Crispin Sartwell

Starting from Scratch with Phenomenology

What I'm struck by as I read these words is the extent to which people were speaking past one another. Of course, I wasn't there, and it is probable that physical proximity—gestures and expressions—mitigated this to some extent. But each of the participants seemed intent on remaining within a circumscribed space, of enforcing a terminology or a set of canonical texts. In fact, it often seemed more like a collection of mini-lectures than a conversation. I mean that as a criticism not only of this particular exercise—which had its moments, since these are extremely smart people who have thought for years about these issues—but of the institutions in which the conversation is embedded.

If the question is the intersection of aesthetics and art history, then we had better focus, among other things, on the degree of specialization required of high-level academics. Once the trainings of two people have diverged for twenty years, so that they're not reading the same things or speaking with the same words or responding to the same set of problems, then it hardly matters that, in some sense, their subject matter is the same. They just are not going to be able to communicate very effectively. They're not going to want to read one another's papers, and so on. Maybe the incomprehension is going to be accompanied by just a little contempt as well.

Anyway, to do my own grandstanding for a moment, I am really not that interested in disciplinary boundaries. I'm not that interested in the border between art and nonart, or between art and religion, and so on. I'm really, really not interested in struggling yet again with categories like the modern and the postmodern. What I'm interested in is what people do and how they experience things. I would have liked to toss questions into this mix about things like gardening, or child-rearing, or hip hop: specific things with regard to which aesthetic and art-historical questions actually arise. Of course in dealing with stuff like that, both aestheticians and art historians will often want to start by ruling in or out: is it art? If it is, then we could at least talk about it in accord with a theory of what art is; it would at least take up a place in a history, and so on.

I had, I must admit, a pretty intensely anti-intellectual response to that conversation. I want to get you out of Soho for a minute, or at least away from Paul McCarthy; I even want to get you away from Kant, who might be the only real touchstone that all these folks recognize. (Though in passing, I think David Raskin asks the right—or *a* right— question: Do we really want to dissolve the world into consciousness, which is where we've been stuck since Kant?) I, myself, would want to start from scratch with a phenomenology of something: What sorts of things do we experience; how do we sort them out; what are the experiences like; and how do we tell the story of those things and of ourselves in relation to them? On that level aesthetics and art history are obviously entwined and mutually dependent, since art history has to figure out what it's a history of and a philosophy of, art has to respond to the actual things that it counts as art as those things unfold historically. The problem is certainly not principled or conceptual; it is, again, professional and professorial.

In this regard, I think the idea of beauty—while indeed insufferably general and vague—is still indispensable. It's still something people use; it still fundamentally informs peoples' practice and experience. It has a history, and that history bears some relation to the history of art and of other cultural practices. We could tell this history in a number of ways. Holding on to beauty is not merely a reactionary gesture or an insistence on reaching back before modernism, though those could also be a valid moments or strategies. But, if you see a perfect rose, you still want to say it's beautiful, don't you? Well, for God's sake, don't let your conceptual commitments keep you from doing so, because even those commitments don't keep you from having the experience. It's an "aesthetic" response, and it is not a merely formalist evaluation.

At any rate, it's at these most general nodes—"beauty" or "art" or "experience"—that disciplines can begin to collapse their divergent histories into one another. However, they have to want to.

Paul Crowther

Aesthetics in Art History (and Vice-Versa)

The Kantian and Hegelian traditions—in their different ways—each held historical factors as partially constitutive of artistic meaning; while the great tradition of German art history from Riegl to the early Panofsky posited that art-historical change centered on issues of aesthetic transformation. The reciprocal dependence of art-historical and aesthetic significance was acknowledged in the seminar by both adherents of both schools, even if it was not fully understood.

The importance of this reciprocal dependence has long been forgotten. In fact, recent developments in art history and aesthetics actively suppress it. In this essay I shall consider some of its ramifications mainly in relation to the limitations of contemporary art history.

A first problem arises from an influential consumerist mind-set whose major manifestation is a (putatively) "antifoundational" cultural relativism. This derives, in large part, from an unquestioning acceptance of the self-contradictory discourses of Foucault, Derrida, and the like.[19] Such relativism has distorted both art practice and the interpretative discourses consequent upon such practice. More specifically, it has reversed the order of dependence between these so that art practice is now understood primarily as a vehicle for the reflection of modes of reception and theory rather than as a mode of making.

This reversal is consolidated by the contentious supposition that Duchamp's readymades center on the creation of something artistically different, rather than something different from art. A supposition of this kind is tacitly racist to the profoundest degree (as well as being conceptually flawed).[20] The reason why is that while, for many thousands of years (and across many cultural boundaries), art has been bound up with the making of aesthetically significant images and forms, the Duchamp precedent seems to demand a redefinition. Rather than being acknowledged as, at best, a marginal Western art-critical strategy, it is seen as the paradigmatic art-creation activity in relation to which all else should be understood. The primacy of making is dismissed with a condescending sneer, or worse. Art per se is taken to amount to little more than ideas, theories, and their contexts of occurrence.

The dominant *contextualist* modes of recent art history have internalized this view with dogmatic insistency.[21] They reduce artistic meaning to factors bound up with the image's documentary and persuasive effects, and the social and other contextual elements which enable these. Apart from the occasional discussion of technique and artists' materials, such approaches are overwhelmingly consumer- and context-oriented.

It might be thought that the frequent contextualist use of such terms as "artistic production" argues otherwise. However, we must recognize that the tacit correlate of production is consumption and that this pairing is itself a deployment of Western consumerist patterns of instrumental reason.

In fact, matters get worse. For, in contextualist terms, production is understood as a composite phenomenon emergent from a broader field of signification. Within this, *the process of making is reduced to a function of its component "signifying practices" rather than understood as a unifying activity which directs those practices*. The upshot is that what is distinctive to the making and meaning of visual images per se is either repressed or distorted. It is recreated as the academic consumer's disembodied fantasy *image* of what making is supposed to involve.

This consumerist distortion has also carried over into the understanding of art history as a discipline itself. Over the past twenty years or so, the key German tradition referred to earlier has been looked at again, and many of its key works have appeared in English translation for the first time. However, the analyses of these texts have emphasized how they enable us to understand the way in which art history has been "constructed" as an area of "discourse." The active core of this tradition—its conception of art as a formative aesthetic activity—is understood not in terms of its continuing relevance for the art object but rather as an idea in the development of art history itself.

What I am describing then is, literally, a Western conceptual *degradation* of the intimate link between art making and its objects. There is also a smug consumerist philosophical complacency in the analytic tradition, associated with the institutional definitions of art, which gives succor to this. It holds that the concept of art has simply changed. It has become an "open" concept which *must* be redefined so as to accommodate a vast range of practices based on material not made by the artist. But against this, while such a change may be true *de facto*, its validity *de juris* is an entirely different matter. All sorts of ethical problems and conceptual difficulties arise, and if a sustained alternative to this occidental smugness is available, it must be grasped with alacrity.[22]

Fortunately, there is such an alternative.[23] A useful starting point for understanding it consists in what might be called *the intrinsic significance of the image*. The ubiquity of the image and decorative forms across vastly different times and places suggests that they have some compelling aesthetic power. Only on this assumption can we explain the extraordinary range of magical and communicative functions which different cultures invest in them.

Contextualist art history might attempt to dismiss this significance as follows: "Art" is a privileged form of representation which reflects and consolidates the interests of white male middle-class Eurocentric patriarchy. Its informative and persuasive power arises through representing visual reality from the viewpoint of this dominant and *controlling* power group. Art's privileged status is due to its provision of luxury commodities which can set their consumers apart from others in terms of social kudos.

Again, however, we must ask what it is about the visual image which supports these and other functions, and, especially, what it is about art which *enables* it to sustain the privileged social status assigned to it? Why should it be taken to be worthy of such kudos? If the kudos is based on aesthetic pleasure being regarded as superior, what is it about such pleasure which allows it to be so regarded?

The problem is, here, that when all the social functions of art and the standard questions of iconography and iconology have been mapped out and analyzed, the fundamental question remains unanswered, namely what is it about the visual image which enables it to sustain such breadth of meaning? What is the basis of its formative power? We are left, in other words, with the problem of the intrinsic significance of the image.

In non-Western art this dimension is especially to the fore. This is not because of some modernist myth of such art's closeness to the throbbing primal rhythms of the universe or whatever, but because it more manifestly recognizes, and acts upon, a very straightforward truth. This is the fact that, in the very act of making an image (irrespective of one's practical intentions and subsequent uses of the image) one literally acts upon the world, and in so doing, changes one's relation to both the represented object and to oneself, and to existence in more general terms.

To put this more technically, *to make a visual image involves acting on reality in a way that changes the existing relation of subject and object of experience at all levels.* This, in the barest outline, is the intrinsic significance of the made visual image. If, therefore (as I have done at great length elsewhere), we can identify the factors and implications involved in more detail, we will have a worthwhile explanation of what is distinctive to the making and enjoyment of visual images. We will have a genuine *theory of the image*, rather than a mere history of its uses and social meaning.

Contextualist art history might respond to all this by dismissing such an approach as "ahistorical." This is indicative of a further problem within contextualism itself. Such art history likes to legitimize itself through a familiar binary opposition between the "historical" and the "ahistorical." The former involves the understanding of events, persons, and activities in their original contexts of enactment, on the basis of institutional, cultural, social, economic, racial, and gender factors. The "ahistorical" attempts to formulate "timeless" truths based on its object of investigation being analyzed without reference to the litany of factors just noted. It goes without saying that, for the contextualists, "ahistorical" is seen as a methodological flaw to be avoided at all costs. (The term "essentialist" is a related sneer.)

Now it might be argued that the idea of image-making having an intrinsic significance over and above its historically specific uses is something ahistorical, and thus, an empty abstraction. But, it must also be noted that the distinction between the historical and ahistorical per se is itself an even greater abstraction. There is a missing term involved, namely diachronic art history—understood not in the derivative sense of patterns of reception, but in the primary one of *chronologically successive transformations of making*.

The contextualist approach privileges the synchronic dimension of history as the authentic mode, and marginalizes the primary diachronic aspect. However, no phenomenon can exist in purely synchronous terms. Its character and significance in a specific place and time will necessarily be informed by factors (direct or indirect) which were in place long before and which may survive long after. Indeed, with some activities and institutions, the diachronic dimension may be of more importance than the synchronic.

Art is a case in point, for what establishes itself as canonic does not do so in arbitrary terms; it offers achievements which exceed the time and place of their creation. To make sense of this we need, therefore, to acknowledge that the "other" of synchronic history is the diachronic, and not the ahistorical. But if this is the case, then we need some enduring factor which is the basis of diachronic transmission in artistic practice.

This, of course, is the role played by the intrinsic significance of image-making (among other factors). In mediating between synchronic and diachronic history, it has a transhistorical rather than "ahistorical" importance. The mistaken accusation of ahistoricality, in other words, ends up by confirming rather than refuting the idea of intrinsic significance.

If, therefore, we are to theorize art in adequate terms, we require a key negotiation between the making of art, its intrinsic significance, and the way in which this is instantiated in a diachronic horizon of historical transmission. It is especially possible to conduct such negotiation on the basis of a redevelopment and substantial extension of Kant's aesthetics and, most notably, his theory of fine art and aesthetic ideas.[24] In his theory, originality is, in part, constitutive of artistic meaning. Hence, insofar as originality is conceptually tied to artistic achievement in the dimension of diachronic history, this allows the requisite negotiations to be made in some depth. Aesthetics and art history find, thereby, a zone of authentic interaction.

Mary Rawlinson

Beauty and Politics

Philosophers tend to position the visual arts at a distance from philosophy itself in a hierarchy of activities. Both Kant and Hegel, for example, in comparing the "aesthetic value of the various fine arts," locate poetry, not painting, nearest to the discursive domain of philosophy. Operating in the ineluctably universalizing medium of language, poetry, in its formalities of style, self-consciousness, and power of nonsensuous representation, approaches the horizon of philosophy. Of all the arts, it is the least dependent upon sensible intuition and the least likely to degenerate into what Kant calls the "merely agreeable." Poetry, however, never actually enters into the discursive domains of science, politics, and philosophy that are said by Hegel to define the "serious pursuits of the dialectician."

Painting, which Kant identifies with landscape gardening, interior decoration, and fashion, is, like music, too "agreeable" to be associated with philosophy. An art is "merely agreeable," Kant argues, if its purpose is "merely enjoyment" and its pleasure attached to "mere sensations." A *fine* art, on the other hand, stimulates a pleasure in presentations that are "ways of cognizing." Its standard is the "reflective power of judgment," not "sensuous experience (*Sinnenempfindung*)."[25]

Though painting is a *visual* art in Kant's own classification, its approach to the borders of philosophy through the precincts of fine art depends on an abandonment of its appeal to sensuous intuition. The visual impressions that it offers—its evocation of a certain texture, a particular light—must be subordinated to its direct appeal, through narrative or formal properties, to the cognitive or moral faculties. To be a *fine* and come nearer to philosophy the painting must invoke a moral idea.[26]

Though distant from philosophy and sharing no borders with it, painting lies somewhat nearer to the discursive discipline than does music, as it "can penetrate much further into the region of ideas." As the art of design, painting underlies all the other visual arts. It provides a site for the demonstration of the idea of the sublime in nature. Its narrative content provides a visual representation or analogue to certain ideas, of justice or piety, for example. Finally, painting and other visual arts, insofar as they exhibit the repeatable form of an artistic style, Kant argues, can be said to be analogous to gesture in speech. In the visual style, the artist gives expression directly to "what and how he has thought"—what Arthur Danto refers to as the artist's "reasons." Thus, the nearer painting comes to philosophy, the less it seems to be painting, a specifically *visual* art, and the more it seems to be discursive argument by other means.

The itinerary of painting in contemporary philosophy has not been dissimilar. With regard to this evaluation of painting, as Diarmuid Costello suggests, the distinction between a modernist aesthetic and a postmodernist aesthetic makes no difference. In the latter, as in Kant and Hegel, when painting comes near to philosophy, it is even taken up into the domain of philosophy as a kind of exemplar, its specificity as painting and its particular sensuous visibility are left behind.

> The painter is looking, his face turned slightly and his head leaning towards one shoulder. He is staring at a point to which, even though it is invisible, we, the spectators, can easily assign an object, since it is we, ourselves, who are that point: our bodies, our faces, our eyes. The spectacle he is observing is thus doubly invisible: first, because it is not represented within the space of the painting, and, second, because it is situated precisely in that blind point, in that essential hiding place into which our gaze disappears from ourselves at the moment of our actual looking. The tall, monotonous rectangle occupying the whole left portion of the canvas within the picture reconstitutes in the form of a surface the invisibility in depth of what the artist is observing: that space in which we are, and which we are. From the eyes of the painter to what he is observing there runs a compelling line that we, the onlookers, have no power of evading: it runs through the real picture and emerges from its surface to join the place from which we see the painter observing us; this dotted line reaches out to us ineluctably, and links us to other representation of the picture.[27]

Here in this famous analysis of Velasquez's *Las Meninas* at the beginning of *Les Mots et Les Choses*, Michel Foucault goes on for some pages to analyze the optics and politics of the scene. Almost nothing is said of its sensuous visibility beyond a mention of the "pink and grey" color of the Infanta's dress, Summarizing, Foucault remarks that this painting constitutes "the representation of Classical representation." It is the representation by visual means of the logic of representation that defines an epoch of thought. Foucault's analysis confirms the painting's location within the borders of fine art. The painting stimulates, not a pleasure in the sheen of the silk or the Infanta's frizzy blonde halo or the burnished glow of the dwarf's skin, not a pleasure in sensuous intuitions, but a demonstration by other means of a philosophical form, what Kant called a "way of cognizing." This postmodern analysis of the work as a "way of seeing" is entirely consistent with the modernism of Kant and Hegel.[28]

Toward the end of the analysis Foucault remarks on the dog lying on the floor in the right-hand corner of the painting, noting the deep reliefs with which it is depicted and "the light playing on its silky hair." Only this object, he suggests, is meant to be merely a thing seen, rather than an element in this logic of representation, and only here in describing the painting does Foucault use a sensuous, textural word like "silky."

Jean Starobinski repeats this Kantian-Hegelian approach to painting as the embodiment of a form of mind in his volume *1789: The Emblems of Reason*.[29] David's *The Oath of the Horatii* serves as symptom of culture, the emblem of revolutionary ideology. Like Foucault in the case of *Las Meninas*, Starobinski analyzes the *Oath* almost exclusively in terms of its narrative content, as a dramaturgical scene. Codes of gender, political equality, and filial sacrifice overlay and reinforce one another in Starobinski's interpretation of the *Oath*, without regard for the brilliant red of the near brother's cockade, the anatomical precision of the father's outstretched calf, or the gauzy sheerness of the mother's headdress and the sculptural effects of her drapery.

And, I hesitate to allude to those infamous shoes. In Heidegger's analysis of Van Gogh's painting one might almost forget that the subject *is* a painting and not the *actual shoes* of the peasant woman or the German soil to which they supposedly belong. In commentaries by Schapiro and Derrida, the question of whose shoes these are continues to burn—the peasant woman's, a city dweller's, Van Gogh's own, or Heidegger's by some miraculous transposition—and the painting serves as the site of contestation for Anglo-American analytic philosophy and contemporary French thought. But the discussions do not say much about the sensuous textures of the painting; indifferent to the controversy, the awkward shoes remain quiet and still, beyond attribution.

So, philosophy valorizes the discursive discipline nearest to its own formality—poetry or literature—distancing itself from the sensuous materiality of objects that might be "merely agreeable." And, when philosophy does approaches painting, it represses specific sensuous visibilities in favor of formal ideas. So, the first thing to be noted about the discussion in "The Art Seminar" is that the apparent difference between philosophy and art history over the status of the work of art is merely apparent. As the discussion demonstrates, both disciplines approach the work either as the occasion for a debate over formal issues of value and judgment, or as the embodiment of an historically determined form of thinking and a symptom of culture which must be interpreted.

Whether art historians or philosophers, the discussants (with one exception) seem to be comfortable with the reduction of the work to the status of an historical artifact. Indeed, there are any number of important questions that are asked and answered by art history from this point of view, many of which are identified in the course of the discussion. What were the conditions of production for this work? Why did this artist choose to represent this body in that way? How does this work represent what Hegel would call the "spirit" of the people who produced it, their *Weltanschauung*? What are the parameters of taste in this epoch and how are they reflected in the valorization of certain works? How did these people in this time and place decide what to keep and what to throw away? However, neither the discussion's contrast between a modern and postmodern aesthetic, nor the difference between philosophers and art historians is relevant here. The reductive analysis of the work as a symptom of culture belongs first to Hegel.[30] Does the work of art exceed this analysis upon which both the philosophers and historians of "The Art Seminar" seem to agree? Once the work is analyzed as an historical artifact exemplifying a "way of seeing" or "way of cognizing," is it exhausted, or is there a remainder not yet exposed in this approach?

Perhaps the anxiety in the discussion over issues of value and the graphic proposal to forcibly excise Kant from the body of aesthetics are themselves symptoms that this historicizing of the work does not altogether get at what matters in art and aesthetic experience. What is it about Kant's approach that is so disturbing? Perhaps, it is that, in spite of his disregard for the specific sensuous qualities of the work, Kant's central idea is that our experience of the work of art makes a difference philosophically. It teaches us something that we can learn no other way. Being clear on two crucial points of Kant's project, then, may open up a new horizon for joining the analysis of the work of art with the questions of philosophy.

1. *Beauty is not a property*. There is significant confusion in the discussion about why Kant takes a philosophical interest in beauty and what he means by it. Danto is quite right that beauty is not a property, but a value, though he himself goes on to discuss beauty as distinct from the gory or the dainty, as if it were, indeed, a property. But, the gory or the dainty can be beautiful. Take Lucian Freud's paintings: the bodies he paints are not themselves beautiful in any conventional sense. What is beautiful is the *paintings*, not the bodies. So, works like Paul McCarthy's that have even a "repulsive" content may be beautiful.

Moreover, in Kant's analysis beauty is not, as Diarmuid Costello suggests, attributed to the subjective or a property of subjective "feeling." Beauty in nature, Kant remarks, belongs to the *thing*, but "artistic beauty is a *beautiful presentation* of a thing." The presentation, embodied in the thing, requires genius and is already something subjective, even before it provokes a feeling in the viewer. Kant does not tarry to wonder about the remarkable capacity of art to present the specificity of an alien other. Rather than focusing on the specificity of style, he moves quickly to render the work of art as the embodiment of a "way of cognizing." Instead of the specificity of style, he focuses on the "aesthetics ideas" which can be detached from the sensuous presentation. Like Hegel, he identifies beauty with spirit (*Geist*), and with the nondiscursive presentation of "rational ideas." Still, his location of beauty in the presentation which supersedes the distinction between subject and object leaves open the possibility of returning to the specificity of style and the alien other that the viewer encounters in it.

2. *Beauty is not an historically determined taste*. Davey and others misunderstand what Kant means by "taste" because they confuse it with subjective preference. Of course, there are historical tides in the evaluation of works of art. Taste, in the sense of what people prefer, is something about which histories can be written. But, this is not at all what Kant analyzes. Davey's confusion stems from his erroneous belief that the artwork has no "extra-aesthetic" purpose for Kant. Indeed, it does. While Kant distinguishes aesthetic engagement from any interest of *utility*—this is, after all, an object for which the subject does not even have a concept—he links aesthetic experience directly to moral interest. We like what is beautiful, Kant insists, in the way that we do, only because "we refer (*Rücksicht)* the beautiful to the morally good." In fact, beauty is the "symbol of morality" and the very purpose of its analysis in the

> *Critique of Judgment* is to provide a bridge between empirical experience and the purely intelligible region of the moral idea.[31] Aesthetic experience overarches the "great gulf" between these two domains precisely because of the phenomenological content alluded to in the remarks by Thierry de Duve that, ironically, elicited so much laughter.

While much of the discussion confused taste with preference, Kant's analysis does focus on the way in which a work of art *compels* our liking. We experience that aesthetic liking quite differently from other sensuous preferences, say for chocolate over vanilla. An essential feature of the experience is that another would be compelled—in the way that I am—to admit the value of the work. We might disagree over the best flavor of ice cream, but it would be rather silly to argue about it: it is merely a matter of personal preference. But, if I say that Motherwell's *Elegy to the Spanish Republic* or the work of Paul McCarthy is lousy art, Danto will want to argue with me about it. And, he will have *reasons* to bring to bear in order to compel me to admit that, though I may not like it, it is good or valuable art. In fact, anyone with a wide experience of art has often been compelled to admit the value of something that he or she doesn't particularly like. So, the work of art exists in a space where our disagreements matter and are not mere differences of preference.

Thus, my experience of the work of art immediately invokes the intersubjectivity of my *own* experience, in the sense that there is *another* implied in it. It is for this reason that Thierry de Duve is quite right to link Kant's aesthetics to political hope. And, it is not, as Nicholas Davey claims, that Kant assumes as given an intersubjectivity "unaffected by tradition, history, or social circumstance."

The apprehension of the sublime, for example, in Kant's analysis explicitly depends on education and cultural formation. What is given in experience is, rather, a kind of challenge. In the distinction between the particularity of preference and the claims of taste or beauty, I am challenged to say why this or that work seems valuable to me in the way that it does. We could name it, in homage to Arthur Danto's account of the rationality of art, "a call for reasons." We merely express preferences, but we argue about value. And there is an urgency to the debate, for it determines, as de Duve remarks, "what we shall keep and what we shall throw away." It determines, as Dominic Willsdon points out, "what gets into the museum," not just into the building, but into the historical record itself—what is not forgotten.

Nicholas Davey is quite right, however, to be suspicious of this linkage of aesthetics and ethics or politics. If we accept Kant's disengagement from the specificity of the work, are we not left with the space of a "common" sense? Is not philosophy's allergy to the specificity of the work of art linked to the idea that the other is essentially the same, like me? Would the turn to beauty, then, not be a form of nostalgia, a return, as Elaine Scarry has pointed out, to the value of fraternity, a politics in which the other is already identified with the "science of man," already marked male, white, and European, "like me?"[32]

Perhaps, philosophy's historical allergy to painting and the visual arts stems precisely from the challenge they pose to this politics of the same.

Plato speaks of a quarrel, an enmity already ancient in his time, between philosophy and art. An attack on "scene-painting" and perspectivism constitute a main theme in Socrates' condemnation of art as a dangerous and soul-corrupting illusion. The figure of truth is drawn in this Platonic metaphysic precisely in contrast to the image of the artist, who is not the mere opposite of the philosopher (*enantion*), but his other (*eteron*): a pretender to the place of the philosopher, who must be put in his place. This figure remains intact throughout the history of metaphysics and we find it in Hegel's text where it is against art that the speculative operations of philosophy are described. Nietzsche names this metaphysical structure which we find in place from Plato to Hegel—in which philosophy opposes the perspectivism of art—the fable of the one true world.

What is at issue for both Plato and Hegel in the philosopher's opposition to art is the problem of the signature. The specificity of style calls into question the generality of philosophical truth. The sensuous materiality of the painting resists in its specificity any attempt to reduce it to a general theory or form. If, as Derrida has remarked, all is not to be thought at one go, it isn't to be painted at one go either. So, the specific differences that arise in the field of painting, the multiplicity of signatures, provide a countermovement to the seemingly inexorable march of the concept of the same or the "in general" as it formalizes and regularizes every domain of life.

It is against this background that there arises the problem of novelty analyzed by Benjamin and Bataille among others. "At a time," Hegel remarks, "when the universal gathers such strength, less must be expected of the individual and he must expect less for himself."[33] At a time when virtually every domain of life is regulated by generalized images and principles, the individual must think of himself as "only an instance" of a general form of consciousness. Similarly, in an age of mechanical reproduction, objects lose their "aura" or become, as Heidegger suggests, "ersatz." The technical possibilities of reproduction qualify the originality of the object and render it at once disposable and subject to substitution. The practical triumph of the concept of the general, its embodiment in systems of production and regulation that ensure the reproduction of the same in every register, seems to imperil the very existence of the painting as a unique sensuous occasion.

But, there is a countertheme woven into the history of metaphysics. In the *Symposium* Socrates recognizes sensuous beauty as initiating the soul's dialectical ascent. Moreover, as Luce Irigaray has noted, in Diotima's speech the concern is much less with the ascent than with a transiting, a crossing of borders, between materiality and the invisibilities of thought.[34]

A beautiful thing causes us to love it. It attacks our eyes and makes us desire it, engendering a longing for its presence. Its representatives, a slide or reproduction, only mark its absence. Its visibility becomes lodged within me and takes up an itinerary of its own. Associations accrue and other impressions are woven into it. It provokes me to travel great distances to see it and to make significant physical sacrifices in order to be in its presence. And, my own physical safety may be worth sacrificing to secure the painting's unique materiality. When it is lost, there is no substitute for the sensuous materiality that has been excised from experience, no more than there is a substitution possible for the dead other.

While philosophy seems to require an "alienation from the sensuous," in fact this countertheme within it recognizes sensuous beauty as a portal, a site of transition or conversion. Inherently unstable, painting provides the scene for violent border crossings, disturbing transitions from sensuous materiality to the invisible idea. The violent interpenetration of these incommensurables defines the work, as Hegel argues.[35] The sensuous beauty of the painting offers the chiasmatic figure of two alien series—material and spiritual—intertwined. A painting, as Merleau-Ponty remarks, "mixes up all our categories—essence and existence, imaginary and real, visible and invisible." It offers the "imaginary texture of the real" in its sensuous materiality and provokes ideas that are not the opposite of the sensible but its "lining and depth."[36]

Moreover, the painting mixes up my experience with that of the other who always eludes me in ordinary experience and whom philosophy has only been able to establish "by analogy" or in virtue of some reductive "in common." Descartes remarks that a theory of painting will always require a metaphysics. It does so not only because it provides a site of transmutation between the visible and the invisible, but also because the painting provides a material field in which the other is encountered as an *immediacy*. Painting offers the transposition of a style of seeing into a material embodiment *from which that seeing can be recovered*. Like a membrane between sensuous material and invisible idea, the painting facilitates a displacement within the subject and the emergence of an actual other.

The painting's evocation of invisible ideas and the way of seeing with which they are associated reveal a style of experience that can be reconstituted from the painting's sensuous immediacy. This experience of the other cannot be reduced to the painting's narrative content, nor, to its instantiation of some institutionalized code, nor its legibility as a symptom of culture. The painting does not offer its ideas according to the logic of form and content or law and instance. In explicating this chiasmatic figure of painting Merleau-Ponty refers to Proust as the one who has gone farthest in exploring the borders of this territory and in demonstrating that these ideas cannot be detached from their sensible appearance.

At the beginning of the fifth volume of *À la recherche du temps perdu*, the great writer Bergotte, who has been the hero's most important philosophical and literary mentor, dies. Ill and ordered to rest in bed, Bergotte comes across an article by a critic on Vermeer's *View of Delft*, a painting "which he adored and imagined that he knew by heart." The critic refers to "a little patch of yellow wall (which Bergotte could not remember) so well painted that it was "of a beauty that was sufficient in itself." Bergotte cannot resist rising from his sick bed to go in search of this beauty. Feeling dizzy and ill, he comes at last to the Vermeer "which he remembered as more striking, more different from anything else he knew, but in which, thanks to the critic's article, he noticed for the first time, some small figures in blue, that the sand was pink, and, finally, the precious substance of the tiny patch of yellow wall … painted by an artist destined to be forever unknown and barely identified under the name Vermeer." Bergotte's dizziness increases and he dies before leaving the gallery, having sacrificed his life for a glimpse of a "the little patch of yellow wall ... precious in itself." Proust insists though "that the idea that Bergotte was not permanently dead is by no means improbable. ... They buried him, but all through that night of mourning, in the lighted shop windows, his books, arranged three by three, kept vigil like angels with outstretched wings and seemed, for him who was no more, the symbol of his resurrection." Just as the perception of the critic generously yielded the pleasure of the "little patch of yellow wall" for Bergotte, so Bergotte's own writing will revive his perception again and again in his readers.[37]

The "little patch of yellow wall" is "precious in itself," not because it is a symptom of culture, the emblem of a form, or the artifact of a *Weltanschauung*. Its value resides in its sensuous immediacy and the evocation of another's perception. It is just that beautiful and compelling yellow laid down by a hand not my own, and nothing else. Before it, the prolixity of philosophy, its desire to turn things into words and the sensuous into a form, is stymied. The little patch of yellow wall, "precious in itself," does not seem to require the supplement of philosophical commentary to exert its claim to truth.

Painting challenges philosophy's understanding of its own figure of truth. In "The Art Seminar," de Duve contrasts the distinction between the particular and the general with that between the singular and the universal, a contrast between instantiation and exemplarity. But, the singularity of the work of art is not only that it cannot be subsumed under a rule. Its singularity does not open up the domain of a "common sense." Rather, it gives rise to an experience of the other as alien, an other than I can know immediately, who is yet not like me. This experience reveals features of experience that are not derived from my own. These features are universal in that they are, via the work, transposable from one experience to another, but they do not imply any figure of the "in general" or "in common." They remain alien to me, even as they are realized in my own experience. Thus, the work of art gives rise to the idea that "the" universal is multiple, a field of transposable figures irreducible to any generality.

The work of art presents truth as contingent, as inseparable from the conditions of its sensuous presentation. Color and line, of just this consistency, laid on just this way, just this once. There is no way of deducing a painting from some general rule, any more than you could deduce Renoir from Turner or Milton Avery from Matisse. It is neither as an instance of a general rule, nor as the emblem of a simple universal that the painting gives access to invisibilities or ideas, but in the irreducible specificity of its contingent materiality.

As contingent, the painting is also unique and irreplaceable. Once, only once, and never again. The reproductions through which it is distributed are inadequate to demonstrate the unreproducibility of the painting.[38] Thus, like Bergotte, we make our pilgrimages at some sacrifice. And, in its sensuous specificity, the painting provokes directly an intimation of our own mortality.

The painting's irreducible sensuous specificity imposes upon me an other than is not merely an instance of a general form, who is not an other *like me*. I find my thought and feeling claimed by a sensuous vision that is foreign to me, just as I am displaced from the narrative position in my own consciousness by the technology of reading. It is in this difference, not by virtue of a hypothetical *sensus communis* or the assumption of some other form of the "in common," that I come to know the other of the painting. And, like Bergotte, I cannot help but feel gratitude at the generosity of impressions offered to me by the work, gratitude for the pleasure of the "little patch of yellow wall."

The artwork achieves epochal effects. Philosophy regularly inscribes as its inaugural gesture an epoche, a dislodging of the subject from the natural attitude of prejudices, assumptions, and conventions. Yet, philosophy proceeds, as Husserl does, for example, as if the mere articulation of the concept of an epoche were sufficient to bring it about, as if the effecting of such an epoche required no work other than stating the task. Displacing me in favor of the other, the painting, like the book, has the capacity to effect an actual suspension of the natural attitude, as the nude in Manet's *Olympia* disturbs us and reveals a whole logic of subjection merely by looking back.

But, what does this critique of the epistemology of art have to do with the question of politics or ethics invoked by Thierry de Duve? In the *Passions of the Soul* Descartes remarks:

> When the first encounter with some object surprises us, and we judge it to be new or very different from what we formerly knew, or from what we supposed that it ought to be, that causes us to wonder and be surprised; and because that may happen before we in any way know whether this object is agreeable to us or is not so, it appears to me that wonder is the first of all the passions; and it has no opposite, because if the object which presents itself has nothing in it that surprises us, we are in no wise moved regarding it and we consider it without passion.[39]

Painting may, as Kant suggested, have an ethical or political effect, but not because of any alienation from its sensuous material, nor in virtue of its narrative content, nor because it conveys as an instance some logical form or cultural complex. Rather painting may have an ethical effect in the power of its specific contingent sensuous material to surprise or provoke wonder. Diarmuid Costello was right that the attribution of beauty to a work is equivalent to Warhol's "Wow!" And, he was right in saying that this experience inaugurates a debate about why a work seems compelling and valuable. But, he is wrong in thinking that this "begs the question." It is precisely this experience of being accosted by the work, being set in motion by it, that lies at the heart of aesthetic experience. It is the reason we value any art, as well as the link between art and politics.

Unique, mortal, and specific, the frivolous excess of a "little patch of yellow wall" opens to me the borders of another alien experience. I find myself displaced by the other who is not like me and whose availability does not depend upon some concept or institution of the commonplace. And, my encounter with the alien other is accompanied by gratitude for the gift of pleasure afforded by the "little patch of yellow wall." As Bataille remarks in his essay on Proust, *The Love of Truth and Justice and the Socialism of Marcel Proust*, "There is something passionate, generous and sacred in us which exceeds the representations of the mind: it is this excess which makes us human." A certain transcendence of the material over words subverts the philosopher's attempt to convert the sensuous material into a discursive property or to render the work anything other than the gift of the other.

Hegel is right to criticize Kant and any moral philosophy that attempts to reduce the sensuous substance of our actual moral experiencc to formal rules and universal principles. Painting suggests a politics that begins instead from my gratitude to other who has gone before, who laid down the surprise, whose generosity afforded me the pleasure of novelty or travel, the pleasure of transgressing the boundaries not only of the sensuous and the idca, but of my own experience. Painting, then, supplies an occasion to escape the fundamental narcissism of ordinary vision, the ineluctable tendency in ordinary experience to see one's self in the other, not the other in his difference. Frivolous and excessive, painting occasions a wonder before the other and a crossing of borders that may be the beginning of ethical life.

Ján Bakoš

Art History versus Aesthetics in East Central Europe

A short notice concerning the art history/aesthetics relationship from an east-central-European point of view:

It is well known that the idea of the unity of art history and aesthetics had already been rejected in nineteenth century. In the name of scientific objectivity and impartiality, Winckelmann's historical normativism was replaced by historical relativism.[40] The expulsion of aesthetics from the realm of art history was justified later by means of a neo-Kantian model of the two families of sciences.[41] Aesthetics was regarded as the systematic discipline and art history as the historical discipline *par excellence* focusing on particularities.[42]

Art historians realized that they were not able to get rid of aesthetic judgment and that they could not avoid projecting the aesthetic norms of contemporary (mostly avant-garde) art into their interpretations of history.[43] Despite that, they were not willing to renounce the divorce of art history from aesthetics. Art historians continued to regard asthetics as part of the philosophy or psychology of reception. Even now, within poststructuralism and deconstructionism they are willing to accept aesthetics only if it conceived of as a history of taste, so that the aesthetic canon is regarded as a historical and ideological construct.[44]

Because it still keeps to epistemological stereotypes of modernism, east-central-European art history has not re-examined or rethought the relationship between aesthetics and the history of art.[45] Art historians and aestheticians in that region ignore one other, and don't ever pose Elkins's topical question "Why don't art historians attend aesthetic conferences?" Consequently, current attempts by some aestheticians and philosophers to blur the borders between art history and aesthetics have either been dismissed or critiqued as ahistorical and antiscientific.[46] The aesthetic implication of Hans Belting's appeal for the re-examination of an anthropological dimension of the history of art (an appeal inspired by the process of globalization) still goes unnoticed.[47]

Alexander Nehamas

Beauty Links Art History and Aesthetics

The hero's corpse in *Death of Marat* is beautiful, Arthur Danto says, not because David always painted beautiful bodies (he did: even the blind, begging Belissarius retains his warrior's musculature) but because, by posing the body as if it were part of a Deposition, David wanted to connect Marat's suffering with the passion of Jesus and thus inspire his audience with revolutionary zeal. This is how beauty and aesthetics find their way into the history of art: as the explanation of how aesthetic features of paintings illuminate historical meaning. Diarmuid Costello, though, will have none of it. He finds talk of beauty almost completely useless in the discussion of art. He argues, no doubt correctly, that to say that a painting is beautiful is most often simply to pay it a vague compliment, which is filled out and becomes telling only when "beautiful" is replaced by more specific terms, like "clunky," "delicate," or "light." Beauty, he asserts, casts no light on art.

Is one of these people right and the other wrong? That would be the case, if they were talking about the same thing, but the answers they give to the question "Why is that beautiful?" are so different that it is difficult to believe that they are asking the same question. For Danto, beauty is one of many distinct features to be found in a painting, coordinate with ugliness, stateliness, or massiveness, the presence of which he wants to explain by means of its contribution to the work's meaning. Costello, though, takes beauty to signify a generic and empty compliment to a painting, which serves its purpose if it starts a conversation, but he wants to replace it as soon as possible with the more specific features that are subordinate to it. Costello asks why *we call paintings beautiful* in the first place; Danto asks why *artists make beautiful paintings* (assuming we have already determined that they are beautiful).

Perhaps these are one and the same question after all, our reason for calling a painting beautiful being that the artist has made it so. Yet, although Danto begins by asking "Why is a work beautiful?" he goes on to explain not the beauty of *Death of Marat* but the beauty of Marat's corpse—and these are not at all the same thing. *Death of Marat* may well be a beautiful painting, but that is not because Marat's corpse is beautiful—there is no necessary connection between the beauty of an element of a painting and the beauty of the painting to which it belongs. We cannot answer Costello's question by pointing out that some of the elements of the painting are beautiful, since in each case the question "And why is *that* beautiful?" can be asked again and demands an answer in which "beautiful" is replaced by a more specific term. But we can never say something like "Because it is supposed to bring to mind the body of Jesus": such answers presuppose that we are already satisfied with our reasons for thinking that it is beautiful in the first place and beg Costello's question.

In fact, nothing prevents a painting that is beautiful—in Costello's sense—from depicting a body that Danto would be right to consider ugly. In many cases, the ugliness of the element may be in part responsible for the beauty of the whole. Ghirlandaio's *Old Man with a Child* is an obvious example: the tenderness with which the man and the child in his arms are looking at each other is poignant precisely because the man's ugly nose does not hinder the tenderness between them. And although it is considerably more difficult to think of an ugly painting that depicts a beautiful body, I believe that John Currin's *Heartless*, like much of the rest of his work, fits the bill.

The beauty with which Danto is struck is, as he has said before, "really as obvious as blue: one does not have to work at seeing it when it is there": Motherwell's *Elegies for the Spanish Republic* stopped him in his tracks the moment he saw them, although he knew nothing about the work at the time.[48] This is clearly not true of the compliment, however vague, that Costello has in mind: it can take time—sometimes a very long time—to find a painting beautiful if "beautiful" is, as he believes, another way of saying that it is good. For Danto, however, beauty is very different from artistic success. The value of *Death of Marat* does not depend directly on the beauty of Marat's body but on its appropriateness to the painting's revolutionary content. By contrast, the beauty of Salgado's photographs of the displaced makes them dissonant and jarring: "If beauty is internally connected to the content of a work, it can be a criticism of the work that it is beautiful when it is inappropriate for it to be so."[49] This suggests that Danto—not unreasonably—thinks that *being beautiful* is identical with *looking good*: both Marat's corpse and Delgado's photographs are undeniably good-looking, but their looks do not by themselves determine artistic value and, as in all cases when they conform to our own standards of what counts as looking good, are just about the first thing we notice about them.

Since the standards of what looks good change over time, what counts as beautiful in this sense is historically conditioned, as both James Elkins and Richard Woodfield suggest: David gives Marat's corpse a set of features and a pose that we (still) easily associate with beautiful bodies.[50] Such standards may be quite widely shared at any particular time,[51] but they are subject to diverse influences over longer periods. One of the reasons the depiction of the naked human body has taken so many forms over the centuries is that the interpretation of the body's shape was often determined by contemporary fashion in clothes. If you look at the shape that a certain period's fashionable clothes give to a body and subtract the clothes, the result is the version of the naked body as each period would like it to look.[52]

Is beauty as Costello understands it—the most general compliment we give to pictures—subject to the same historical conditions? Of course, tastes change; different paintings, painters, and genres become more or less prominent at different times. And, what belongs to history, especially to the history of art, has a profound effect on what counts as looking good as time unfolds. Elkins makes an interesting point: Marat's corpse may appear beautiful not only *in order to* call the Deposition to mind but also because it actually *does*.

Still, it is generally easier for people at some particular time to agree about the beauty of Marat's body than about the pictures each judges to be beautiful as Costello understands that judgment. Standards for establishing what looks good are more widely shared than standards for determining the artistic worth of pictures. And along with that synchronic difference goes a diachronic one. The artistic value of *Death of Marat*, like its historical meaning, need not change when different kinds of bodies (and different ways of representing them) come into fashion, as they inevitably will. We could still understand that David was trying to appeal to the revolutionary masses, and even that he was successful, even if Marat's body did not move us as, presumably, it still does. What that requires is an understanding of David's intentions and a sense of what his audience would have considered to be a beautiful body, whether or not it strikes us as such. In the end, the question whether Marat's corpse is beautiful is a question about David's intentions (and his abilities).

We are ready to assume, for example, that both gods in Cranach's *Apollo and Diana*—one painfully gaunt, the other disproportionally bottom-heavy—are represented as beautiful and so take the painting as an indication of the influence of Renaissance humanism on Cranach's later work and not as a criticism of paganism. Although you may not find Apollo's body attractive,[53] you may still be able to understand and perhaps admire the painting. You may even be moved by it: you may find the painting beautiful—but you will not for that reason find that Apollo is good-looking. In the end, art historians do not need to bring their aesthetic preferences into their practice in order to take account of the features which Danto is so right to emphasize: all they need is an understanding of the aesthetic preferences of others.

Nevertheless, people—even art historians—are moved by paintings and find some of them beautiful. Personal taste plays a much bigger role in this kind of judgment and although taste is itself historically conditioned, there is much more room for individual variations when it comes to the paintings we find beautiful than there is when we are concerned with the paintings (or the elements in paintings) that we find good-looking. More important, we not only expect such variations—we value them; they matter to us in ways that differences about Marat's body don't. I will probably not mind much if you don't find Marat's body attractive, and despite our disagreement we can still go on to discuss the painting, its sense, and its worth—you may still be moved by the painting. But if you are not, if you don't find *Death of Marat* beautiful, and you are someone whose taste and judgment I respect, I will certainly have second thoughts, either about my judgment of the painting or about my respect for yours. Such disagreements are significant to us. At the same time, however, no matter how much I want us to agree on some particular case, I will never want to agree with you about everything: that sort of convergence would not only be impossible to understand, but also repulsive. It could only come about if one (or both) of us made it a lifelong project to imitate the other, an unending effort to renounce our individuality. And just as I would not want anyone to share every one of my judgments, I would also not want everyone to share any one of them. What we find beautiful is an expression of our taste and character, and we want both to be distinctly *our own*.[54]

It is impossible to find any features that are common to every painting that people find beautiful and explain why that is so—neither features of its elements, like the beauty of Marat's corpse, nor features of the work as whole, like the lightness of Twombly or the silence of Gober—it is not even possible to justify the judgment of any particular work. Nothing that we say about a painting, no matter how detailed, will ever imply that the work is beautiful, that is, that someone else who notices the same features will have to agree that it is. Kant was the first to make that issue central to aesthetics: "There can … be no rule in accordance with which someone could be compelled to acknowledge something as beautiful. Whether a garment, a house, a flower is beautiful: no one allows himself to be talked into his judgment about that by means of any grounds or fundamental principles."[55] His explanation was that the judgment of beauty, although he claimed for it "a universal voice," depends only on the subjective pleasure one feels when the cognitive faculties—understanding and imagination—are in harmonious "free play." A more likely reason is that, as Costello puts it, the judgment of beauty is an invitation to discussion and "critical exchange." That is, it is a prospective judgment, the expression not of a conclusion regarding a work but of a suspicion, a guess that spending time with it, making it in some way a part of one's life, will be worth the trouble. But neither a guess nor a suspicion can anticipate what (if anything) the work will eventually disclose and, since as long as we still find the work beautiful we will still feel that there is more to it than we have seen already; we will be unable to say what beauty is "gesturing toward." It is only if we are no longer moved by a thing's beauty that we feel we have seen all that was worth seeing about it, and by then we will no longer care about what made it beautiful in the first place: we will have moved on to other things, and it is their beauty that now promises that there is more to them than we have seen so far.

I agree with Costello that critics rarely say that works of art are beautiful and that, if they do, what they say is not particularly helpful—a point that Wittgenstein made about aesthetic terms in general: "It is remarkable that in real life, when aesthetic judgments are made, aesthetic adjectives such as 'beautiful,' 'fine,' etc., play hardly any role at all. ... The words you use are more akin to 'right' and 'correct' (as these words are used in ordinary speech) than to 'beautiful' and 'lovely.'"[56] I also agree that the words "This is beautiful" are useful mostly in beginning a conversation and are likely to disappear once that conversation is under way.[57] But I don't think that the important issue is whether the act of *saying* that something is beautiful is or is not helpful in the discussion of art: what matters is whether the phenomenon of *judging* or *finding* things beautiful has a place in aesthetics or the history of art. It is only if we look at what happens when something actually strikes us with its beauty, whether or not we give our reaction expression in language, that we will see that it has a place in both.

Wittgenstein is, once again, helpful: "What are expressions of liking something? Is it only what we say or interjections we use or faces we make? Obviously not. It is, often, how often I read something or how often I wear a suit. Perhaps I won't even say: 'It's fine,' but wear it often and look at it."[58] If when I find a painting beautiful I look at it often, then to find it beautiful is to make it a part of my life; and (although that may not have been the point Wittgenstein had wanted to make) I do so because of the suspicion, or the hope, that to spend time with it and try to find out why I am attracted to it will make life better than it would be without it. This group of beliefs, feelings, dispositions, and activities need not be expressed in language, and every explanation I give for it is bound to be wanting and incomplete, especially if it involves the formula "This is beautiful." It will produce a different orientation to the world and will manifest itself in a large variety of activities, some of them conversations about the painting and a few among those, perhaps, beginning by means of that formula. Aesthetics fashions the very shape of our lives.

So far I have assumed, with Costello, that judgments of beauty and judgments of artistic value come more or less to the same thing. In fact, though, these are different judgments, and their differences are important. I have no trouble recognizing the value of Rubens or Renoir—the mastery through which Rubens's works contain vast crowds without being crowded, or the delicacy that animates the skin of Renoir's girls—but their work leaves me unmoved. I believe they are outstanding and important painters and I often return to them for these reasons, but I don't find their work beautiful. I see why others might, but it is Velasquez and Manet that I would rather look at. I admire Rubens and Renoir, but I don't love them—Renoir, in particular, I quite dislike.

There is an obvious response to such embarrassing self-revelations: they express, for better or worse, my aesthetic preferences—my taste—but they are, like aesthetics as a whole, irrelevant to the history of art. Yet Thierry de Duve is right: what enters the museum and what does not, what becomes part of the history of art and what disappears from it, is often determined by choices based on aesthetics; art history, as he says, "is the evidential record of previous aesthetic judgments." Meyer Schapiro attributed a different social significance to the stonework of Souillac, and made the sculpture as he interpreted it part of a different history of art, not only by means of seeing that an example of sin has replaced the judging Christ in the central arch of the tympanum in the Church of Sainte Marie but also by noting that the demon changes his appearance as his power over Theophilus increases, "assuming a more predatory character by an astonishing conversion of the features into flamboyant, centrifugal, tentacular curves. ... The lines of the Devil's snout and jaw flow into the curves of the capital surmounting the column, and thus to the bowed, not opposed head of Theophilus."[59] Schapiro's interpretation is as solidly aesthetic as

Rosalind Krauss's account of the abstract, nonfigurative, "preobjective" character of Richard Serra's *Shift*:

> As one moves over the grounds of the work, the tops of the walls are in gradual but constant transformation. From being the lines along which one sights as one stands above them and looks down, thereby establishing one's connection to the distance, the walls change as one "descends" the work to become an enclosure that binds one within the earth. Felt as barrier rather than as perspective, they then heighten the experience of the physical place of one's body. Without depicting anything—this nearby human figure, that distant tree—the walls' linear/physical network articulates both a situation and a lived perspective. And it does this in the abstractest way possible: by the rotation in and out of depth of a plane.[60]

Both descriptions could be answers to the question "Why is this beautiful?", whether or not it has been explicitly asked, and both are incomplete. Both articulate their authors' reasons for wanting to spend some of their time and energy with these works, and both surely fail to exhaust those reasons: whoever is still struck by these works will feel that there is more to them than anyone has been able to articulate so far. Their beauty can be completely described only when, as Plato in the *Symposium* was first to see, it has ceased to attract and has given its place to another; and even then, it is not so much the description that is complete as it is our interest that has disappeared.[61]

I said earlier that aesthetics fashions the shape of our life. To find things beautiful is not just to stand before them feeling some inexpressible tingle or to contemplate them passively during some idle moments. It is to want to interact with them, and our interactions are a large part of our life—different things would have made us live differently; they would have led us to become different persons. To find something beautiful is to desire to know it better, to learn what makes it beautiful, and—again, as Plato saw—that desire is kept alive only by a sense that it has not yet captured everything that it wants, that it has not yet answered the question "But *why* is it beautiful?" Plato called that desire *eros*—love—and said that its object was beauty. So, beauty is neither the property of looking good nor an empty compliment: it is simply the object of love. What we find beautiful—persons or objects—is what we want to make part of our life because we love it—not just because it is interesting, important, or even a great work of art.[62] It is what moves us, and what, as we pursue it through life, gives our lives direction and shape and helps us become who we are.

Whatever the difficulties of such an approach to beauty, it is not right to describe it, as James Elkins does, as "a nostalgic attempt to return to elements of a modernist or even premodernist aesthetic." Nor can it support Costello's claim that "what is too often meant by 'a return to beauty' is, implicitly, returning to a broadly *formalist* conception of the aesthetic: one that focuses, crudely speaking, on how things look, and the feelings this induces, *at the expense* of the kind of cognitive engagement works elicit in their viewers." Beauty as I understand it has nothing to do with formalism: both Schapiro's and Krauss's accounts, which I take to be elaborations of an aesthetic judgment, are vastly more complex.[63] The return to the beautiful, as I understand it, is not a step back, but an acknowledgment that beauty and aesthetic vocabulary more generally have always played, and continue to play, a central role both in life and in that part of it that is the history of art. It is not so much a call to adopt new (or old) values and vocabularies, but an effort to reveal the values and vocabularies we have been using and continue to use. The very idea that beauty and thought (or knowledge) are opposed to each other, which is based on a misinterpretation of Kant, is a modern invention that ignores the great Platonist tradition that counts both beauty and love among the starting points of learning. We can preserve the insights of that tradition—that beauty is the object of love and that to love something is to desire to come to know it better than one knows it already—without accepting the metaphysics that dictate the conclusion that the final object of love, the one truly beautiful thing, is the otherworldly Form of Beauty that only a very few people are privileged to see. We can even give up the idea that the love of beauty can only culminate in philosophy: it would be good enough if we agreed that it leads, among other things, to a better, more self-conscious art history.

Ciarán Benson

Eavesdropping

I read this debate with the sense of an outsider eavesdropping on a sometimes recondite private conversation. Territorial sensitivities, in these circumstances, can seem somewhat beside the point of inquiry. What I find myself looking for is a clear statement of the key questions prompting the inquiry. By the time I had reached the end of the exchange, I had come to recognize much that I was familiar with, and some positions that puzzled me. In what follows I will make brief reference to instances of both.

My own starting position is partly shaped by a version of pragmatist aesthetics—I admire John Dewey's aesthetics and William James's psychology—coupled with an aspiration for the kind of synthesis that, I believe, should characterize a broadly based "cultural psychology."[64] Here are a few of the issues that attracted my attention: From the beginning of the dialogue, I was struck by the absence of an underlying consensus on what constituted key distinctions, and by what I discerned to be the need for a lexicon of words and phrases that could be shared across the disciplines. Let one example suffice: Arthur Danto begins by speaking of "aesthetic properties." Richard Woodfield immediately follows by agreeing with Danto while himself speaking of "artistic properties." Surely these are not the same kind of property.

I take the category of the "artistic" as referring to the working point of view of a *maker* of art, whereas that of the "aesthetic" refers to the perspective of the *spectator* or "re-maker" (which of course includes the maker when the artist becomes observer of his or her own work). Why is this an important distinction to respect? It is necessary for the sort of question more likely to be asked by those interested in the higher levels of psychological aesthetics than by art historians or by more formally oriented aestheticians. In its pristine form the question might be put like this: Why does this work *matter to me*, or to anyone else, and why does it matter *in this way*? This kind of question will be familiar to readers of the late Richard Wollheim, for instance.[65]

Given this concern, a simple statement like Danto's "I found them beautiful before I knew they were elegies" is the kind of response that resonates with me. So much is happening psychologically and culturally in that simple verb *found*. I take it that art historians of the more traditional kind would feel that their discipline could, among other things, reconstruct "complex works to arrive at an understanding of how they originally looked and were taken in by the viewer."[66] Paradoxically, what is often absent from these kinds of art-historical accounts is an account of the historical contingencies of the psychologies themselves which are recruited to characterize "viewers." Important though the work of a Gestalt psychologist like Rudolf Arnheim is for such accounts, together with the insights of his neuroscientific successors, they are far from sufficient for describing, let alone explaining, the empirical varieties of "viewing" that typify different historical times and distinctive cultural "worlds."[67]

It will come as little surprise that I found myself identifying with Danto's critical approach in this debate. There is no doubt that the ways in which the objects and events that are called "art" come to matter to me are deeply enmeshed with how I have come to make sense of the world. The ideas that constitute my sense-making are historically and culturally contingent. The notion that a universal, ahistorical, acultural psychology can offer an adequate account of the impact of "reasons in general" on the functioning of specific aesthetic properties in the workings of particular art objects/events seems very suspect to me.

The historical perspective which traditional art history takes for granted in its own identity should also be required of any psychology that it recruits to account for the higher functions of the makers and viewers of art that such history concerns itself with. To the extent that it relies on ahistorical, acultural psychologies in its reconstruction of the higher functions of the "artist/viewer" it falls short in this specific aspect of its remit. Danto is right to stress that (an appropriately broad) aesthetics can guide art history into the historical *meanings* of works, and that that begins with the "initial aesthetic response" of those who make and remake those meanings. The issue of what different qualities of an artwork *do* that other qualities don't is a fertile question for a psychologically grounded aesthetics. An adequate psychological aesthetics must make its contribution at this same juncture.

My puzzlement at some elements of the exchanges revolves around the concept of "feeling." I take feelings to be foundational for consciousness, and therefore for the work that art does. I assume—and may well be wrong in this—that Danto's "finding" Motherwell's paintings "beautiful" before knowing that they were elegies to the Spanish Republic, was constituted by feelings of one sort or another. This leads to questions of how important are "feelings" in the practice of art history, and if they are important—diagnostically? evaluatively?—what kinds of feelings are they? And how subjectively distinct are "feelings" and "reasons"? Susanne Langer, as I recall, wrote somewhere of thinking as being the brain's way of feeling.

Thankfully, if belatedly, "feeling" and "emotion" are resurgent topics in current psychology and neuroscience. But they need recasting in quite fundamental ways. I note Dominic Willsdon's endorsement of the utility of these terms and, by contrast, Costello's more problematic analogy of form/content to feeling/cognition. In the case of artistic and aesthetic thinking, the initial phenomena are complex—they are, that is, amalgams of many *kinds* of affective and cognitive processes. The *a priori* distinction of "cognition" from "feeling" is in this case unhelpful. Equally, I would take issue with David Raskin's conflation of two problems. I can easily, and with good empirical support, accept that "what the world is like" is (with qualifications about "like") how it appears to me. This I can do without becoming ensnared with the following proposition concerning art's possible "picturing" of "reality":[68] Idealism is not a necessary consequence of holding the first position.

In conclusion, for someone like myself who is interested in the cultural and psychological dimensions of art, a core and rather obvious question for this debate is "Why is art historical knowledge valuable?" Following from this is a conviction that the sorts of historical knowledge that art historians should be happy to include in their brief must include accounts of why art *mattered* to those who made the art, and to those who remade it and continue to aesthetically remake it. The contribution of philosophical aesthetics to this task is surely an application of the general role of philosophy: to provide the means for sifting productive questions from unproductive ones by creating distinctions and by argumentatively testing these categories in dialogue with "the real."

Wendy Steiner

Aesthetics and Art History: An Interdisciplinary Fling

I would not lay money on the prospect of a happy union between art history and aesthetics. They are separate disciplines after all, constrained by distinct traditions; they formulate different sorts of questions and answer them in methodologically incompatible ways. The proposal to merge the two would sound as wrongheaded as a move to marry their parent disciplines of history and philosophy, were it not for the seeming bond of the word "beauty."

Since the 1990s, when "beauty" started turning up in the titles of books, exhibitions, and conferences, "theory" has been retreating and aesthetics gaining ground. Meanwhile, art history, which for generations had ignored the whole topic of beauty, has been forced by artists, curators, and the general culture to take it on. No doubt marriages have been founded on less commonality than an interest in beauty, but in this case it seems prudent at least to counsel a long engagement.

The current proliferation of beauty scholarship illustrates this claim. I think James Elkins errs, then, in marshaling it for his "seventh model" of the art history–aesthetics merger: "in it, a rediscovery of aesthetics by art historians would be a nostalgic attempt to return to elements of a modernist or even premodernist aesthetic. A certain support for this reading could be found in the recent spate of work on beauty by Dave Hickey, Elaine Scarry, Wendy Steiner, and Alexander Nehamas." The only art historian in this group is Dave Hickey. Alexander Nehamas is a philosopher and classicist, and Elaine Scarry and I were trained as literary scholars. We could hardly be cited as examples of "a rediscovery of aesthetics by art historians." If instead we are to be seen as prompters of this rediscovery, our disciplinary differences should be noted.

Further, our relation to our disciplines is peculiar. Though the four of us are chaired professors in our respective departments, from a disciplinary standpoint we are odd ducks. (I think my colleagues would not take offense at this description.) Our oddness lies not in our simultaneously practicing art history and aesthetics—we don't do that—but in our relative independence from disciplines. Our scholarship instead is problem driven. What connection can be drawn between the experience of beauty and behaving justly (Scarry)? What has been the rhetorical force of beauty, i.e., the institutional work it has performed (Hickey)? What connection is there between beauty and the good life (Nehamas)? And in my case, why has beauty, so marginalized in modernism, become so topical in contemporary culture? In approaching this problem, I certainly discuss Kant and paintings (as well as literary works), but aestheticians and art historians would be the first to deny that I have faithfully merged their views, methods, and interests. Instead, I have focused on a problem that happens to touch on several disciplines, describing those touches while largely ignoring the dictates of the disciplines touched.

Moreover, it is an error to describe these "beauty books" as encouraging "a nostalgic attempt to return to elements of a modernist or even premodernist aesthetic." Mine at least is a direct critique of modernist thinking, and it argues equally vehemently that feminism (among other factors) has made it quite impossible to return to premodernist approaches to beauty. What evokes the specter of nostalgia is the very interesting historical fact that beauty—an extraordinarily rich complex of ideas, values, and long-standing symbols—was largely driven out of high-art discourse for much of the twentieth century, whereas it is now on everyone's lips. But in speaking the word again and remembering when it was in common use before, we are not necessarily yearning for the good old days.

Figuring out what "beauty" might mean at this point in history and why it is being so frequently evoked is anything but an exercise in nostalgia. It is forward-looking, sometimes almost oracular, demanding an awareness different from that of a critic, an art historian, an aesthetician, or an arts practitioner. Outside these disciplines, "Kant" might not appear as a sacred text, but rather as the source of fuzzy, inconsistent, and even politically retrograde precepts. The modernist disdain for beauty and pleasure—aided and abetted by art historians and critics—might look like a blight rather than a sign of superior sensibility. And, *pace* Diarmuid Costello, the predicate "beautiful" might no longer be critically uninteresting for telling us "more about how a work disposes a viewer than about the work itself." When it comes to beauty there might be no such thing as "the work itself," and the disposition of particular viewers might turn out to be precisely what critical interest is.

James Elkins wonders whether "art history might be the acid that corrodes aesthetics." But art historians are not the ones wielding this acid; their own discipline is equally threatened by the carbolic effects of recent beauty scholarship. For this very reason, the "return of beauty" may ultimately have little permanent effect on art history or aesthetics, never mind effecting their merger. The two disciplines, briefly attracted, will reasonably and usefully proceed along their separate paths, perhaps fortified by the knowledge that it is better to have loved and lost than never to have loved at all.

Matthew Rampley

Art History without Aesthetics: Escaping the Legacy of Kant

The past twenty or so years have seen an unprecedented degree of critical reflection on the historiography of art, its philosophical implications, its guiding presuppositions, and its relations to other fields of academic discourse. This has been paralleled by a remarkable growth of interest in the history of the discipline. The discussion about the relation of art history and aesthetics is another example of such a process of reflection. What is remarkable about this reflection is the extent to which it relies on a hypostatized notion of art history; authors who have built up a reputation as commentators on the discipline frequently do so without reference to a single example of art-historical discourse. The foregoing debate is a case in point. There is plenty of reference to specific authors of aesthetic theories, but none to any art historians, save a rather lapidary discussion of Michael Baxandall who, on such occasions, stands as a signifier of enlightened "progressive" art history.

Why does this matter? Because the discussion about art history and aesthetics seems more to be about art *criticism*. Danto has, to be sure, made some grandiose claims about the history of art or, more specifically, about the *end* of the history of art, but these have been generated from critical reviews about the artists of the 1980s, Julian Schnabel the most notable among them. An art critic such as Danto is, of course, entitled to employ aesthetic concepts, and these have been central to Western criticism since Diderot. It is otherwise, however, with art history.

There have been many who have emphasized the role of aesthetic judgment within art history. In 1963 James Ackerman argued that the main characteristic of art history was the existence of a distinctive sort of primary datum—works of art—which marked it off from other historical and humanistic discourses. To cite Ackerman:

> The social and political historian uses artefacts of the past in order to reconstruct in imagination a human situation he cannot directly experience. The art historian, by contrast, uses what he can discover of past situations to supplement a direct experience of the artefact.[69]

A similar claim was made by Kurt Badt eight years later.[70] This was probably the last time such a view of art history could be upheld and be taken seriously, for it rests on a reified notion of art. There has, to be sure, been a long tradition of such reification in art history; the numerous variants of formalism present obvious examples, as do the various kinds of positivist art history. Ackerman combines these two, viewing the artwork as a "datum" and then emphasizing the centrality of style as a category of analysis. Paradoxically, while art history has moved on, debates about the relation between art history and aesthetics remain trapped within an image of the discipline that would have been reassuring to scholars of Ackerman's generation, but unrecognizable to contemporary writers. What are the reasons for this?

I think the principal cause is that reflection on the historiography of art and its history has been dominated by a renewed interest in the aesthetics of Kant. This means that critical writing on the historiography of art has been ensnared within the epistemological dramaturgy of the relation between subjects and the objects of their cognition. Historical accounts of the discipline have consequently tended to privilege figures—Alois Riegl, Heinrich Wölfflin, Erwin Panofsky—who similarly took their point of departure from Kantian and neo-Kantian aesthetics.[71] It is within this framework that aesthetics seems important for art history. Art history need not be thought of in this way, however. As Ernst Tugendhat has argued, attention to the discursive basis of knowledge means that the model of cognition based on a subject-object relation is open to interrogation and reformulation.[72] For Tugendhat it was one of the breakthroughs of so-called analytical philosophy, when the object-oriented conception of "traditional philosophy," as he terms it, was replaced by a concern with rules of discourse, and with conditions under which certain statements might be held to be true or not.

Those involved in debates regarding the constitution of art history would do well to take note of this shift. I am not necessarily arguing for some form of analytic art history. What I am arguing for, however, is the need to think about art history in terms other than the relation between a discourse and artworks as primary "data." Many others have, of course, already reached a similar set of conclusions, albeit by different routes. For Marxists, the position of writers such as Ackerman is open to the charge of reification; artworks are only the visible remainder of a much more complex cultural practice that involves a specific kind of experience and a particular set of institutional norms, structures, and constraints.

The critique of the reification of art by traditional art history has most usually been associated with the radical art history of the

1970s and 1980s. In many respects, however, in spite of its stress on the socially mediated nature of artistic production, dissemination and consumption, radical art history failed to move away from the fundamental orientation toward art-historical "objects." T. J. Clark, Norman Bryson, or Griselda Pollock, to name perhaps the most prominent representatives of radical art history, were still ultimately concerned with the interpretation and elucidation of artworks. Although embedded within an attention to social and cultural frameworks, their writings were often comparable to the close readings associated with formalist analysis; Clark's reading of Manet's *Olympia* is the most striking instance.[73] There have been other histories of art, however, that have attempted with greater rigor to shift from the consideration of artworks to the analysis of art as a broader social phenomenon, and these have not necessarily been motivated by Marxist, feminist, or other radical politics. As early as 1938, the conservative Catholic historian Martin Wackernagel published a pioneering microsocial analysis of the Renaissance, *The World of the Renaissance Florentine Artist*.[74] Wackernagel examined in detail the conditions that infused the *Lebensraum* or milieu of the artist, ranging from the agencies of patronage to the social situation of the artist, including questions of social class and class consciousness, social environment, the business practices of artists, working practices in the studio, and professional status. The term *Lebensraum* had unfortunate connotations, and consequently few followed Wackernagel's model, ceding the territory to sociologists; the closest recent equivalent to Wackernagel's notion of the artistic *Lebensraum* might be Becker's concept of the "artworld."[75] This opens up the field to a reconsideration of the term "art," which is clearly not limited to artworks. At its most immaterial, it might be conceived as an autopoietic system of ephemeral communicative events, as in the work of Niklas Luhmann, where the materiality of works of art is, at best, of secondary importance.[76]

I am not arguing that art history should be remodeled as a branch of sociology, but I am highlighting the fact that there exist other kinds of art history in which the question of the role of aesthetics might well seem irrelevant. It could be objected that while art history can distance itself from the orientation toward individual artworks, it will nevertheless ultimately have to confront aesthetic questions when it comes to consideration both the aesthetic values that governed the art worlds of the past, and also the kinds of aesthetic judgments historically passed on individual artworks. However, from the standpoint of the art historian this is primarily a matter of historical rather than aesthetic analysis. The best way of conceiving this is in terms of the "methodological philistinism" espoused by the British anthropologist Alfred Gell.[77] In the same way that, for Gell, the anthropology of religion entails suspension of belief in the religious structure under examination, so the anthropology of art should require a detachment from aesthetic response or indeed from belief in art objects as a privileged category of analysis. This stands in place of the traditional anthropology of art which, Gell contends, is "essentially geared to refining and expanding the aesthetic sensitivities of the Western art public by providing a cultural context within which non-Western art objects can be assimilated to the categories of Western aesthetic art appreciation."[78] Judgments in the anthropology of art are thus conducted at a metalevel that subsumes aesthetic values and responses, but is distinct from them. Methodological philistinism is driven by Gell's equation of anthropology with *social* anthropology. In other words, the interest in art is an interest not in aesthetic artifacts, but in the nexus of social relations within which the production and consumption of artifacts takes place. Paradoxically, I find myself in agreement with Arthur Danto, although not for reasons he would recognize. Exploration of the role of beauty or melancholy in the paintings of Picasso or Modigliani is undoubtedly more interesting than simple affirmation of their qualities, but such an examination has to be recognized as an historical judgment rather than an aesthetic one. If it becomes the latter, it can play no part in art-historical analysis.

It is also important to address the potential criticism that ultimately, when selecting artworks for analysis, aesthetic judgments inevitably come into play. I see no reason why judgments about art-historical significance should entail judgments about aesthetic quality. This was already being argued for by Alois Riegl a century ago, and it is worth recalling that a predecessor of Riegl in Vienna, Moritz Thausing, famously expressed the desire for aesthetic terms to be banished from the domain of art history.[79] This was admittedly in the name of an equally problematic positivism, but it foregrounds the existence of a long tradition of alternatives to an aestheticized art history.

One final comment: The debate about the relation of art history to aesthetics is not explored with the same intensity in the domain of contemporary literary theory and criticism. There is a straightforward reason for this; literary texts are much less amenable to aesthetic reification than physical works of art on display in galleries and museums. In this respect it is also notable that the art history/aesthetics discussion revolves around the work of artists who produce "traditional" artworks: Picasso, Modigliani, David, and Gober. What relevant aesthetic judgments could be made about the work of Stanley Brouwn, Chris Burden or Keith Arnatt? It is unfortunate that the debate has not managed to break out of this basic museological limitation. "Dainty," "dumpy," or "affect" might well be appropriate qualities to ascribe to artworks, but I leave that for the aestheticians and the art critics to decide.

Keith Moxey

Aesthetics Is Dead: Long Live Aesthetics

The discussions held at Cork on the relation between aesthetics and art history are fascinating. Having been involved in a Clark

Art Institute conference that attempted to bring aesthetics, art history, and visual studies together, I am familiar with the ways in which these disciplines, which would appear to have so much to do with one another, tend to pass each other like ships in the night.[80] The ambition to make them address each other, at least long enough to understand why it is that they neglect each other, affords us insight into the nature of the intellectual culture in which we live. My own way into this topic has to do with my suspicion of the "grand narratives" on which aesthetics and art history have so often relied. I am concerned that the infinite variety of human experience is necessarily neglected when it is reduced to orderly categories by means of philosophies of art or philosophies of history based on universalizing notions of subjectivity.

For example, what intrigues me most about the transcript is the complete absence of any reference to the ways in which processes of postcolonial development or globalization impinge on the debate about the relation of aesthetics to art history. Indeed, I read this absence as a symptom of what must be left unsaid in any encounter between forms of interpretation that represent the universal and the particular. Where one (art history) is deeply immersed in the empirical particulars of the time and place under consideration, the other (aesthetics) seeks to develop general theories that might encompass the nature of human response. One often conceals its philosophical assumptions in the object of study, while the other depends on philosophy for its raison d'être. The circumstances confronting both disciplines in the context of a heightened consciousness of both the proximity and difference of other cultures serves to dramatize the tensions that have traditionally distinguished them. Philosophies of art are confronted with the limitations placed on their theories by the recognition of cultural difference, while art history finds the philosophies of history that have motivated its narratives in the past increasingly provincial and inadequate.

In his reflection on Kant's third *Critique*, Jacques Derrida suggested that arguments about aesthetic value depended on the "frame" brought to the discussion.[81] Any question concerning, say, the "beautiful" is necessarily based on the presuppositions that motivate it. If we accept his point, we operate in an intellectual context that is inevitably going to have difficulties with any concept that aspires to universality. Historical developments in the past fifty years—not unrelated to Derrida's philosophical position—have seen the rise of political movements, such as feminism, gender studies, ethnic studies, etc., that have challenged the grounds on which claims aspiring to universal applicability are declared. Following their lead, I would disagree with Thierry de Duve who defends Kant when he argues: "In claiming universal validity for personal judgments and feelings, people attribute those capacities to others, and so on universally. There is room for disagreement, but in making aesthetic judgments we postulate human faculty: that of agreement, *sensus communis*." To this vision of aesthetic judgment I would oppose that of Nicholas Davey when he writes:

> [T]o go back to Kant is to return to a model of aesthetic judgment which supposes that discourse about art is possible (though difficult) because it is based upon a shared intersubjective *a priori* framework of aesthetic judgments which are unaffected by tradition, history, or social circumstance. Against this, however, it is surely the fact that we view an artwork from different historical and social perspectives that gives to art its richness of content, that enables us to learn from the artwork, and that allows us to view both the art work, ourselves, and others *differently*.

What is at issue in the Cork transcript is nothing less than the limits of interpretation. Derrida and the political movements mentioned above laid the foundation for a recognition that a subject's position matters; that in interpretation it is not only the object under scrutiny that makes a difference, *but the nature of the subject who does the scrutinizing*. Such a position is crucially important in trying to understand the implications of the economic and cultural forces informing the processes of globalization. Whereas some interpretations insist on regarding these developments as a manifestation of a single principle that is identified with historical necessity, others would argue that there are a variety of factors at work. Marxist cultural critics, for example, have suggested that the dominant capitalist model of economic production condemns us to live in an age of growing homogenization. Others argue that the ever-increasing integration of economic markets and the massive export of the industrial production of the wealthy nations of Europe and the United States to the undeveloped world (outsourcing) results in cultural hybridization and a rising awareness of the incommensurability of the world's cultures.

Among those who would interpret our present circumstances in the light of a narrative that is universal in its ambition is Fredric Jameson,[82] who argues that globalization is an unmitigated disaster because it represents the triumph of capitalism. In this view, differences between the cultures of the world are gradually but systematically being eroded by the power of multinational corporations and their industrial products. When regarded from the standpoint of the producer, the notion of the "global village" becomes a metaphor for the international reach of these enterprises.

Opposing this dire prediction are thinkers such as Arjun Appadurai[83] and Néstor García Canclini,[84] who insist that the cultural interaction and economic integration characteristic of the postcolonial moment cannot be understood in these terms. Against the concept of the capitalist producer, they both focus on the consumer. They argue that the Marxist thesis, while affording us useful insights into our present predicament, privileges the agency of the producer at the expense of the consumer. Appadurai stresses the role of the imagination as a means of negotiating the political and social implications of cultural encounters. He refuses to reduce the cultural to the economic. Similarly, García Canclini suggests that consumption is the location where the consumer's agency is exercised. Rather than being determined by the operation of market forces, the consumer actively engages them in a dialogical play that affords him or her a degree of power in the determination of a particular form of life. In one account, a Coke bottle is a Coke bottle is a Coke bottle, regardless of where in the world it is produced and consumed; on the other, the significance of the Coke bottle and the purposes to which it is put vary according to the consumer's varying cultural circumstances. Whereas in one culture the bottle is disposed of as soon as its contents are consumed, in another the empty bottle enjoys a variety of different functions that endow it with cultural meaning long after it might otherwise have been consigned to oblivion. Where in one context the disposal of the Coke bottle may be regarded as an indication of the reckless consumption of natural resources and the destruction of the environment, in another the bottle's capacity to serve, for example, as a dispenser for a variety of cooking ingredients, endows it with a significant role in a domestic economy. Needless to say, the cultural value or nonvalue ascribed to the bottle profoundly alters its significance in the eyes of those who acquire it.

Can it similarly be claimed that aesthetic judgment is locally determined and cannot be decided on the basis of a comprehensive theory? If so, what implications does this have for the project of philosophical aesthetics? David Summers's important book *Real Spaces* is a spirited assertion of the continuing need to approach our understanding of the art of the world's cultures on the basis of all-embracing principles that depend on an assumption of intersubjectivity.[85] It may, however, be possible to envision another position which involves a profound rethinking of the concept of aesthetics itself. From this perspective aesthetic judgments would have local or transcultural (rather than intercultural or universal) validity. Rather than seek to articulate the qualities that make a work of art interesting to all people—an ambition based on an Enlightenment notion of subjectivity—aestheticians might attempt to analyze the bases on which different cultures privilege one set of artifacts above others. Such a view has the advantage of not having to confront the question of whether or not it matters that the intellectual origins of the theories used in this process are "Western" or "non-Western." The idea of hybridity, so useful in approaching other aspects of postcolonial culture, helps us conceive of the imaginative new forms of interpretation required by contemporary circumstances. Rather than a philosophical system, studies of this kind would offer anthropologies of aesthetic judgment.

Nonuniversalizing aesthetic judgments would appear to be increasingly valuable to an age that has seen the rise of "visual studies."[86] Whereas this new academic field has often been viewed with suspicion by art historians for expanding the boundaries of the study of visual culture beyond the parameters usually imposed on objects by accepted ideas of aesthetics, it seems to me that this project affords renewed importance to our capacity to articulate ideologies of value. Rather than simply foreclose the question of what may or may not be considered "art" on the basis that art history exists to serve the established canon of Euro-American art, one that depends on the application of the aesthetic theories of the late eighteenth and early nineteenth centuries, the discipline could be re-envisioned as seeking to articulate the grounds on which people make the discriminations that allow them to privilege some artifacts above others both in the past and in the present.[87] Were aesthetics to accept that its judgments have less than universal validity, its relation to art history would no longer be haunted by the gulf that distinguishes the universal from the particular. There is no reason why both forms of interpretation might not work together in articulating ways in which to account for the infinite variety of aesthetic choices implicit in the cultural practice of the past and the present. The world is old and it is big. *If Aesthetics is dead: long live aesthetics!*

Christine Wertheim

Why Kant Got It Right

In "The Art Seminar," Nicholas Davey outlines three different senses of the term "aesthetics." For the Greeks, *aisthesis* referred to the activity of seeing well, and grasping what one saw. In the Enlightenment, the term became attached "to discourses about sensibility and taste as well as to debates about how the beautiful might be judged." Lastly, there is a twentieth-century usage "which speaks of a Marxist, feminist, or a phenomenological *aesthetic*," where the power of art is deemed to lie in its capacity for making visible "the horizons of meaning or *Weltanschauung* out of which the work had initially sprung." Given that none are mutually exclusive, even if their outcomes are different, Davey asks why we keep returning to the second, Kantian usage in which all attention is focused on "the concept of the beautiful." For Thierry de Duve, the answer to this question is simply that Kant "got it right." "Why," he responds, "would you want a new theory if you have a satisfactory one? That doesn't happen in science." I agree with de Duve on this point, but for a different reason. Kant did get something right, but this was not, as de Duve says, that "in making aesthetic judgments we postulate a universal human faculty: that of agreement, *sensus communis*," we could potentially lay the "foundation for democracy and peace on earth." Kant was not right about this even if, as de Duve rightly states, this is merely an ethically necessary *hypothesis*, rather than the assertion of a supposed *a priori* fact.

Mary Rawlinson elaborates this point in her essay in "Assessments," emphasising that for Kant the potential for *sensus communis* evoked by art does not depend on any notion of a universal taste based on a fraternity of preferences, but on the intersubjective element of experience that art highlights—"the sense that there is *another implied in it*" (emphasis mine). For Rawlinson, this conclusion depends on Kant's argument that the material specificity of the artwork is not opposed to the generalized ideals or concepts philosophy normally valorizes. Rather, the value of art's "beauty" lies in its capacity to throw a bridge between the concrete particularity of the material realm, and the abstract generality of invisible world of ideas. This it can do, Rawlinson says because the painting's singular

> evocation of invisible ideas and the way of seeing with which they are associated reveal a style of experience … [that] cannot be reduced to the painting's … instantiation of some instiutionalized code, nor its legibility as a symptom of culture. The painting does not offer its ideas according to the logic of form and content. … it cannot be subsumed under a rule.

The artwork is absolutely "singular": even "multiples" such as by Warhol are singular in their being different from reproductions in print, according to Rawlinson.[88] But this "singularity"

> does not open up the domain of a "common sense," rather it gives rise to an experience of the other as alien, an other that I can know immediately.

In other words, the artwork—she specifically cites the case of painting—provides a field in which the other is encountered not as the unnamable other-ness of some Lacanian style analysis, but rather as a real, particular, individual entity—an *I* who is simply one of the many-others. *This* is the *sensus communis* to which art gives rise, not the figure of the "in general" or "in common," but the community based on a concrete and always wonderously suprising experience of the other's difference, their "Wow!" that I come to know through my encounter with their art. The value of beauty, Rawlinson assserts, is that it enables us to "escape the fundamental narcissism of ordinary vision, the ineluctible tendency in ordinary experience to see one's self in the other, not the other in his difference," and thus to experience "the gift of the other."

I am deeply indebted to Rawlinson for making this point so clear. However, for me what Kant gets most right is not his elaboration of the beautiful, but his musings on the sublime: for whatever the nature of human community, *individuals* are innately contradictory—they are beside, not at one with, *themselves*—and it is in his theory of the sublime that Kant deals with this issue, which is, at least initially, purely an instance of "form." Furthermore, it is my contention that it is only on the basis of its claim to invoke the sublime that modern art is accorded the status of an *institution:* hence its emphasis, however, ill-informed, on form. Without this claim, art is either, as Rawlinson states, a means for community-building, (a form of personal play-therapy or a branch of the entertainment industry), or it is another resource for propaganda, something badly needed by those not in control of the "official" media, especially in America. Both these functions are worthwhile, and a work may serve both at once. But neither of them constitutes an item or event as *Art*; that status is, at least in the modern era, guaranteed only by its claim—not even its success—to induce a sublime experience in its audience. The promised experience is not one that is commonly agreed upon or of certain sense. Nor is it a meeting of otherwise completely different minds; it is a snarkish and paradoxically equivocal non-sense that confronts us, not with the universality of (clear) understanding, or the space we share with others, but with *limits*—limits of understanding, limits of ourselves, and even limits of "space." Is it perhaps the realization of these limits that constitutes the human universal? In other words, if art qua art has a special function in modernity, it is because it is the one nonmilitarized zone of our culture where we can still confront these limits.

In order to clarify what is at stake here, I shall use the term "Aesthetics" to highlight the technical and limiting non-sense in which I want to use it, and the uncapitalized "aesthetics" when referring to as it is used in discussons on "beauty." I do not claim that these are the only ways the term may legitimately be used. As Davey and Rawlinson show, it has many meanings. I simply want to clarify the sense that I find most useful, a sense not referred to by either Davey or Rawlinson. I shall thus give a brief outline of Kant's project as I see it, before concluding with some remarks about how this might be useful for the discipline of art history.

In summary, Kant was drawn to a discussion of the Aesthetic through his self-fulfilling proof of the limits of logic.[89] To Kant this task was of the utmost importance, for in his view, the subject, as opposed to a calculating body, only arises when the given, and hence un-free, resources for sense- and decisison-making, i.e., logic, are exhausted, and the mind is forced beyond the bounds of its given nature to make "free" choices and invent "original" ideas. In other words, for Kant, the human mind is divided into two levels. The first, understanding, is the subject-less, automatous, sense-making logical apparatus with which we are born, the apparatus through which we give form to our experiences. (Though for Kant the terms "form" and "logic" are isomorphic, they are not for me; I shall use the phrase "forms of logic" to refer to his categories of understanding.) As we might say, the forms of logic are hardwired at birth, or even at conception. (Kant had no developmental theory of how this "program" comes into being. He focused exclusively on its fully matured state.) But this hardwired logic program, which Kant believed he could grasp through an analysis of the categories of language, has its limits. According to Kant, there are, as a simple matter of fact, *some experiences that understanding—the forms of logic—simply cannot process.* These experiences he christened by the name of the sublime, referring to Burke and Longinus although he went substantially beyond them with the specificity of his claims for the experience in relation to overall mental behavior. When the mind has a sublime experience it passes from understanding into a new region, one that is not controlled by logic. This is what Kant called "reason." It is in this new region of reason that both subjectivity and "freedom" lie, freedom from instinct, and freedom from the forms of logic.

In Kant's speculative analysis, when a calculating body endowed with understanding/logic finds itself confronted with something it can't process, a gap opens in which the experience as an event in itself is cut off from the *agent* of the experience, and for the first time the mind thinks of and speaks to *itself* as an "I," in the self-originating performative utterance "*I* do not understand what is happening to me." In other words, for Kant, the self-conscious subject only comes into being at the limit of understanding/logic when the mind splits itself completely from its object in experience, and confronts *itself* as an object. From that point on, if the mind wants to make sense of experience, it must either withdraw from the strangely splitting sublime encounter and return to the realm of understanding where self-consciousness lies, or stay with its split self by making up—literally *inventing*—categories to define the strange event that is the happening of Itself. *Nothing* governs these startlingly new ideas (I would wish to use the term new "forms" here, but Kant wouldn't), which Kant called "concepts of reason" to distinguish them from the categories of the forms of logic in the understanding. These ideas are "free" even if, as he believed, they are universal. They are exactly the same ones—e.g., God, the Good, etc.—that arise spontaneously in the mind of all free agents. (I do not wish to enter the debate about the universality of such concepts except to state that I don't believe in it.) What matters here is that, for Kant, Aesthetics is the discipline that sets out to explore this realm where the sense of experience cannot be analyzed, deduced, and "proved," as he believed is the case for the categories of understanding, because it is beyond comprehension by the forms of logic.[90] There are two parts to this task: finding ways to actually evoke such experiences, and developing means for transmitting something of them to others. (They can no longer be conveyed even as language, if it continues to adhere to the rules of grammar, which are govered by the deeper laws of the forms of logic.) These two tasks are not the same, though the latter is often confused with the former. (Wordsworth's descriptions of his sublime experiences at Tintern Abbey do not induce an uprushing of the soul in me, though his poems convince me that he really felt something like a new man out there in the dank English countryside.) The question is then, *what methodologies would best enable us to carry out these sublime tasks?*

As so many have pointed out, for Kant, the sublime *absolutely cannot be explored through art*, for the simple reason that whatever is man-made is clearly comprehensible by man, and thus not beyond the limits of understanding. For Kant only contemplation of the vastness of nature, such as an apparently infinite mountainscape or a storm at sea, can induce experiences strong enough to overpower understanding. Hence, for him, hiking and sailing were the best methods for performing the first evocative part of Aesthetics. (In more pro-active America we might translate this into huntin', shootin' and fishin', which if we stick to the mythical dimensions of a whale hunt, is not such a bad translation.) Paul Crowther has demolished this part of Kant's argument, showing that there are at least four ways in which man-made items can overwhelm understanding: by being incomprehensively large, such as the Great Wall of China; by being incomprehensibly small, such as the painted dust-sculptures of Hagop Sandaldjian; by incorporating an incomprehensible amount of labor, such as the Bayeaux tapestry; or by being incomprehensibly complex, such as your average VCR.[91] In line with this last hypothesis, Baudrillard has suggested that, as a single continuous man-made "installation," the whole of contemporary society is now so complex, vast, and incomprehensible as to induce a permanent sublime in us all. (Another name for an ongoing sublime is trauma. At least this is the theory of trauma in Freud, and for this reason, in Freudian theory, representations are not "bad" intrusions that sever us from a desirable immersion in the immediacy of experience, but "good" mediators that rescue us from the overwhelming presence of the unnamable "Thing.")

As for the second task of Aesthetics—developing means for transmitting something of the sublime experience to others—Kant had very little to say on the subject (and of course, he had no way of mechanically reproducing it, as with a film of an on-rushing train), except that, like everyone else he did his best to transmit something of his own experience of it without really offering much in the way of directions for how to make such transmissions effective (beyond requiring that such transmissions defy the laws of classical logic). For Kant this meant that the transmission itself must in some way partake of the infinite. This is why he believed man-made products can't do it: for Kant, infinitudes cannot be manufactured. Irrespective of our capacity for unlimited manufacture, today we know that the limits of logic lie not in infinitudes but in paradoxes, and it is to this that we must now turn if we wish to link Aesthetics to art and its history.

For Kant the difference between the sublime and the beautiful is that whereas the beautiful is constituted by a balanced and harmonious. i.e., logical arrangement of its parts—a kind of relational stasis that induces a sense of peace and equilibrium in which every part feels as if it's in its proper place—in the sublime we sense an impending "crisis," for suddenly the sum of the parts is incomplete, inconsistent, contradictory, or ambiguous. That is to say, the "whole" formed by the parts cannot be assigned a clear value because it fails *both* to conform to the laws of classical logic—identity, noncontradiction, and excluded middle—*and* to present itself as a completely disordered mess. In other words, the sublime encounter induces the experience of a liminal zone, between (what has traditionally been seen as "absolute") order and complete disorder, that exceeds the bounds of classical logic—and hence the (Kantian) Understanding. If then—as Rawlinson accurately states of the beautiful—the sublime is a "value," not a "property," it is that value which cannot be defined through the binary oppositions of traditional Western thinking.

This is why we may regard the sublime as "ir-rational," but only if we use the term in its technical, i.e., mathematical sense, to designate a value that, while being ungraspable from within a certain specified system—for example, the system of whole-number ratios—may nevertheless be counted from the perspective of another, wider, more subtle complex of relations, for example one that includes numbers with infinite decimal expansions.

At least for the Western subject, sublimity is critical, for we, it seems, cannot easily bear the sense of potent uncertainty that arises when the parts of an experience neither clearly add up to a harmonious whole, nor clearly fall into a disordered heap; we cannot make sense of the more subtle region of experience onto which the sublime opens. It is this, its capacity to gesture beyond the binarism of classical logic, and toward an entirely different kind of thinking-acting-being predicated on uncertainty and equivocation (not its community-building beauty, however much this is predicated on real encounters with others), that entitles art in modernity to erect itself into the institution of Art; it is Aesthetics, not aesthetics, that is at stake in the relationship between art history and philosophy. Of course, this is ideally part of a much longer analysis: but for these purposes I will end by simply pointing to several moments in the discussion where these issues are occluded.

When Arthur Danto says that the basic issue for an art historian is to discuss such questions as, "Why is the Grünewald altarpiece repulsive?" he refers to aesthetics, not Aesthetics, though the altarpiece itself clearly has a sublime dimension. Indeed, I would argue that it is one of the most sublimity-inducing artworks in the Western canon; whatever one might think of them, Grunewald's stark juxtapositions of light and dark, flesh and spirit, beauty and repulsion, are clearly meant to evoke a region beyond the logic of the either/or. I'm not sure that the same could be said of McCarthy, however much I like his work. A task for an Aesthetically-minded art historian might be to enquire whether *Bossy Burger* is technically sublime or not; Thierry de Duve's suggestion that "it stages disgust at a remove" might be a place to begin.

Approaching the problem from an entirely different perspective, John Hyman proposes that there is a fundamental difference between art history and philosophy because the former deals with particulars and the latter with universals. It seems to me that this division is somewhat tendentious, for it is not a foregone conclusion that in the subtler realms of the sublime such a distinction is relevant. I don't say it isn't. I merely note that we shouldn't take it for granted. The point of the sublime is that, being a value, it can be investigated by many disciplines and many media, precisely because it is a product of "form."

This brings me to my final point, the problem raised by Diarmuid Costello concerning the "opposition" between beautiful, aesthetically charged, form-oriented modernist practices based on "how things look"; and those supposedly anti-aesthetic postmodern or "conceptual" modes that privilege "cognitive engagment." Costello is right to question this opposition, for the sublime is a cognitive event, yet it is induced precisely by *form*, albeit this has nothing to do with the strict separation of media, but as I have said with the *logic of sense.* We can, I believe, produce a different model for the encounter of art history and aesthetics if, as James Elkins so eloquently suggests, "we run *around* aesthetics and into something wholly different," that is, into Aesthetics.

Eva Schürmann

Art's Call for Aesthetic Theory

The notorious gap between art historians and philosophers, which is evinced once again by the conversation documented in this volume, is not unlike the problem famously formulated by Kant: conceptions without intuitions are empty and intuitions without conceptions are blind. Not that it would not be objectionable—as Kant perfectly well knew and went on to demonstrate in the *Critique of Pure Reason*—if there were such a thing as a pure conception without any kind of intuition, and vice versa. But however provisional or artificial the distinction between concepts and visual perceptions, thinking and seeing, might be, it nonetheless highlights differences in figure-ground constellations, that is to say: it shows what in each discipline is prior and what is background. It makes a crucial difference if, on the one hand, one is chiefly concerned with forming concepts and elaborating critical definitions, or if, on the other hand, one's basic enterprise is to look at particular works in order to find out as much as possible about their visual features. And even if an art historian temporarily refrains from notions such as form and style to focus on, say, the circumstances of a work's production, he or she still stresses the singular art work. By contrast, it is telling that a philosopher can, under certain circumstances, work very well without opening his or her eyes to the concrete givenness of a specific work.

And yet it would be a simplification to say that art historians are mainly concerned with the particular—in the sense of uniqueness and singularity—since almost every exponent of the discipline is worried about what is generalizable in a single work, be it the social and historical context or the ascription to a broader artistic movement. Precisely with his considerations about "art-in-general," Thierry de Duve showed how very general an art-historical approach to the particular became in case of modern art.[92] An art historian without any systematic account of the role and function of art would be a mere philological researcher. There are many ways of practicing art history and of dealing with an art work, but none of those ways contents itself with a simple description of what is to be seen there.

Although things lie differently with the philosophy of art—since important and influential theories indeed consisted in very abstract conceptual formulations, for instance those of Schelling or Schopenhauer—it would again be too easy to think of philosophy as exclusively directed toward the general and the universal. Philosophers are not merely subsuming the particular beneath a general heading when they scrutinize which general is the most suitable for grasping the sense of a singular. Even the generalistic attitudes of some contextualization theories—for instance Luhmann's concept of art as a system or Bourdieu's hypothesis about the normative impact society has on what is considered to be art—eventually entail important insights into a single artwork's embeddedness in a greater configuration and thereby contribute to a better understanding of its connectedness. And as art historians cannot help but generalize, philosophers inadvertently stumble into art-historical territory when they have to refer to individual works in order to explain their ideas.

So apparently distinctions between the general and the particular do not lead very far.

But to stress an art historian's talent for visual discernment and a philosopher's gift for conceptual astuteness still helps to point out the different priorities and salient features of both disciplines in order to get an idea of the systematic reasons for differences and misunderstandings.

I suppose that most philosophers would find rather troubling the genetic and historical link Thierry de Duve draws between Paul McCarthy and Matthias Grünewald "via Bruce Nauman, back to Dada, and then even further, back to Courbet." They would be irritated not because it is McCarthy or an issue of disgust (or because they would think that Grünewald is incomparatively stronger than McCarthy) but because it is as incautious as it is bold to juggle with such strong philosophical-historical assumptions and to suggest such a far-reaching genetic continuity without justifying the implicit normative assertions at work in such an approach. That is not to say that such a thesis would not be interesting and worthwhile to argue within the context of art-historical discussion, but for someone with both a different academic socialization and a strong claim for conceptual justification it is just not plausible.

On the other hand, it is not difficult to imagine that most art historians would be rather bored by the philosopher's exegetic worries about what Kant meant or by the philosophically very important difference between the general and the universal. That difference would not be of any applicable relevance to their concerns.

Now, if this is so, then we could say: long live the difference! Both are right to concentrate on their own concerns. They just have different critical agendas and are dealing with incomparable issues and Hyman is quite right to recommend each to remain on their own patch. We should then rather concentrate on developing an account of their incommensurability.

I suppose this would be true and sufficient, if there were not the matter of aesthetics being precisely the intersection and intertwining of questions crucial to both disciplines. Intersection does not mean that things are helplessly confused, but that a philosophical theory of art and an art-historical account of art occupy, indeed, very much the same ground. They do so all the more since art itself became philosophical. Not only since Duchamp's readymade, but already with paintings that make their own media a subject of discussion (Turner, the Impressionists, etc.), art started to ask philosophical questions that have to be reflected in terms of aesthetic theory. Duchamp's bicycle wheel persistently asks: what distinguishes an artwork from a nonartwork? Jasper

Johns's painting raises the very intricate question: is it a flag or is it a painting? Magritte makes us nervous by incessantly questioning the difference between the medium and the mediated. And so does Josef Beuys by shifting the boundaries between art and life. Those questions became, in part, more important than the single work. This becoming-philosophical of art that Danto repeatedly pointed out—for instance when he described Warhol as a philosopher[93]—is the reason why it would be absurd if art historians were to content themselves with leaving aesthetics to philosophers.

For it is art itself that makes claims for aesthetic theory. With its development toward self-reflexivity, it calls for the approximation of art and philosophy. We need this discipline for art's sake and we would be very wrong to resign ourselves to inherited disciplinary boundaries and differences. What Adorno appropriately called art's dependency on commentary makes aesthetics an indispensable enterprise that requires skills philosophers and art historians can best provide together. Philosophy yields insights into what could serve as a common denominator of art's great diversity, disclosing thereby the shared aesthetic ground for various research projects. Art history can render such insights more specific with regards to concrete instances by taking into consideration the historical origins, settings, and circumstances of individual works. Only together can philosophical concepts, in their capacity to disclose previously unnoticed connections, and art-historical approaches, in their historic considerations and visual perspicacity, ensure that we come closer to art's salient features.

Aesthetics, not in the narrow sense of either Kant's theory of aesthetic judgment or of any kind of ideologically overdetermined reading, but as an approach that seeks to develop theoretical distinctions while remaining devoted to what Jim Elkins has emphasized as the irreducibly visual and ungeneralizably singular character of works of art. One has reason to think that it is precisely this irreducibility that can scarcely be conceptually determined and that is in itself something unknown, as Elkins pointed out.[94] But then we are to understand *how* indeterminate and unknown it is. It is the work's "incomprehensibility that needs to be comprehended," as Adorno said.[95]

We could have learned from the Greeks the very notion of *theoria* as a form of intellectual vision. Likewise, this is what some versions of phenomenology could have taught us. Aesthetic theory is already based on concepts as well as on intuitions, that is to say, on their inseparability. For the antinomy of conceptions and intuitions is in itself a concept. Kant provided the insight into their very connectedness and mutual condition. And significantly this is also an insight provided by art, as Adorno has rightly emphasized: "art," he wrote, "is no more concept than it is pure intuition, and it is precisely thereby that art protests against their separation."[96] It is art, therefore, that urges us to collaborate in forging aesthetic conceptions that are not only not empty, but seeing.

Harry Cooper

Ugly Beauty (with Apologies to T. Monk)

If aesthetics is for artists what ornithology is for the birds (Barnett Newman), where does that leave art historians? Poisoning pigeons in the park (Tom Lehrer)? But seriously, leaving the birds out of it, what is the interest or utility of aesthetics for art historians? Specifically, what use do we have for the concept of beauty?

Although the word "beautiful" composed itself on my keyboard once or twice, I don't think I've ever typed b-e-a-u-t-y until just now. This supports the idea that art historians are more concerned with the particular, philosophers with the general (John Hyman). Adjectives vs. nouns, or local explanation vs. eternal truth. Such are the traditional distinctions, and they deserve shaking up. Thus it was refreshing to see a philosopher (Arthur Danto) decrying transhistorical judgments while an art historian (Thierry de Duve) made absolute claims like Kant "got it right." And why shouldn't art historians take philosophical or even aesthetic positions? Trying to bury our aesthetic responses under a pile of archives, hoping to avoid the personal and the universal at once, we end up in futile contortions.

That said, I agree that the "return to beauty" has been regressive, not so much because it returns us to formalism (Diarmuid Costello) as because it restores a naïve conception of the imagination that ignores phenomenology and semiotics. As a modernist, the question I ask is not "Does it possess beauty?" but rather "Is it successful?" or "Is it good?" or at least "Is it better or worse than another work?" There is a considerable dose of the relative in these judgments—some measurement against the stated or implied goals of the work, some consideration of the limits and possibilities of the particular language it employs or the kinds of responses it triggers—as well as a more basic judgment of aesthetic quality. I suppose that that judgment relies on a greatly expanded, perhaps exploded, conception of what is beautiful, one that takes into account all the solicitation of ugliness, shock, and difficulty that has been the trademark of the avant-garde since Gustave Courbet. This is not an "aesthetics-at-large" (Dominic Willsdon): for the self-conscious, mock embrace of the everyday in modernism enforces the category of art all the more fiercely. As for b----y, I prefer to keep a respectful (or is it an embarrassed?) silence.

Adrian Rifkin

An Aside: or Something on Not Joining In

[Adrian Rifkin's text took the form of an interlinear commentary on the seminar conversation. Here his remarks are preceded by a couple of lines from the conversation, to give them their contexts.—Ed.]

James Elkins: Let's take as our starting point that art history, considered as a discipline, is largely disconnected from aesthetics, and that that disconnection is not well theorized by either discipline. And so let me suggest that we talk about different models for the relation between the fields: let's try to gather some models, and see what features they have in common.

Adrian Rifkin: As if one were joining in the conversation muttering alongside as a guest invited late and rather ignored, but thus privileged to have heard the whole conversation before it has begun, but, at the same time, as if from another planet—the planet of theoretical heterotopias where notions like modernity were, at last, coming slowly to be forgotten and replaced by more sophisticated and yet more simple concepts of the esthetico-historical; a not-quite now, but in many ways like it had been in the eighteenth century, in texts, such as those of the Comte de Caylus for example, where aesthetics and history walk hand in hand: or even more like the sixteenth century, with Vasari, where the whole system of historical and aesthetic knowledges set each other in action in the peculiar dynamics of beauty and historical progress in their conceptual interaction, and where pictorial surface, sculptural gesture and anecdote confirm each other's probability as evidence for a judgment on art; and where—on this not-quite now planet—gender and sexuality and both general and particular understandings of otherness and self-otherness had already, and will continuously become a part of the episteme. At the same time this once and future place is not only like the eighteenth or sixteenth century but quite like now, today, with its burgeoning of new ways of writing out the aesthetic relation, that might in one case form a Foucauldian attention to the way a subject speaks or remains silent, a fittingness of a discourse to what it is we call art and the ways that it is made and seen, an acting out of a relation to the object or the moment (Dominic Willsdon almost touches on this, but Gavin Butt puts it very well in his introduction to *Beyond Art Criticism*); or it might be a way of lying close to art and listening to its murmurings of time and times and its coagulation of materials as an attention to all the possibilities of attending to itself, a non-structure that is sometimes spun out between re- and de-territorialisation (odd here to reference the desolate Jean Clair and not the productive and inventive Jean-Louis Schefer, or Deleuze): or a certain (almost) resigned yet totally invested engagement in what is given to see, the complex temporalities and spatial differences of the given in its unfolding of political disagreements, histories of the subject and their imbricated historical densities, Derrida, Rancière, Kristeva, Bal, Fisher, and Didi-Huberman, in their various ways.

Why are all the interventions that follow so afraid of oxymoron and catachresis, those twin discursive ideals of a momentary desublimation of theoretical categories? Maybe a reading of Bersani on the Nineveh Lion Hunt or Graham Hammill on sexuality and form, or even the good old warhorse of Lacan's Kant with Sade will help us to answer this? Though it—this paralysis or fear—is not a conundrum, nor is it an enigma. But what is the Kantian sublime and its aftermath if it is not a catachresis? This is what I would mumble under my breath, were I present, and even more … the adverted reader could fill it out for me. Below, in so many passages, I find myself utterly lost with all these matters of "historians already inside history (of art)," "using" aesthetic words, constrained models, words as aesthetic predicates; gory as an alternative to beautiful is an especially constrained and even strained example, and really strange in a discussion of Christian figurations; I am lost because, for better or for worse, I do not know what all of this concerns, what it regards, or rather, if I were to set out from Bourdieu, I would know all too well! Something to do with holding to the limits of a field?

Arthur Danto: There is this wonderful statement J. L. Austin makes in "A Plea for Excuses": he says we won't make progress in aesthetics until we give over talking about the beautiful and sublime, and start talking about the dainty and the dumpy. So start with dumpy, if you like, and pick a work where dumpy is not a criticism, but goes instead to make a certain kind of point. Or take the delicate; *we do use that term … or take* clunky. *Diarmuid, we talked about your favorite painter Philip Guston: his paintings are—*

AR: Here I want to recall a distant situation, just to suggest and elaborate upon how tiresome I find Austin's senior common-room chat, however much I love his writing; but you can hear the chat—"oh, that dumpy girl at Somerville" or "that plump boy at Merton." The incident took place at the then Tate. I was chairing a discussion between Thierry (he may recall it) and Boris Groys on "the return of beauty" which incidentally, but unkown to me, was the launch for the Phaidon volume on Jeff Wall. Despite of our rather careful preparation over lunch, the conversation was not going very well: and, in an attempt to focus, we looked at two slides that I had pulled out just in case we might need them. One was a photographic scene of Wall's, a *grande machine* of the kind that people like to call history painting, the other was a well-known Soviet painting, *Death of a Commissar*, and I asked which was the more beautiful. I don't want to prolong the anecdote, but I thought these things, or rather think them again while reading this conversation: the *Death of a Commissar* was beautiful in its striving for an elegiac formality, its straining to bring affect and symbol into alignment through saturated red and physiognomy, and it was touching its patina of political outwornness, of history's disillusions. The Wall I had carefully selected to appear relatively weak at the level of the figures, and even weaker at the level of the figural. On the other hand, in its matching of contemporary aesthetic expectations, the public almost certainly found Wall's light-box effects more beautiful and less quaint than the canvas; but anyway these aesthetic projections are overdetermined or hypercathected, and constitute an excess to judgment. (Poor Kant, always right and always inadequate, it is that textual strain which makes his texts so beautiful). In effect, despite the title of the Tate discussion, the beautiful began to look like a minor issue in the situation, and not to be rescued by recourse either to Kant or to objects as a focus for intellectual energies and demands. At the same time neither de Duve nor Groys rose to the bait, though the latter clearly opted, spasmodically, for the painting. So despite the diverse beauties of the two images, the situation itself was ugly. Not dainty, nor dumpy, just plain ugly, and I scuttled off as soon as I could decently end the session without making the audience feel they had been short-changed. But to the point, neither dumpy nor dainty could be substituted within the framework set out by the beautiful and the ugly; Austin was being silly, and his suggestion even further underlines the need to think of the beautiful or the ugly as situational and thus as potentially interchangeable. I saw a small Wall at the Whitechapel centenary show, the one of a sink with a lovely diagonal, and from in front of it one could, at the same time, see a Mondrian and a Kenneth Martin, each work wonderful in itself: seen together, the situation was itself beautiful—certainly not the opposite of dumpy, anything but slim—I would say it was affectively rather fat; but its beauty did not take the form of a judgment; rather it appeared an historical and aesthetic location in which the relations of aesthetics and art history (diagonal vs. vertical, order and chance, hand and mechanism, modernity and its post) themselves unwound and could be sloughed off as redundant categories of modernism's own redundancy; something like the uncanny. The situation in the Tate, on the contrary, remained plain ugly, and maybe because of the very constraints of aesthetic discourse we had accepted as our agenda. (Here I find that I have used some common words such as, overdetermination, cathected, and affect, that are largely lacking in the discussion that unfolds—as if neither Marxian nor Freudian language had ever entered into the vernacular of cultural discourse, until rather too late with Anna Dezeuze, and then within a discussion of its vulgar "usefulness.")

Diarmuid Costello: [. . .] Beauty, when predicated of works of art, needs to be invested with meaning by further explanations and elaborations. On its own it's empty as a judgment about the work.

But perhaps this is just a certain Kantian bias on my part manifesting itself, albeit in a rather perverse way, given that when one calls a work of art beautiful one isn't really predicating a determinate quality of the work at all, at least not for Kant, so much as saying something about the feeling it elicits in the viewer (and, of course, raising a normative claim off the back of that feeling). Perhaps this is why I find the idea of beauty unhelpful as a critical term; because it tells you more about how a work disposes a viewer than about the work itself.

AR: Of course here is a good instance of beginning to see how silly Austin could be, but pulling back from the insight in order to save the terms of debate that guide the conversation—beauty is not critical, "dainty" is more *useful*, as if this "critical/useful" were a significant difference; but where, oh where, is the difference between the "work itself" and "how it disposes a viewer" that is slipped in so easily as if it were an embedded fact of art? This missed chance rather reinforces my point about the fear of irregular and unexpected outcomes, but also suggests that while the missing is tied up with an apparently rigorous procedure, this itself is haunted by category errors: predicate = solution. Oh the mid-forged manacles of this aesthetic framing; catachresis be thou my guide!

Nicholas Davey: [. . .] The Kantian aesthetician is invariably interested in the artwork in and for its own sake. *It is not attributed any extra-aesthetic purpose. The art historian is, arguably, interested in the artwork for what it points to beyond itself. It is for this reason that an art historian will clearly be interested in the third sense of the term* aesthetic *(what an artwork brings us to see of its world).*

AR: Jesus, this is really muddled, every phrase is the trace of some categorial confusion—disciplined in seeing well and attentively is either a pleonasm or nonsense, and evades the historical character of discipline as a notion.

Thierry de Duve: Why go back to Kant? … I'd say with a leap that Kant's Critique of Judgment *formulates a transcendental—I say transcendental, not utopian or anything like that—foundation for democracy and peace on earth. [*Good-natured laughter.*]*

AD: That's exceedingly noble. […]

AR: In effect this is more than noble or not the same as noble and points to something we need to recognize—that a philosopher's reading of Kant is not necessarily the best one; Thierry's reading of Kant is just fine, as a reading through cognitive viability, through rendering a text operational as a text rather than as an object of exegesis, in relation at least to an access to the judgment and its respect, an impeccable liberalism in response to an especially tautological and authoritarian intervention. He responds to the symptom of a longing for a hypostatized professional reading, for the reinstatement of dogma, and a lesson on the lesson. Yet, leafing through Paul Gilroy's pages on the exclusions of Kant's democracy, the "negro," the "jew," and so forth, it's both difficult to see how one can really think Kant quite this way unless one wishes to think neither difference nor sameness as the grounding of the ungrounding of all kinds of aesthetic discourse in its situations as an accomplished discovery.

Arthur Danto: I don't know why we keep wandering off the path that James has set. The basic issue is: Why is it important for an art historian to discuss questions such as, "Why is the Grünewald altarpiece repulsive?" Repulsive *is an aesthetic term. … Take Paul McCarthy, for example. He is systematically disgusting. The question is: Why? What does that contribute to what he is doing? We don't have to worry about the meaning of disgust because it is part of our discourse—everyone agrees on that. But why does McCarthy make a point, let's say in his masterpiece* Bossy Burger, *of creating an experience so disgusting that it is hard just to stand and look? The parallels between Grünewald and the video* Bossy Burger *are intriguing, and that is where aesthetics and art history can come together.*

AR: Nonsense, frankly, philosophers without a sense of the epistemic outcome of theories of sexuality can hardly see that the grounds of comparison here—in relation to disgust—are tendentious or feeble without that, without something which is not art-historical but disgust-historical; this is one reason why Danto's work on Mapplethorpe invariably misses the issues, elaborated as it is from a blinkered heteronormativity. McCarthy certainly lives out, and wonderfully, a crisis in the dead end of just this heteronormativity that is of almost no interest at all for Grünewald; in this case the comparison is as inappropriate and weak an anachronism as the playing out of the "ugly" or the "repulsive"; it's not on the same ground of presence; nor indeed does one have to find the Grünewald any more disgusting than the environment of its original cathexis, which might rather lead to an empathetic reading—in the end there is theology as well as aesthetics, suffering as well as and in beauty, textness or textuality, that even Kant and Grünewald might share.

Martin Donougho: [...] One art historian whom philosophers do read (and who shows himself to have read philosophers) is Michael Baxandall. He is wonderful at showing the dialects of concepts such as commensurazione, *as well as the history of ideas such as* affect. *One realizes the world was different then, so that maybe we should think about the present differently as well.*

AR: Here is a lovely lapsus; the world was indeed different when Baxandall wrote what he did, and while there are powerful elements of conservation in his writing, against the iconoclasms of the moment, he precisely made no compromises with a closed dialectic, but rather "overcame" aesthetics and history through a particularizing of the sensuous in the work of art and its being made. In effect his attention to history was subtly of an oxymoron, in that the attention in itself, in its kind, was profoundly anachronistic and of our present. Now, if we are to put Kant back in his place, then we should bid farewell to anachronism? Pity.

Thierry de Duve: [...]My political philosophy is to keep the realms of the artistic and the religious separate. It is the achievement of the Enlightenment to keep thinking*—cultural thinking, artistic thinking—from the domination of religious thinking. This is why Kant is the most enlightening philosopher in the Enlightenment, and why he is so useful and timely now, politically as well as intellectually.*

AR: Noble again, but due to the perspective he misses the point, as they are not separate, only appearing to be in the narrow enlightenment. I just feel odder and odder on this planet. The rest is silence, of a kind.

David J. Getsy

Other Values (or, Is It an African or an Indian Elephant in the Room?)

Lurking behind this discussion of art history and aesthetics is the question of values. "Value" is a much-derided term, yet is at the foundation of both aesthetics and art history. It has two related definitions for the present purposes: (1) the overall desirability or purported "intrinsic" worth of the work of art—that is, the starting point and scope of aesthetics, and (2) a principle or belief held as a criterion for evaluation. At the outset, Arthur Danto rightly noted that "beauty is a value," alluding to the long-standing equation between the central object of aesthetics and its moral and ethical connotations. It is this issue of values, however, that quickly fell by the wayside in the conversation but that offers a possible hinge between aesthetics and art history.

What, we need to ask, are those values that underwrite positive and negative evaluations? In other words, what are the assumptions behind aesthetic criteria? In the classical ideal as formulated in Enlightenment aesthetics, the beautiful, for instance, was determined by those cultural values to which it was defined as being analogous. Stability, wholeness, balance, harmony, and other traits were seen to make up or contribute to beauty. One must recognize that those elements that constituted this classical ideal are also all species of the related value *order*, and this version of the beautiful privileges beyond all else the rational and the orderly. As has been repeatedly argued and proven over the subsequent centuries, however, there are many other paths to aesthetic engagement or even to the beautiful. To state it simply, fluctuating values produce other aesthetic criteria.

The problem of the historical relativism of aesthetic criteria was brought up in the roundtable, but there remained a glaring absence. This omission—the elephant in the room—was the fundamental issue of aesthetics in different cultures. There was next to no acknowledgment of cultures other than contemporary America or Western Europe, yet both historically and within our own historical moment there is overwhelming evidence for such *different* aesthetics.[97] Does aesthetics transcend cultural difference, even when individual qualities such as harmony, balance, or the like are read dissimilarly in the constitution and reception of visual things across cultures? African, Asian, Oceanic, Inuit, hybrid, and other cultures all create visually distinct objects informed by well-worked-out values. Putting to one side the important question of whether or not these cultures have a definition of "art" as is employed in the European tradition, one can nevertheless not fail to see that their visual products more often than not evince independent, unique, and even alien (to us) aesthetic concerns. It is a basic point—one that I am surprised that I have to make—yet it found no place in this debate about the proper places for aesthetics and art history.

Attempting to apprehend the constitution of cultural values and examining their transposition into aesthetic criteria, one gains not just a reminder of difference but also a stronger basis from which to understand one's own position. For, despite the protestations and disapprobations of those who take it upon themselves to be "defenders" of value or values, neither is as stable, neutral, or universal as is so often claimed. Values are amorphous in definition and perpetually in flux. Yet they can also be formalized or marshaled defensively in reaction to some perceived threat. Recognizing other values, their histories, and moments of contact between value systems helps to illuminate how our own have come about. Scattered throughout Kant's aesthetics, for instance, are counterexamples or comments on cultures *outside* Europe (for instance, the Iroquois). The growing pressure of contact with, and awareness of, non-European cultures contributed to the increasing codification of aesthetic criteria in the Enlightenment. Aesthetics, that is, has very often been entangled with the problems of cultural difference.

In order to place aesthetics in a more global network, the multiple values that inform its evaluative criteria need to be recognized for their particularity. This is where art history can make its contribution. It has begun (but by no means fully succeeded in) trying to understand the historical, geographic, and cultural contexts that determine visual production and its receptions. By contrast, aesthetics (at least as it seemed to be defended in this panel) appears too closed off and too irrelevant to the complexities of history and of global cultures. This does not mean we should throw out aesthetics. Quite the contrary, a globally and historically attuned aesthetics would allow us to see more precisely the work of art and its receptions in relation to varied historical and cultural situations—even our own.

Michael Kelly

The Aesthetic / Art / Art History Triangle

Judging by some of the language used in the roundtable discussion convened at the end of the "Re-Discovering Aesthetics" conference to explore the relationship between aesthetics and art history, I would have to say the relationship seems rather strained. There was talk of *disconnection* (between the two disciplines, imagined to occupy different "patches"), or *use* (of art history by aesthetics, or was it the other way around?), or *dissolution* (of the concepts of aesthetics by art history). Even the talk of a *confluence* of the two fields, though intended to be positive, still sounds forced. If I were a marriage counselor examining this language, I'd likely recommend that the parties see a divorce lawyer. Instead of taking such a dramatic step, however, I'd rather reexamine this language and propose a (tenth) model for the aesthetics/art history relationship based on the working relationship between the philosophy and history of science, two disciplines that in many universities around the world enjoy a civil union, if not a sanctioned marriage.

In recent decades, the philosophy of science has joined forces with the history of science, and they have done so while focusing their energies on the concrete practices of particular sciences such as physics or biology. This does not mean that the *philosophy* of science has been abandoned (to history, say), for many of the central concepts in the philosophy/history/science triangle—causation, time, explanation, and the like—are the same as those that have dominated traditional philosophy of science. But it does mean that these concepts have been historicized in the sense that they no longer have quite the same content or scope as they once did because history now provides their context and even content. Although these concepts may no longer be considered timeless, they continue to enjoy the same privileged roles in contemporary science (and they are often said to be still universal).

Something similar will happen, I believe, if aesthetics enters a working relationship with art history, and if, at the same time, they focus on art (a similar relationship could be established, or may already exist, between the other arts and art-related disciplines). Familiar concepts will continue to be discussed—beauty, meaning, form, interpretation, sublime, and the like—but such discussion will be enriched by historical understanding and contemporary practice as well as by philosophical insight. Here, too, aesthetic concepts (distinctions, principles, and the like) will no longer be considered timeless; rather, they will be historical (though some would say still universal). As such, these concepts will be better suited to render intelligible the art practices and aesthetic experiences that are themselves historical.

The (tenth) model here thus involves a triangular relationship: aesthetics/art history/art. In the light of this triangle, some of the language in the roundtable discussion that otherwise suggests a strained relationship between aesthetics and art history will become more constructive. For example, it was said that art is broader than aesthetics or, as Anna Dezeuze put it, aesthetics lags behind art. Yet Diarmuid Costello claimed that "the aesthetic" is broader than "the artistic." How can both claims be right? They can be because, as Richard Woodfield, Nicholas Davey, and Thierry de Duve point out in varying ways, there are different notions of "aesthetic" operating in the two claims.

In the first claim, aesthetics is a subdiscipline of philosophy sometimes determined (as to its interests, concepts, and the like) more by the demands of the discipline in general than by those of art. That is, some contemporary (analytic) aestheticians tend to follow the lead of cognitive science or the philosophy of language while more or less ignoring contemporary art—which is, however, as absurd as expecting philosophers of physics to follow the same leads with little or no regard for quantum mechanics. In the second claim, the aesthetic no longer refers to a subdiscipline of philosophy but rather to everyday life, to what Dominic Willsdon calls "aesthetics-at-large," which is broader than art because there are more objects and activities in everyday life that have aesthetic properties than there are objects or activities that we would call artistic. So aesthetics qua discipline may be narrower than art, yet the scope of the aesthetic is indeed broader than that of the artistic.

If understood in the context of the triangular relationship between aesthetics, art history, and art, however, these different senses of aesthetics can begin to inform and guide one another. Aesthetics needs to be broadened, on the philosophy/history/science model. And aesthetics-at-large needs to be refined so that we can better understand the philosophical impact of, say, the 9/11 memorials created on the streets of Manhattan. Arthur Danto recounts that it was such memorials that got him back into aesthetics (as distinct from the philosophy of art) because he saw people turning to beauty in a time of loss. From this observation he argues that it is clear that beauty remains necessary to life (as a value, like truth and goodness) even though it is just as clearly no longer necessary to art. This way of expressing the philosophical point here separates life and art in a way that many—philosophers as well as artists—may resist, arguing instead that whether or not the 9/11 memorials are art (they hardly need to be "elevated" to art status given how effective they were, and continue to be), they set the standard for what any art dealing with 9/11 must aspire to. However we work out these points, we now have a framework—aesthetics/art history/art, with a focus on the contemporary—for reflecting on them philosophically.

At the same time, such clarification of the narrow and broad senses of aesthetics will offset the anti-aesthetic tone in the roundtable discussion and, more generally, in contemporary art theory. As Diarmuid Costello argues, "a narrow modernist conception of the aesthetic has overdetermined the anti-aesthetic bias of postmodernism." Once the disciplinary sense of the aesthetic is properly taken in its (art) historical context, then, as Thierry de Duve has demonstrated, even Kant, typically thought to embody the paradigm of narrow aesthetics, is now, through the concept of aesthetic judgment, the inspiration for a view that the field of art includes "everything and anything today." If Kant can be understood so that we can in turn be liberated from Kantianism once "aesthetics" is calibrated to "the aesthetic," then I think it will be possible to break free of the false dilemma—modernist aesthetic or postmodernist anti-aesthetic—that constrains contemporary art history as much as aesthetics.

The aesthetics/history/art triangle will also help us to make sense of the contemporary debates about beauty. I am not convinced that the history of aesthetics ever uniformly adopted any universal concept of beauty (at least one with any content) that many critics of beauty are trying to displace, since philosophers from the very beginning of aesthetics, such as Hume, spoke about the beauties and blemishes of art together (and "common sense" was not necessarily universal in any strict sense). But I recognize that some such universal concept has had a strong cultural and intellectual influence and it does have some contemporary advocates. So the concept of beauty does need to be deconstructed, and art history can help philosophers shake any lingering allegiance to universal beauty, just as visual studies theorists are helping art historians do the same. I welcome all this. But I would add that such deconstruction is the basis for a healthy, rather than a tense relationship, even though there may be some tense moments. For example, the exchange about beauty in the Cork roundtable between Arthur Danto and Diarmuid Costello is exactly the kind of discussion we need to see more of, so long as the parties recognize, as these two do, that they are in the same game: making aesthetics relevant to the understanding of contemporary art.

Of course, all that I've said concerns only one half of the relationship between aesthetics and art history, but that is because I am a philosopher. Just as there are multiple ways of understanding aesthetics, there are undoubtedly multiple conceptions of art history. I cannot speak as well to these conceptions, but I agree with Thierry de Duve that art history without aesthetics is inconceivable because all art historians engage in aesthetic judgments. But perhaps a better word here would be "unacceptable" rather than "inconceivable," at least in the case of aesthetics. For although aesthetics without art history is indeed conceivable, (since some contemporary aestheticians writing on the visual arts all too often still try to go it alone), aesthetics without art history is no longer acceptable on philosophical or historical grounds because we have a better model to work with. We should wholeheartedly adopt this philosophical model and thereby reconfigure the relationship between aesthetics and art history via the mediation of art.[98]

It should not be difficult to follow this new model for aesthetics for several reasons. First of all, two prominent figures in recent philosophy of art—Nelson Goodman and Arthur Danto—began their philosophical careers working in the philosophy of science. Danto was influenced specifically by the work of N. R. Hanson, who himself was a pioneer in the field of the history and philosophy of science (for example, he founded the Department of History and Philosophy of Science at Indiana University in 1960). By his own account, Danto brought this same combination of philosophy and history to the philosophy of art when he first began writing about art in the 1960s. In even more recent times, several philosophers of science—Lorraine Daston, Peter Galison, and Bruno Latour—are now also writing on art; coming from the science side, they are bringing their model of philosophy and history to art. At the same time, several art historians—Caroline A. Jones and Barbara Maria Stafford, to name only a few—are working from the opposite direction to the same basic aim.[99] What I am proposing here is that philosophers working in aesthetics join the dialogue that these philosophers and art historians have already begun and to which the participants in the Cork conference have contributed to as well. So I thank the organizers of "Re-discovering Aesthetics"—James Elkins, Francis Halsall, Julia Jansen, and Tony O'Connor—for opening up another phase of this dialogue.

Margaret Iversen

Beyond the Aesthetic/Anti-Aesthetic Position

The conversation came into sharp focus for me when it turned to the question of the anti-aesthetic. What greater testimony could there be, I thought, of the continuing pertinence of philosophical aesthetics for art theory and practice than this negative self-understanding in relation to the aesthetic? I would have liked the discussion to dwell on this subject at greater length, so I will take up the topic here. Some time in the 1950s or 1960s, Duchamp's example, which had been suppressed by the Greenbergian paradigm, began to resurface—first in the work of Jasper Johns and Rauschenberg and later in the work of Robert Morris and others. This increasingly radical anti-aesthetic position, culminating in conceptual and postconceptual art, was bound to precipitate conservative reactions, including the recent revival of talk about the beautiful. Yet, as Elkins notes, there have always been artists and critics who, unhappy with either position, have tried to negotiate a path beyond them—to "think outside the opposition," as Elkins puts it.[100]

It's not surprising to find Robert Smithson's name emerging in this context. Both Elkins and Costello cite Stephen Melville's work on Smithson's practice as an expanded field that acknowledges itself as part of a wider system. Jeff Wall also remarks on Smithson in his paper, "Marks of Indifference." He notes Smithson's unusual reception of minimalist sculpture, such as Donald Judd's, whose specific objects "appeared to erase the associative chain of experience, the interior monologue of creativity." Wall suggests that "Smithson's exposure of what he saw as Minimalism's emotional interior depends on the return of ideas of time and process, of narrative and enactment, of experience, memory and allusion, to the artistic forefront, against the rhetoric of both Greenberg and Judd."[101] What Wall is describing here is Smithson's effort to think a way around the stalled antithesis of modernist aesthetics vs.

minimalist anti-aesthetics. Who but Smithson would have thought of describing Judd's steel and plexiglass boxes as "uncanny" and "on the verge of disappearance"?[102]

In all his work, but perhaps most emphatically in *Spiral Jetty* (1970), Smithson aimed to reformulate the terms of the opposition by developing what I call "an aesthetic beyond the pleasure principle." He was assisted in this project by Anton Ehrenzweig's *The Hidden Order of Art*, where a psychoanalytic conception of creative "dedifferentiation" is seen as a necessary prelude to composition and framing.[103] For Smithson, the artist's job was to endure temporarily the suspension of boundaries between what Ehrenzweig called the self and the non-self, and then return to tell the tale: "The artist who is physically engulfed tries to give evidence of this experience through a limited mapped revision of the original unbounded state."[104] Form that has not emerged out of an experience of unbounded dedifferentiation is "empty," that is, a purely formal repetition. Yet equally, pure dedifferentiation that has not been artistically transposed is unintelligible: "if art is art it must have limits."[105] Smithson effectively "displaces" the aesthetic/anti-aesthetic opposition onto a dialectical movement of destruction and composition animating artistic practice.

Both Smithson and Robert Morris were influenced by *The Hidden Order of Art*, but Morris promoted a more uncompromising, one-sided, insistence on antiform.[106] Smithson's more nuanced reading of the book meant that, unlike Morris, he always emphasized the necessary relation between the two poles of the dialectic of form and antiform. His reply to Michael Fried's famous critique of the future of art conjured up by Tony Smith's night ride on the unfinished New Jersey Turnpike is basically that the ride should not be understood as a finished work of art, but rather as a necessary preliminary, an experience of unboundedness, of antiform, that must then be presented in some legible way by the artist.[107] It strikes me that Smithson's account of his pedestrian meandering through Passaic, New Jersey was offered as a downbeat alternative to Tony Smith's sublime, formless trip.[108] The poor monuments of Passaic may seem remote from the concerns of philosophical aesthetics, but I take them to be his way of sustaining the free play of the imagination in a cold climate.

Michael J. Golec

Warhol's "Wow!"

There are two ways to take the general conversation initiated by James Elkins in "The Art Seminar." First, we can take the issues raised in conversation to articulate that we have an impoverished art history that refuses to account for aesthetic judgments. And, second, we can observe that there exists an impoverished aesthetics that disregards the history of art. All of the panel participants address these two issues. But, it is, to my mind, Diarmuid Costello's admission that locates a gap in the penurious disciplines of art history and aesthetics:

"I generally find the idea of beauty unhelpful in discussions about art, because when one says '*x* is beautiful'—which one rarely does in engaging with actual works of art—it is essentially a way of expressing a honorific judgment; it functions as a kind of placeholder, or short-hand way of saying, 'That work is good.' As such, it has about as much content or substance as a judgment as Andy Warhol's 'Wow!' It just isn't informative." Costello's formulation—that both "*x* is beautiful" and Warhol's "Wow!" equals zero information—strikes me as a productive place to begin thinking about the historical specificity of voicing, or giving voice to, an aesthetic judgment. I happen not to agree with his proposition that the anonymous, or overly generalized, "*x* is beautiful" is the same as, or is equal to Warhol's "Wow!" The distinction is crucial for both art history and aesthetics.

No doubt, the anonymous and general judgment "*x* is beautiful" isn't informative. Nevertheless, I beg to differ with Costello on his point that the articulation of an aesthetic judgment by an historically significant artist lacks information. Indeed, Warhol's "Wow!" is a "placeholder." But the artist's declaration isn't *merely* that; it doesn't take the place of, or mark the absence of, a more expansive analysis of an artwork (even if Warhol had been willing to go into more detail on anything). It is, rather, an *historical* placeholder. By this, I mean that Warhol said, "Wow!" at a specific moment, in front of a specific object. To determine the historical place of Warhol's aesthetic judgment, we must listen for the difference between his voice and the ahistorical (because anonymous) voice that states "*x* is beautiful." And in listening, we should be willing to acknowledge that Warhol's expression of aesthetic interest is both informative and meaningful.

Granted, there is certain deadpan anonymity to Warhol's "Wow!" His use of the hipster, gum-popping term to express his immediate apprehension and appreciation of something has a common tone; that is, everyone says, "Wow" about something likeable, even pleasurable. I don't believe, however, that it is the same anonymity as that expressed by "*x* is beautiful," which is anonymous in the sense that we do not know who is speaking. When Warhol says, "Wow!" we hear the voice of a person who made particular kinds of artworks, who collected certain kinds of artifacts, and who expressed interest in other artists. In this sense, the commonplace anonymity of "*x* is beautiful" can be distinguished from the historical specificity of "Wow!"

Perhaps this is what Arthur Danto means when, in response to Costello's remarks, he paraphrases J. L. Austin on "the dainty and the dumpy." Danto's comment implies that we can have access to information that we might gain from "dumpy" when the term is used to "make a certain kind of point." This access requires that we attend to the context in which the word is uttered. There is, to my mind, no reason that "Wow!" can't be examined in light of its use to make "a certain kind of point." The focus would have to be on what kind of point is being made when a Warhol says, "Wow!" We can have a better sense of the point made, and the potential information that it holds, if we have an idea of the person. Stanley Cavell has something to say on this when he remarks on the relationship between the human voice and judgments of value. It isn't simply the case, as Cavell explains, that creatures that speak can make judgments. Rather, "only a creature that can say something can say something in particular."[109] There is a particularity to the voice, a vocal grain, that says something meaningful and that, in its intentionality, points us toward something. If this were not the case, then we would have to accept that a judgment like "Wow!" is voiceless in the way that "*x* is beautiful" is voiceless.

What then does an acknowledgment, or a hearing, of Warhol's voice point us toward? Warhol's "Wow!" introduces, as Husserl might say, and as Nicholas Davey says, "horizons of meaning." "Wow!" stamps the artwork with intention; the voice marks, and remarks on, the embeddedness of a cognitive-perceptual moment in the artwork and in the viewer. Put in another way, aesthetic judgments are of something (they are intentional), just as artworks are of something. The intentional moment and its response are voiced in "Wow!" I don't want to misinterpret Davey, but I'm fairly certain that he suggests the possibility of artworks being open to such an aesthetic experience when he comments on the "horizons of meaning or *Weltanschauung* out of which the work had initially sprung." Warhol's "Wow!" makes others "see," or voices what is visible for others to see.

The challenge for both the art historian and for the philosopher of art is to listen for, and acknowledge the meaning voiced in "Wow!" In Warhol's case, voices were his companions. In *The Philosophy of Andy Warhol (from A to B and Back Again)*, Warhol says, "But I didn't get married until 1964 when I got my first tape recorder. ...When I say 'we,' I mean my tape recorder and me."[110] What strikes me as significant about Warhol's statement is that he considered the recorded voice to be a companion, as a presence that accompanied him to the Factory, to parties, to openings, and throughout the course of his day. Perhaps, like Warhol, art historians and philosophers of art too might take seriously the distinctiveness of voices in art history and aesthetics.

Michael Newman

Ideas and Contexts in Art History

In considering the various and often vexed relationships between art history and aesthetics, it is not a matter of whether art history or philosophy "subsumes" art more or less adequately. Rather, art—whether one considers the work as event, sensation, or experience—tests the limits of both philosophy and of the discipline of art history, no doubt in each case differently. Indeed, their different stances with respect to the work of art serve to distinguish philosophy and art history from one another.

The major challenge that philosophy poses to art history, I believe, lies in something that doesn't seem to have been discussed in "The Art Seminar": that is, the use of periodization. In the German and Anglo-Saxon traditions, history is subdivided into periods which then provide "contexts" for the interpretation of art. This may proceed according to the to-and-fro of a hermeneutic circle, whereby the experience of art and its documents can change the way in which the historical period is understood, and vice versa. Nonetheless, the "closure" that makes the discipline possible—and there is no discipline of thought without some kind of closure—has largely been that of the historical period. This is reflected institutionally in syllabi, and in hiring according to period of specialization, thereby reproducing the primacy of periodization in the definition of art history. Although originally intended to introduce a methodological rigor, this approach has been something of a disaster for the discipline. A periodized art history provides a part of the story, but not necessarily the most important part.

Philosophy, in its different relation both to itself and to the work of art, may provide a way to challenge the dominance of periodization in art history. It would therefore be a matter not of importing concepts from aesthetics into art history, or replacing art history with philosophy, but rather of a philosophical transformation of art history itself.

I am not at all arguing for "transcending" history toward "eternal" aesthetic values, but rather for a rethinking of history itself, on the basis of a distinction between "history" and "historicity." The philosophy of art may throw into question the conception of history as "context": the artwork "in" history is "historical"; an alternative way of understanding the artwork is not as "in" history but "as" history, perhaps as a form of initiation. A beginning is an event. This does not mean that the event (and at a metalevel, the conception of the artwork as event), cannot itself be contextualized (as "modernism," for example). Both philosophy and art history are concerned with the edge or border between event and history, but they come at it from different directions: philosophy from the universal claim of the event; art history from the context or actuality into which the event is absorbed. This leaves us with the question of the relation between "event" and "object." Would it be the case that philosophy is able to think of the artwork as event, while art history is restricted to the categories of the object, its qualities, and its context? I think we need to problematize the opposition.

One way of doing this would be to suggest that, if the artwork is initially considered as an "event," then its mode of becoming goes to the root of the constitution of the object. Rather than artworks being limited kinds of objects, the object is a limited mode of the artwork. And this in turn must radicalize art history, since it could no longer understand that with which it is concerned as an object in the limited sense. Either art history has to begin with the event that always exceeds any historical contextualization—philosophically this would be close to Alain Badiou[111]—even though there is obviously no "contextual" access to this excess. Or, it must transform the notion of the object, from the bearer of qualities which may be aesthetic or historical or both, to something closer to the idea of the object that Bruno Latour derives from the etymology of the Germanic *Ding*. According to Latour, the idea of the "thing" combines the way people are gathered around a matter of concern, and their representation of that object. The event-dimension is always already objectified, but that object cannot be reduced to the referent of representations or the bearer of qualities, since it is also the very gathering of (and not simply that which gathers) those who are concerned.[112] Where and how, then, is the "thing" of art constituted? What and where are the public, social, and institutional spaces in which art becomes a matter of concern?

We could say that criticism is the practice in which the art becomes a matter of concern. Does art criticism "mediate" between art history and philosophy, as Arthur Danto suggests? The first question to ask is: if it does, how does it mediate? As a mediation between the universal and the particular, as the "application" of concepts? Or as the search for the concept of the particular through judgment? Second question: couldn't we see criticism not as mediating, but as dividing or differentiating art history and philosophy, and doing so on the basis of something about the artwork that may be assimilated to neither? Perhaps criticism is both mediating and differentiating, which puts it in a difficult, contradictory position: criticism is set to work by the very excess that it "reduces": the universality that it desires in its judgment inevitably is brought down to the partiality of a particular social group.

Art history, for Thierry de Duve, is the record of past aesthetic judgments and the "transmission" of tradition, which now includes the tradition of the avant-garde. We have to take account of the fact that art history as a discipline arose in relation to a *crisis* of transmission. This is well attested by Aby Warburg—the Warburg

Institute was supposed to be the place where transmission (specifically of the classical tradition in the Renaissance) would be studied, but also performed.[113] This was necessitated by a crisis in transmission that Walter Benjamin attributed to a crisis of experience in modernity. Art history cannot be understood simply as a means of transmission, since it is precisely a symptom of its failure.[114] Therefore art history no less blocks transmission than assures it, usually both at the same time. This paradox would be particularly acute when it comes to the transmission of the "avant-garde," which surely is the art of the break, of the interruption of tradition. How do you transmit the interruption of transmission without reducing it to continuity? Precisely by the false continuum of historicism that Benjamin deconstructed? In this situation, Benjamin may be understood as the "critic" par excellence.

Diarmuid Costello suggests that Kant's third *Critique* overdetermined subsequent debates, especially in the last couple of decades of the 20th century. It is interesting to note that "critique" has virtually disappeared as an approach in art criticism, except perhaps when written by philosophers. The philosophical input into criticism that seems to grab the specialist public's imagination now comes rather from Deleuze and his followers. Deleuze seems to me to be elaborating not critique but a new kind of materialism—or at least a new spin on a very old atomist materialism, which is actually to be found in the pre-Kantian origins of criticism in the 18th century, in Diderot. Aesthetics would revert to its older reference to sensation, rather than judgment based on a feeling that would already be a determination or "territorialization" of a sensation. (I suspect that this contemporary emphasis on sensation has something to do with the encroachment of new media on everyday life, and is both a response to, and reaction against, the hypermodernity of the digital.) Deleuze's book *Francis Bacon: The Logic of Sensation* is an exemplary piece of philosophical criticism, and one that makes no reference to judgment or critique.

A question remains of *where* criticism takes place, in a metaphoric as well as a practical sense. For criticism to have a project, as opposed to declining into promotion or reverting to art history or theory, it requires a public space, one that it contributes to creating. Dominic Willsdon contrasts the art of Gonzalez-Torres to street memorials, the former being acceptable in a museum, the latter not. But what of an artist who makes street memorials? I am thinking of the nonmonumental "monuments" to philosophers (Spinoza, Deleuze, Bataille) by the Swiss artist Thomas Hirschhorn. Art practice is not separate from philosophy, art history, and art criticism: there are all sorts of "feedback loops" at work. The very discipline that explores the conditions of possibility for the constitution of object-domains may itself become the object of its object, whether that be art history or art practice. This is inherent in the philosophy of art from the beginning, in Plato, the "artist" of the dialogue excludes the artists from the city. Hirschhorn takes up Plato's paradoxical position from the side of the artist, throwing the relation of inside and outside into question, as he does with his installations. We need a topology that would complicate the opposition of inside and outside, and thereby also the relations between artwork, philosophy, history, and criticism.

Gregg M. Horowitz

Aesthetic Knowing and Historical Knowing

To comment on the significance of a conversation that you did not experience first-hand is always a tough job. When the subject of the conversation is the relation between aesthetics and art history, commentary becomes so deliciously self-reflexive that it is easy to believe that James Elkins had a trap for philosophers in mind when he designed the assignment. I do not mean to say that the task has not been pleasurable. The transcript offers so many spontaneously expressed provocative ideas that it would be churlish to be ungrateful for the opportunity to have listened in.

The sense of being trapped arises instead from the fact that what has been withheld from me, but is nonetheless as utterly palpable as the persistent embodiment of my absence from the scene, is precisely the experiential—which is to say the aesthetic—aspect of the roundtable itself. Because I have such restricted access to the embodied thinking that went on that day, I find myself in an unintended alliance, perhaps even a conspiracy, with the historical side of the conversation.

The most frustrating moments of powerlessness occur when Elkins, in his role as moderator, sums up intellectual accomplishment by summarizing a previous line of inquiry. Had I been in attendance at the roundtable I likely would have experienced these moments of synthesis as helping "us" to gather up the diverse wildflowers of the discussion into little bouquets of illumination. On the page, however, Elkins's summaries serve as reminders to the reader that he is merely a reader and neither a participant nor an auditor, that he is perceiving no cocked eyebrow, shrugged shoulder, or glowering glance, no low grumble, indiscreet whisper, or sharp intake of breath. Not one perceptible nuance of phrase or gesture remains to memorialize the individual perspectives of the participants as they were swept up into the monument of group achievement. The reader can only struggle to glean from the transcript of the event traces of those phenomena that, had he been an auditor, he at least would have glimpsed or overheard or taken in only unconsciously but that, in any case, are as crucial to the dialectical progress of an argument as any well-scored points. This loss of aesthetic experience may be the price we pay to have historical records, but it is no less a loss for all that.

But exactly what sort of loss of experience is this? As I have already suggested, it is not necessarily a loss of pleasure. Reading quietly and alone has its own pleasures, such as untrammeled speculation about the motives of the "characters" in the script, and I suppose it is a matter of taste whether one values such pleasures more than those of audition. But if reading a transcript of the conversation does not entail a loss of pleasure, why do I feel the need right off the bat to ward off the thought that pleasure, pain, and their fate are the principal stakes in aesthetic experience? I must confess that I would have dropped this concern with pleasure and pain altogether were it not that the participants at the roundtable largely treat aesthetic qualities as bearers of pleasure or displeasure the significance of which is captured not, paradoxically, in feeling them, but rather in understanding how they make other perceivers feel. This is why Arthur Danto proposes that art historians ought to discuss aesthetic qualities when the question of how those qualities affect viewers is internal to the meaning of the artwork that bears them, right alongside the work's representational qualities. But it is also why judgments of aesthetic quality are perpetually in danger of becoming, as Diarmuid Costello puts it, mere signals of the emotional states of perceivers that are "uninformative" about works themselves. The only plausible counterexample to this emotive regard for aesthetic qualities arises, oddly, in the course of the discussion of beauty. While one might be inclined to think of beauty as the aesthetic quality most vulnerable to purely hedonic interpretation—the one most like the Warholian "Wow!," as Costello suggests in his disagreement with Danto—Danto rightly reminds us that "beauty" is also the name of a basic value, right up there with truth and goodness. Beauty is something that can help guide one's life, can help, indeed, to figure out how to live it as a life.[115] But this thought, that beauty, and perhaps some other aesthetic qualities, mark fundamental moments of personal or cultural valuing, which is to say moments of *affective knowing*, is, strangely, never picked up in the roundtable. Even Nicholas Davey, who helpfully reminds us that for the Greeks *aisthesis* was normatively bound up with knowledge and acknowledgment, permits "the aesthetic" to drop back into the realm of the noncognitive by mistakenly attributing to Kant the view that an aesthetic interest in the artwork—an interest in it, in and for its own sake—necessarily entails a denial that the artwork is also a site of knowing. The aesthetic, in short, persistently, maybe even resistantly, remains a stalking horse for arational affectivity, in a way I am sure Kant, with his interest in disinterested *perception*, would repudiate in a flash.

I will take up the issue of aesthetic valuing directly in a moment, but let me press my point about the cognitive significance of aesthetic experience by returning to the matter of what is lost for me in not having aesthetic access to the conversation at the roundtable. Three times in the transcript, noise in the room is noted as significant, albeit without attribution to any specific speaker. I am thinking of when the reporter records laughter in the room. But why record this and none of the sneezes and paper-shuffling and assorted hems, haws, and excuse me's that no doubt punctuated the discussion? Hard to say for sure, but the laughter in question seems to convey to the absent reader something crucial about the meaning of what has just been said by the speaker, something that is manifestly over and above what the recorded "mere words" convey but that is nonetheless essential to grasping what was said. This is especially complex and moving when the laughter in response to Thierry de Duve's claim that Kant provided a transcendental foundation for peace on earth is described as "good-natured." Had de Duve gone momentarily soft in the head, or did he actually believe that Kant successfully established a basis for neighborliness and democracy with philosophical tools alone? The transcription of the laughter tells me that the answer is both. That there was laughter means that the audience registered immediately that de Duve had said something absurd, but that it was good-natured signifies both that the absurdity was not the belief that peace on earth is a good thing (were it a room full of war-mongers the transcription would have noted their barking and braying) and that de Duve himself had somehow gently signaled that he knew (or sort of, or almost knew) there was something a touch silly, maybe even a little politically old-fashioned, in his flight of unguarded optimism. Crucially, then, the good-natured laughter tells me not merely something about de Duve's manner of speaking. It tells me also what he said. It bears meaning, in other words, and not just local color.

My interpretation of this meaning is, to be sure, speculative, and so I could be off-base in all of my inferences. But that worry makes my point: what the *transcribed* laughter makes abundantly clear in its indeterminacy, and in the indeterminacy in which it bathes the words it surrounds, is that what goes missing when one is not there to experience the discussion is an entire mode of access to the multiple "valuings" of the conversation, to, that is, the different and intersecting ways it was perceived. The loss of the aesthetic dimension, then, even if necessary for creating an intelligible record for later commentators—let us call them "historians"—is also, and at the same time, the loss of the experience of a means of knowing. And this loss strikes me as all the more glaring in the context of commenting on this roundtable because, notwithstanding the aesthetic being one of the poles of the discussion, the problem of aesthetic knowing is not reflected in the discussion itself. Perhaps it is the privilege of aesthetic access that its immediate force makes one able to forget the massive mediation that goes into making it possible? Perhaps, in other words, the speakers did not shape their words in light of the demands of posterity? Good for them! But in any case, all that remains for the reader is a transcribed record, a contribution to history, in which the aesthetic phenomena which bore the historical moment have been corroded, leaving pure knowledge—which is to say, radically partial knowledge—as their monument.

But have I not, in fact, come around to the thought with which Elkins closes the roundtable, that the acid bath of history, and of art history in particular, dissolves the claims of the aesthetic? Has it ever happened otherwise, he asks, as if the corrosion of the aesthetic by the art-historical were itself a philosophical necessity? At first glance this seemed a puzzling summative question. The most that seemed to have been achieved dialectically at the roundtable in the agon between aesthetics and art history was a standoff between two claimants who are obviously related but nonetheless cannot find their common ancestor. Whence the corrosive relation? Why does Elkins recommend a grisly renewal of the dismemberment of the body of poor old Kant, as if his corpus were, in fulfillment of John Hyman's counterhistorical wish, still a unity more than two hundred years after his death?

On reflection, however, I think I see at least some of what motivates Elkins's question, and why it is in a way a perfect summary of the conversation. But my insight is dim, so I must proceed deliberately. Art historians, as they are depicted (largely by themselves) in the roundtable, are driven by a disciplinary *will to know*. Like all disciplined states of knowing, art history dissolves what it confronts so it can digest it in its own terms. And that's fine, of course, for it is an old saw that understanding requires an analytic decomposition of its object. But one would think that the object of art-historical understanding is artworks themselves and not aesthetic experience. If the undigested artwork is the source of both the challenges to, and the achievements of, art history, why should the existence of another discipline be in need of dissolution? Perhaps aestheticians think that art is not for knowing but for feeling, thereby standing in the way of the art-historical will to know? But that cannot be right, since then aestheticians would be know-nothings, and from know-nothings knowers have nothing to fear. So, again, why would aesthetics need to be corroded by art history? The demand makes sense, I think, only if aesthetics were perceived as the obstinate preserve of *another way of knowing* art, a way that, because genuinely other to disciplinary historical knowing, yet nonetheless a way of knowing, impedes the disciplinary will of art history. Put the other way around, art-historical analysis of artworks would remain incomplete, and so the discipline's will to know would remain frustrated, only if an alternative discourse of art has a cognitive claim on us and so points to an object of knowledge that remains historically uncomprehended. Is there something that we can know about art when we experience it aesthetically which would reveal thereby an intrinsic incompleteness in the standard historical understanding of art? If so, then aesthetics would need to be dissolved by art history, understood as a formation of a disciplinary will to know, for exactly the same reasons that the last traces of religious belief need to be dissolved by dogmatic skepticism. In both cases, the claim to be another discourse of knowledge would need to be gutted in order for the one true secular discourse to unfold itself in all its glory.

Now, I am just as uncomfortable with my comparison between aesthetics and religion as I hope others are. It seems to depict aesthetics as a redoubt of arationality resistant to the authority of historical knowledge. But my aim is the exact opposite: to underscore that the inheritor of the religious mantle of affective dogmatism is the ahistorical belief that there is only one true discourse, and thus to call into question the basis for the absolute distinction between historical knowing and aesthetic affectivity. The pure pleasures of affective arationality are, regrettably, alien to me, but there seems little doubt that, when they get united with dogmatic conceptualization, they become a very powerful engine of unreflective historicizing. De Duve comes close to making this point when he observes that the blind spot of art history is its seeming incapacity to historicize itself. Art historians do not seem to see their discipline's own social function, as de Duve puts it in a Nietzschean vein, as a conservator of cultural traditions. I would expand on de Duve only by noting that the enterprise of art history as a discipline of knowledge may not be able to redeem this blindness because the condition of its possibility as a discipline of *specifically historical* knowing is the *specifically historical* disappearance of the context of production of the works that it enables us to know. At that moment of disappearance, the prosthesis of historical knowledge becomes necessary to grasp the meaning of the works. This also suggests, however, that the vast history of disappearing contexts on the beaches of which abandoned works are washed up is not itself comprehensible by the disciplinary historical gaze.

All philosophical huffing and puffing aside, the point I am trying to make is really a simple one: art can be known historically only when it has survived the disappearance of its historical moment of production. But this simple point creates an aggressively complicated aporia: while art can be known historically because it is a made thing, it could not in principle have been made to survive in contexts its makers could not anticipate. The artwork "itself," which is the object of historical explanation, is then nothing but art stripped bare of its normatively commanding context of production. Art history, thus, becomes historically possible at just that moment when its exclusive claim to ruthless discursive control of the meaning of its targeted historical vagrants is intrinsically unsupportable. The work is what has survived its context; it is, to (mis)use a point made by Martin Donougho, unsituated. And set adrift from their contexts of production, artworks live by leaking meanings that their makers never knew they contained. These meanings that artworks contain but that can only be disclosed in decontextualized and decontextualizing perception (what Kant called disinterested perception) are the objects of aesthetic experience. Aesthetic experience is thus a means of knowing, but what it enables us to know is the unconscious of the humanly made, i.e., historically made, object. The contentious way to put this point would be to say: the denial that artworks have meanings that can only be known when historical knowledge loses its privilege to overrule aesthetic experience, i.e., the denial of the pact between vagrant meanings and aesthetic judgment, is regressive, unreflective, a remnant of the religious ideal of one comprehensive discourse. But to make a point contentiously when the conversational opportunity for contention has passed is rude. So I will just say this: what the aesthetic experience of art enables us to know and what the discipline of art history enables us to know need not be the same. Yet both are modes of knowing. This is simply another way of saying that the rights of judgment remain untrammeled.

I would like to be able to bring Freud, Benjamin, and Adorno to bear on this issue, for despite their having developed powerful arguments for the need to historicize historical knowing in order to comprehend its function for us, the spirit of their auto-critiques is almost entirely absent from the conversation. But instead let me conclude by saying that the need to criticize historical knowing rests on nothing else but an acknowledgment of the deeply historical nature of our practices *and knowledge*, and that the question must be raised within art history about the basis for such an acknowledgment. I do not invoke the spirit of the critics of historicism in order to attack historical knowledge; rather, we must criticize dogmatic historicism in order to understand how historical knowledge is possible. In the case of art history in particular, coming to grips with the vagrant object, the object that is hypercathected with meaning because it has lost its normative context yet continues to be meaningful, is one such crucial condition. But the vagrant object is the object of aesthetic experience in which we affectively value what cannot be known *right now* and what thereby calls for understanding *in the future*. The future of art history as a discipline of knowing thus depends on a future for aesthetic experience. This Benjaminian idea does not entail that art history needs to become aesthetics any more than that aesthetics must become art history. Rather, the crux of the matter is the continued entwining of distinct futures for knowing art, and for knowing what art knows. I comfort myself with the reminder that several art historians, such as T. J. Clark, Michael Fried, and Rosalind Krauss, seem to grasp well enough that the nonreifying history of works that have slipped their contexts of production depends on the capacity to experience artworks aesthetically. So I am not standing on ground occupied only by aestheticians when I say that it is hard for me to imagine that art history could ever finally digest aesthetic experience without thereby losing its capacity to help us understand art. Indeed, the auto-critique of aesthetics, too, depends on our ability to historicize it by bringing the tools of art history to bear. Such historicization, however, has nothing to do with what people in the past used to "feel." Instead, it has to do with whether we can perceive what was known in the past that has escaped the clutches of normative history. It depends, in other words, on whether we can aesthetically experience artworks.

Stephen Melville

Reckoning with Kant

I find it hard not to think of the context in which these remarks will appear as the world of the character Martin Heidegger describes, in "The Age of the World Picture," as "the research man." It is a leading feature of this character that he is in a certain sense always on the move and nowhere at home, but in another way he is at least based in what the philosopher clearly sees as a university radically transformed. As he puts it:

> The effective unity characteristic of the university, and hence the latter's reality, does not lie in some intellectual power belonging to an original unification of the sciences and emanating from the university because nourished by it and preserved in it. The university is real as an orderly establishment that, in a form still unique because it is administratively self-contained, makes possible and visible the stirring apart of the sciences into the particularization and peculiar unity that belong to ongoing activity.[116]

It seems to me that Heidegger sees here a particular problem—the emergence of what Bill Readings called "the university of excellence"—notably early and apart from the GI Bill, globalization, incentive-based budgeting, and other things we often adduce in explanation of the contemporary university.[117] And I cite Heidegger here because I want to start by emphasizing how very strongly the intellectual questions that animated the roundtable at Cork and that find a certain continuation in the present volume are also questions of the university and its inhabitants—institutional and professional questions, questions of, for example, curriculum, and so questions of what we expect art historians or aestheticians to know and how we expect them to come to that knowledge. To evoke a now-vanished model that still shadows much of our teaching: a university undergraduate curriculum that places a premium on some vision of a core humanistic knowledge both argues—gets students in the habit of thinking—that philosophy and art and history and literature might all have something fairly intimate to do with one another, and also imposes on the disciplinary specializations that stand on that foundation some general curricular obligation to it (if your core makes Aristotle and Kant and Marx fundamental, it's harder to have a Philosophy Department that organizes itself primarily or exclusively around contemporary philosophic idioms). Conversely, if you set your foundation—as my university among many, many others currently does—in a kind of sampling from otherwise noncommunicating specializations, it will be more nearly up to the student to decide whether and how any of these things might have anything to do with any other, and the main curricular obligation imposed on any given department will merely be to be adequate to the way it chooses to introduce itself.

All that's obvious enough but may be useful in underlining the extent to which the things we might find ourselves saying in general intellectual conversation about aesthetics and art history can—and I think should—be translated into direct institutional questions: Should an art history student know something about aesthetics? And if so, what? And when? And where? What about the aesthetician? If we think the art historian should know Kant, is that because Kant represents a certain moment in the history of taste or in "the literature" of Enlightenment (a period term art history interestingly mostly doesn't know; we have only a messy, nearly unthinkable item we settle for calling "the 18th Century." Is that another question?) or perhaps of Romanticism? Is it because we think Kant belongs in some significant way to the history of art history, taking one important step toward the modern possibility of the discipline? Or is it because we think what Kant says about art, or beauty anyway, is important, is something art historians should deal seriously with? At what level do we expect an art historian to be able to deal with the characterization of Clement Greenberg as "a Kantian," and how far do we want that art historian to be able to pursue as complex a footnote as Michael Fried's comment, in "Art and Objecthood," that "in a discussion of this claim with Stanley Cavell it emerged that he once remarked in a seminar that for Kant in the *Critique of Judgment* a work of art is not an object"?[118]

If we take it seriously that the university Heidegger mourns in 1938 and whose nostalgic tug I sometimes also feel is genuinely gone, one might well think that whatever unity the university might now claim for itself is going to have to come not from its overarching wisdom and self-understanding but somehow out of its very disciplinary scattering. And this can't just mean caulking up the fissures between our fields—if that were enough we would not have lost our faith in the grounding capacity of "the humanities"—but must instead point toward a more complex kind of interdisciplinarity, as if every discipline taken to or at its limit had within itself the capacity for a particular interdisciplinarity, a capacity to discover within itself something like

> the terms of a possible university. A department might then wish to cease imagining itself as coinciding with a discipline and choose instead to play host to such parasites as its particular environment offers. We might be surprised by the intellectual models—and conversations—we'd have on our hands then.

I don't of course mean that this is only art history's business; it might be philosophy's as well, and all my questions rewritten for that place. Rewriting them that way might, however, prove more difficult: arguably, art history knows itself to be partial in ways philosophy doesn't or at least doesn't know sustainedly and clearly. No one, to my knowledge, has proposed that art history might have special access to the unifying core of the university, although that thought has certainly been known to philosophy, and literary study has had its moments of bearing that burden in the name of national culture. In any case, it is to art history that I am attached, and I have no real choice but to write out of that attachment (and that's the case even if—some in my department would surely say this—my attachment to art history is first of all and absolutely determinatively a detachment from philosophy).

If art history has never been a bearer of any particular vision of the university, one cause is certainly that it is a late-comer to the university, taking up the place prescribed for it in an institution already in movement toward the one in which we now teach and write. Especially in the U.S. it is as if invented precisely for that institution, formed up in advance for the world of "the research man."[119] There's good reason, I think, to attribute much of this work of invention to Erwin Panofsky. Panofsky uses, very effectively, his attention to the Renaissance to create art history as a humanistic discipline that defines itself in large measure by its relation to the sciences, particularly as we imagined them in the 1920s and 1930s. He does this by setting a particular relation of distance between the subject of the art historian and his or her object, by discerning a particular need for method in negotiating that distance, and by shifting the Kant that matters to art history from the *Critique of Judgment* to the epistemologist of the first *Critique*. Some art historians have lately taken a considerable interest in tracing out how this all came to pass—sometimes as a matter of direct intellectual history and sometimes in ways more deeply interior to art history itself; it seems fair to say that our interest in these matters arises in part at least from the sensed pressure of visual culture (or visual studies) on the discipline and so a need to review, perhaps rethink, art history's claims to disciplinary specificity.[120] One very general thought here would be that Panofsky's foundations for art history are already those visual culture will come to claim as its own (in this way, visual culture would actually owe very little to "theory," and everything to already existing ideas of distance, method, and objectivity), and that this may oblige an art history that wants to insist upon the distinctness of its object to return to versions of art history that show some greater capacity to think about that (as, for example, with Riegl and Wölfflin) and also to take a sharper interest in those forms of contemporary art history that claim a fundamental allegiance to criticism. Michael Baxandall has certainly been the most explicit about holding art history to be a particular mode of art criticism, but it seems distinctly uncontroversial to subscribe both Michael Fried and Rosalind Krauss to some version of this view. Joseph Koerner must, I think, hold it as well. Most social historians of art would, I think, not enroll themselves under this banner, but T. J. Clark is surely committed to it, and one might suspect that Tom Crow is as well. Indeed, the more one works through whatever list one may have of art historians who seem to have made truly major contributions to the field, the harder it may become to think of any who cannot be said to hold this view. This may lead one to slightly rephrase the issue: it's not a question about to whom this view can be plausibly attributed, but about how far one or another writer renders this fact of his or her work thinkable (or, conversely how far the work itself dissembles this fact, holds it beyond or outside its own thought). I take this rephrasing to be implicit in the shape of Baxandall's claims in this area—not that the art historian *should* be a critic, but that an adequate account of explanation in art history, adequately attended to, reveals art history as criticism.

To say this is to say that art history is, among other things, a continual testing of its object-domain, and it is surprising to me that there is, in the roundtable, no terribly sustained discussion of the notion that aesthetics might have something fairly considerable to do with picking out or delimiting that domain. There are, of course, positions within philosophical aesthetics that set out precisely to rule this thought out—the whole family of "institutional theories of art" responds, with quite varying levels of sophistication, to this impulse, and it is certainly not the only such stance within philosophical aesthetics. It's not my purpose here to argue one way or another about the rightness of such theories—but I do very much want to underline how far art history's disciplinary identity (what I tend to call its "objectivity," its having a principled or proper object) as well as its understanding of its own central procedures and claims is at stake in such arguments.

Thierry de Duve remarks, in response to a comment about the usefulness of Kant, "Say you throw yourself out of the window, and you land on the sidewalk. Is Newton useful to you? You have just obeyed the law of universal gravity, that's all." It seems to me that the actual force of the remark vanishes into the laughter and applause that greeted it. Or perhaps it's more accurate to say that the force gets lost between a particular uncertainty in its address (that it is directed all at once to Arthur Danto, whose comment provoked it, to anyone in his or her encounter with a putative work of art, and toward art history insofar as art is its essential object and, so to speak, medium[121]), and its rapid recruitment by Jim Elkins into "the provisional list of models," which is precisely what the remark itself aimed to decline.[122]

De Duve's right; we don't want Kant's aesthetics—if we do indeed want it, something I assume at least for the purpose of these remarks—we want it for its ability to show us how to do or get something but presumably also for something more like orientation: It can't help us avoid the sidewalk, but it can help us understand why there aren't choices about what happens to us when we jump out windows; it can, for example, show us, or seem to show us, how it is that history of art doesn't get done apart from criticism, and maybe that will be enough to stop us from flinging ourselves out of certain windows in hopes that flight will somehow happen. The force of de Duve's remark depends, first of all, on being clear that beauty, as Kant proposes it, is not a concept and so is not parallel to the other cases it tends to get treated with in the discussion (delicate and dumpy and clunky and so on; repulsive is perhaps a special case, evidently visceral, but then, even guts have their histories). It's notable too that Kant does not, on the face of it, expect that the primary instance of our finding and calling something beautiful will be a work of art; it is, for reasons intimately bound up with the nature of the judgment itself, some natural sight—a sunset, a flower, a particular landscape in its fall of light.

That we don't always see this clearly suggests, among other things, that our view of Kant has been blocked by the rather different figure of Clement Greenberg standing in an artist's studio and turning his thumb up or down while repeating Kant's name. What we need to see is something more like ourselves walking somewhere and being struck by something particular enough to give voice to words uncertainly—say, undecidably—balanced as if between their aim at an object and their expression of our being struck. If we recognize this situation as one we have in fact passed through, then we'll know also that what we may have said—what one of us will have said—may very well not have been "that is beautiful." I don't imagine we never say that, I do suspect that more often than not we say something significantly less articulate than that—like "wow" or "oh" or "look." I take this reduction of the explicit judgment to something less propositional as a mark of the peculiar logical status Kant grants to this judgment. And just as the judgment is quick to surrender, and perhaps has trouble rising to, proper logical form, so also its most ordinary tone is also not that of explicit judgment; in particular, Kant says that it is not said by "I" to "you," which is why in working through this example I've played with "we" and "us" and "one" as I have. When I say whatever it is I say before that particular flower or sunset, I'm not communicating anything and am in some sense content to be overheard. The "universal voice" is, Kant seems to me to be saying, one that is genuinely a voice—in that sense inevitably someone's, issuing from one mouth rather than another—but even I, pronouncing my words, more nearly overhear than speak those words. Judgments of this kind are upset by dissent just because that throws their voice as it were back into mere communication between distinct subjects, refusing the deep sociability it had assumed.[123] That's not a problem we have when you disagree with my characterization of one form or another as "clunky" or, for that matter, "pretty." And if we stick to Kant's claim that beauty is not a concept, we see that there is no fixed or fixable relation between clunkiness or delicacy or prettiness and beauty; Kant's no help that way, although he may help us understand how we are taken with this clunkiness, why it feels like a discovery of something.

But now we have in fact begun slipping our way into Guston's studio, which evidently has something to do with why we are now trying to gather up certain words around the thing we are seeing and are no longer simply content with an unanchored and vanishing voice. Kant seems to me to suggest strongly both that we are more or less always crossing this line, and that it remains nonetheless a line worth remarking: we cross it when in front of that sunset we say something like, "Look at the purple there almost underneath the orange" (I think I've sometimes said things like that on the Oregon coast). Arguably we've already betrayed both the line and the capacity to cross it even with that first "wow" or "oh" or "look"—somewhere there may be creatures who simply drink beauty in, but they will in the event say nothing and will take no interest in art except, as it were, by accident. As if to say: where there are judgments of beauty, there will be art with all its failures and betrayals and discoveries. As if also to say: without beauty, we would be creatures capable of no more than meaning (call that "culture," imagining art then as something that emerges peculiarly against culture's grain but not separable from its conditions).

It seems to me important in reading with Kant that one cannot, in fact, get to something worth calling his thought of art without entering some appeal to the sublime. I think we need that to understand the difficult repetitions of "als" that mark §45's first paragraph, which is why that remark on art and beauty can only be made at this point in the text.[124] I also read this section in absolutely intimate connection with the ones that follow on genius. Here too I'll favor a distinctly low-temperature reading: "genius" amounts—and here I'd claim to be following Kant's scenario with a certain imaginative closeness—to whatever it is that shows when in roomful of more or less perfectly competent imitators and imitations the teacher remarks of one bit of work, "That's promising." Kant's account of how "promising" work is possible draws very directly on the account of the sublime—both are matters of the discovery in one's self of a capacity not hitherto knowable as such, awakened in the encounter with an external object, and distinguished by the way in which that encounter forces bare seeing to metaphorical or other transformation of its object. My choice of terms in which the teacher might be imagined to register this event is meant to underline Kant's insistence that what shows here is in some way exemplary, not a following of ... but a to-be-followed, and so also something in need of securing—first of all by the student artist him or herself (there is the real risk of nonsense, of something that only looks like promise, like promising).[125]

But nothing in Kant lets me get much beyond this further gathering of my orientation. If I should become persuaded that what there is to hear in Kant's "als"—the identity it both asserts and swerves from—is best heard, retuned, in Hegel's accounts of the speculative proposition,[126] I will feel as if I've found a way to go on within that orientation but in terms that I can no longer anchor directly to it.

This is then not particularly "a defense of beauty." No more, at least, than Newton's apple or de Duve's flung professor is a defense of gravity. It is, of course, intended in part as a defense of art history—an attempt to show something of its peculiar orientation or its medium, the conditions under which it can claim an object at all (the way you might say what it is to make an airplane or a building, what conditions such things cannot but admit). As such a defense it has certain consequences for how one conceives the overall shape of the discipline (one might, for example, be less willing to accept Panofsky's imagination of it), and to the extent that this depends on working through a particular relation to aesthetics, it may be more or less interesting in relation to the various issues raised at the roundtable.

Probably most of all it means to be an "intervention" (I somehow always like this word better in French) in that conversation—by which I mean that it tries to recall that conversation to the concreteness of our actual practices and institutions. And it does so because I am persuaded—by Hegel among others—that if we begin our conversations by positing a disconnection, our models and theories or theorizations can only end by reproducing it.

Notes

1. Jane Forsey, "The Disenfranchisement of Philosophical Aesthetics," *Journal of the History of Ideas* 64 no. 4 (2003): 581–97.
2. Jacques Rancière, "Le ressentiment anti-esthétique," *Magazine Littéraire* (November 2002): 21.
3. Georges Didi-Huberman, "La dialectique peut-elle se danser? " *Magazine Littéraire* (November 2002): 45.
4. Robert Filliou, cited in *Robert Filliou: génie sans talent*, exhibition guide (Villeneuve d'Ascq: Musée d'art moderne Lille Métropole, 2004), 4.
5. J.L. Austin, *Sense and Sensibilia*, reconstructed from the manuscript notes by G.J. Warnock (Oxford: Oxford University Press, 1962), p. 3.
6. J. Hyman, *The Objective Eye: Colour, Form and Reality in the Theory of Art* (Chicago: University of Chicago Press, 2006).
7. See *(Re)Discovering Aesthetics*, eds. Francis Halsall, Julia Jansen, and Tony O'Connor (New York: Columbia University Press, 2006) for an edited selection of current debates on the recent deployment of aesthetics. The following statement is a synopsis of the editors' ongoing discussions of this topic.
8. See my review of *Encyclopedia of Aesthetics*, ed. Michael Kelly (New York and Oxford, 1998) in *The Art Bulletin* 83 no. 3 (September, 2001): 559–63.
9. Woodfield, "Aesthetics at the End of the Century: Dessoir's Project," *Aesthetics and Art in the 20th Century*, ed. Ipek Tureli (Ankara, Turkey: SANART, 2002), 81–86.
10. For America see special issue of *The Journal of Aesthetics and Art Criticism* 51 no. 2 (Spring, 1993), titled "Aesthetics: Past and Present—A Commemorative Issue Celebrating 50 Years of *The Journal of Aesthetics and Art Criticism* and the American Society for Aesthetics."
11. Stace, *Meaning of Beauty: A Theory of Aesthetics* (London: Grant Richards and Humphrey Toulmin, 1929), 85.
12. Frank Sibley, *Approaches to Aesthetics: Collected Papers on Philosophical Aesthetics* (Oxford: Oxford University Press 2001), 14.
13. Sibley, *Approaches to Aesthetics*, 22–30.
14. Sibley, *Approaches to Aesthetics*, 135–41.
15. Sohm, *Style in the Art Theory of Early Modern Italy* (Cambridge: Cambridge University Press, 2001); Lewis-Williams, *The Mind in the Cave* (London: Thames and Hudson, 2002).
16. See Peter Lamarque, "Reflections on Current Trends in Aesthetics," *Postgraduate Journal of Aesthetics* 1 no. 1 (April, 2004), online at www.british-aesthetics.org/DesktopDefault.aspx?tabindex=6&tabid=63.
17. Kivy, *Philosophies of Arts: An Essay in Differences* (Cambridge: Cambridge University Press, 1997).
18. V. S. Ramachandran and William Hirstein, "The Science of Art: A Neurological Theory of Aesthetic Experience", *Journal of Consciousness Studies* 6 (1999): 6–7.
19. The conceptual inadequacies of poststructuralism are discussed throughout my book *Philosophy After Postmodernism: Civilized Values and the Scope of Knowledge* (London: Routledge, 2003).

20. These claims are defended at length in a paper entitled "Defining Art, Defending the Canon, Contesting Culture," *British Journal of Aesthetics* 44 no. 4 (2004): 361–77.
21. Among the key contextualists are Griselda Pollock, T. J. Clark, Norman Bryson, and Kevin Moxey.
22. These are explored in more detail in my "Defining Art."
23. The idea of the image's intrinsic significance is outlined in Part 3 of my "Cultural Exclusion, Normativity, and the Definition of Art," *Journal of Aesthetics and Art Criticism* 61 no. 2 (2003): 121–31. It is also the major theme of my recently completed book *Theory of the Image: Aesthetics at the Limits of Art History*. For a discussion in a broader context, see my *Transhistorical Image: Philosophizing Art and Its History* (Cambridge: Cambridge University Press, 2002); chap. 4 is especially relevant.
24. This task has been central to all my work in aesthetics. In addition to the foregoing references, see for example, chap. 4 of *Critical Aesthetics and Postmodernism* (Oxford: Clarendon Press, 1993); and chap. 4 and 10 of *Art and Embodiment: From Aesthetics to Self-Consciousness* (Oxford: Clarendon Press, 1993).
25. Kant, *Critique of Judgment*, trans. Werner S. Pluhar (Indianapolis, IN: Hackett Publishing Co., 1987), §44 and 53.
26. *Critique of Judgment*, 326.
27. Foucault, *The Order of Things* (New York: Vintage, 1970), 4.
28. While the discussion attributes the identification of a work of art with its *Weltanschauung* to Gadamer and Heidegger, their position derives from Hegel's analysis of the work as embodying and reflecting the "spirit of a free people." For Hegel art is an emblem of the historically determined form of mind that produced it. See, "The Spiritual Work of Art," in Hegel's *Phenomenology of Spirit*, trans. A.V. Miller (New York: Oxford University Press, 1979), VII.B.c.
29. Jean Starobinski, 1789: *The Emblems of Reason*, trans. Barbara Bray (Charlottesville: University of Virginia Press, 1982).
30. Taking beauty as a property and confusing it with preference, the discussion also becomes ensnared in a false dichotomy between the historical and the philosophical, between historically conditioned judgments and universal claims. Philosophemes are themselves historical terms. The history of philosophy is not merely literary, but conceptual, as Hegel demonstrates. Thus, philosophemes exhibit, what we may call after Derrida, a "paleonymic" effect. I cannot make "beauty" mean anything I like: it has an historical density that prescribes a particular conceptual itinerary. To make it mean *otherwise* constitutes a substantial philosophical labor and is always a matter of redirecting, deflecting, turning, rather than stipulating a new definition on a clean slate.
31. *Critique of Judgment*, §59. See also the discussion of the "great gulf" that is bridged by judgment in the introduction, IX.
32. Elaine Scarry, *On Beauty and Being Just* (Princeton, NJ: Princeton University Press, 1999), 93–95. Scarry identifies beauty with John Rawls's definition of fairness, "the symmetry of everyone's relations to each other." Beauty leads, she argues, to a conception of justice as "equality" and to the

political ideal of fraternity. Thus, she assumes that the specific difference of the other can be reduced according to a logic of the same. Of course, ethical urgent relations are generally ones of inequality—doctor/patient, parent/child, teacher/student, boss/worker. And, the logic of fraternity invokes a supposedly generic moral subject that is already marked masculine, that, as philosophers from Hegel to Irigaray remind us, cannot be divorced from the sexual difference and the division of labor that it prescribes.

33. *Phenomenology*, Preface, 45. See also, Walter Benjamin, "The Work of Art in the Age of Mechanical Reproduction," in *Illuminations* (New York: Harcourt, Brace, Jovanovich, 1968), and Georges Bataille, "Letter to X, Lecturer on Hegel," in *The Bataille Reader*, eds. Fred Botting and Scott Wilson (Oxford: Blackwell Publishers, 1997).
34. Luce Irigaray, *An Ethics of Sexual Difference*, trans. Carolyn Burke and Gillian C. Gill (Ithaca, NY: Cornell University Press, 1993).
35. *Phenomenology*, "The Abstract Work of Art," paragraphs 706 and 707.
36. Merleau-Ponty, "The Intertwining of the Chiasm," *The Visible and the Invisible*, trans. Alphonso Lingis (Evanston, IL: Northwestern University Press, 1968).
37. Perhaps, the value of the critic is not so much his ability to situate a work historically or to diagnosis it as a symptom of culture or "way of seeing," but the way in which his or her knowledge and perception teaches us to see what, despite all our looking, we have not yet seen.
38. Works comprised of multiple instantiations, like Warhol's various portrait series, for example, seem to contradict this claim about the singularity of the work, but there is no mistaking my poster for his print.
39. Descartes, "*Passions of the Soul*," in *The Philosophical Writings of Rene Descartes*, vol. 1 (Cambridge: Cambridge University Press, 1985), article 53.
40. See the recent book on the history of German art history, Hubert Locher, *Kunstgeschichte als historische Theorie der Kunst* 1750–1950 (Munich: Fink, 2001).
41. For example, W. Windelband and H. Rickert's distinguishing between "ideographical" and "nomothetical" sciences.
42. Max Dvořák, "Über die dringendsten methodischen Erfordernisse der Erziehung zur kunstgeschichtlichen Forschung," *Die Geisteswissenschaften* 34/35 (1913/4).
43. See further Hans Belting, *Das Ende der Kunstgeschichte?* (Munich: Deutscher Kunstverlag, 1984), 21–22, 38–43.
44. Keith Moxey, *The Practice of Theory: Poststructuralism, Cultural Politics, and Art History* (Ithaca, NY: Cornell University Press, 1994), 39–40.
45. It is symptomatic that no attention was devoted to the question at the first Congress of Czech Art Historians. See, "Self-reflection of Art History," Prague, 25–26 September 2003.
46. *Compelling Visuality, The Work of Art In and Out of History*, eds. Claire Farago and Robert Zwijnenberg (Minneapolis: University of Minnesota Press, 2003), can be regarded as the latest attempt to bridge the gap between historical and aesthetic approaches.
47. Hans Belting, *Bild-Anthropologie*:Entwürfe für eine Bildwissenschaft (Munich: Fink, 2001); for globalization see Michael Zimmermann, "Art

History as Anthropology: French and German Traditions," in *The Art Historian: National Traditions and Institutional Practices*, ed. Michael Zimmerman (New Haven, CT: Yale University Press, 2003), 173.

48. Danto, *The Abuse of Beauty: Aesthetic and the Concept of Art* (Chicago: Open Court, 2003), 89–109.
49. Danto, *The Abuse of Beauty*, 113.
50. The case of Motherwell's *Elegies* is more complex. My reaction to these works when I first saw them was very different from Danto's: I found them nearly incomprehensible, I could make nothing of the large black forms of which they consisted, and I suspect that mine is not an uncommon reaction. To immediately see these forms as beautiful surely takes much greater familiarity with modernism and painting than I (in contrast to Danto) possessed at the time. Once familiarity is in place, it may take no time to be struck, as Danto was, by their beauty the first time one sees them.
51. That may well be the general conclusion that can be drawn from various psychological studies of the judgment of "the beauty" of faces that seem to suggest that transcultural judgments of attractiveness show significant convergences. See Michael Cunningham et al., " 'Their Ideas of Beauty Are, on the Whole, the Same as Ours': Consistency and Variability in the Cross-Cultural Perception of Female Physical Attractiveness," *Journal of Personality and Social Psychology* 68 (1995): 261–79; Doug Jones and Kim Hill, "Criteria of Facial Attractiveness in Five Populations," *Human Nature* 4 (1993): 271–96; Judith H. Langlois et al., "Infant Preferences for Attractive Faces: Rudiments of a Stereotype?," *Developmental Psychology* 23 (1987): 363–69; Judith H. Langlois and Lori A. Roggman, "Attractive Faces Are Only Average," *Psychological Science* 1 (1990): 115–21.
52. Anne Hollander, *Seeing Through Clothes* (Berkeley: University of California Press, 1993), chap. 3.
53. Compared to female figures, the male figures of which such things can be said is surprisingly small: the disparity raises interesting questions in its own right.
54. I try to offer a more detailed account and defense of this view, and of several of the claims I make without much argument below, in "A Promise of Happiness: The Place of Beauty in a World of Art," *The Tanner Lectures in Human Values*, vol. 23 (Salt Lake City: The University of Utah Press, 2002), 189–231.
55. Kant, *Critique of the Power of Judgment*, trans. Paul Guyer and Eric Matthews (Cambridge: Cambridge University Press, 2000), 101.
56. Ludwig Wittgenstein, *Lectures and Conversation on Aesthetics, Psychology and Religious Belief*, ed. Cyril Barrett (Berkeley: University of California Press, 1967), 3. According to James Taylor's notes, however, Wittgenstein (also?) said, "It would be better to use 'lovely' descriptively, on a level with 'stately,' 'pompous,' etc." That would bring his view closer to Costello's position, the more specific terms replacing the generic predicate.
57. In fact, any aesthetic term—even the most negative one—will do: "repulsive" is as good as "magnificent" for that purpose.

58. *Lectures and Conversations*, p. 12. Rush Rhees's notes read: "If I like a suit I may buy it, or wear it often—without interjections or making faces."
59. Schapiro, "The Sculptures of Souillac," in his *Romanesque Art: Selected Papers* (New York: Thames and Hudson, 1993), 119.
60. Rosalind Krauss, "Richard Serra, a Translation," in her *The Originality of the Avant–Garde and Other Modernist Myths* (Cambridge, MA: MIT Press, 1986), 267–68.
61. Plato, *Symposium* 209e–212a; and see my essay " 'Only in the Contemplation of Beauty is Human Life Worth Living' (Plato, *Symposium* 211d)," forthcoming.
62. Still, I can't imagine that something can be acknowledged as a great work of art unless it has struck some people as beautiful. Try to think of great art that no one has ever loved. And it is important to remember that love's contrary is not hate (with which love can surely coexist) but indifference. Can any great art—at least art that has been recognized as such—have always been nothing but the object of indifference?
63. That is also true of Danto's identification of beauty with good looks, which asks, as we have seen, what contribution beauty makes to a work's historical meaning. I think that even Dave Hickey's view avoids that accusation: to think of beauty as a rhetoric of visual figures that "enfranchise the beholder by exhibiting markers that designate a territory of shared values, thus empowering the beholder to respond" and "valorize the content of the image, which, presuming its litigious or neurotic intent, is in need of valorization" is far from anything that would be acceptable even to the most generous formalist. See Hickey, "After the Great Tsunami," in his *The Invisible Dragon: Four Essays on Beauty* (Los Angeles: Art Issues Press, 1993), 57.
64. Ciarán Benson, *The Cultural Psychology of Self: Place, Morality and Art in Human Worlds* (New York: Routledge, 2001).
65. Richard Wollheim, *Germs: A Memoir of Childhood* (Baltimore: Waywiser Press, 2004).
66. Mark Roskill, *What Is Art History?* (London: Thames and Hudson, 1976), 12.
67. Arnheim's is the psychological account used by Roskill, for example.
68. See, for example, Antonio Damasio, *The Feeling of What Happens: Body and Emotion in the Making of Consciousness* (New York: Harcourt Brace, 1999).
69. James Ackerman, "The Nature of Art History," in Ackerman and Rhys Carpenter, *Art and Archaeology* (Princeton, NJ: Princeton University Press, 1963), 130.
70. Kurt Badt, *Eine Wissenschaftslehre der Kunstgeschichte* (Cologne: DuMont, 1971).
71. See, for example, Michael Podro, *The Critical Historians of Art* (New Haven, CT: Yale University Press, 1982); Michael Ann Holly, *Panofsky and the Foundations of Art History* (Ithaca, NY: Cornell University Press, 1985); Mark Cheetham, *Kant, Art, and Art History: Moments of Discipline* (Cambridge: Cambridge University Press, 2001).
72. Ernst Tugendhat, *Traditional and Analytical Philosophy: Lectures on the Philosophy of Language* (Cambridge: Cambridge University Press, 1982).

73. See T. J. Clark, *The Painting of Modern Life* (London: Thames and Hudson, 1985), 79–146.
74. Martin Wackernagel, *The World of the Florentine Renaissance Artist*, trans. Alison Luchs (Princeton, NJ: Princeton University Press, 1981). First published as *Der Lebensraum des Künstlers in der florentinischen Renaissance: Aufgaben und Auftraggeber, Werkstatt und Kunstmarkt* (Leipzig, 1938).
75. Howard Becker, *Artworlds* (Berkeley: University of California Press, 1982).
76. See Niklas Luhmann, *Art as a Social System* (Stanford, CA: Stanford University Press, 2000).
77. See Alfred Gell, *Art and Agency* (Oxford: Oxford University Press, 1998).
78. *Art and Agency*, 3.
79. Moritz Thausing, "Die Stellung der Kunstgeschichte als Wissenschaft," in Thausing, *Wiener Kunstbriefe* (Leipzig: Seeman, 1884),1–20.
80. *Art History, Aesthetics, Visual Culture*, eds. Michael Ann Holly and Keith Moxey (Williamstown, MA: Sterling and Francine Clark Art Institute, 2002).
81. Jacques Derrida, *The Truth in Painting*, trans. Geoff Bennington and Ian McLeod (Chicago: University of Chicago Press, 1987).
82. Fredric Jameson, "Notes on Globalization as a Philosophical Issue," in *The Cultures of Globalization*, eds. Fredric Jameson and Masao Miyoshi (Durham, NC: Duke University Press, 1998), 55–77.
83. Arjun Appadurai, "Disjuncture and Difference in the Global Cultural Economy," in *Modernity at Large: Cultural Dimensions of Globalization* (Minneapolis: University of Minnesota Press, 1996), 27–47.
84. Nestor Garcia Canclini, *Consumers and Citizens: Globalization and Multicultural Conflicts,* trans. George Yudice (Minneapolis: University of Minnesota Press, 2001) and *Hybrid Cultures: Strategies for Entering and Leaving Modernity,* trans. Christopher Chiappari and Silvia Lopez (Minneapolis: University of Minnesota Press, 1995).
85. See David Summers, *Real Spaces: World Art History and the Rise of Western Modernism* (London: Phaidon, 2003) and James Elkins's review in *Art Bulletin* 86 (2004): 373–81.
86. For a thoughtful overview of this new field as well as the philosophical issues it raises, see James Elkins, *Visual Studies: A Skeptical Introduction* (New York: Routledge, 2003).
87. For a similar proposal see Ella Shohat and Robert Stam, "Narrativizing Visual Culture: Towards a Polycentric Aesthetics," in *The Visual Culture Reader*, ed. Nicholas Mirzoeff (London: Routledge, 1998), 27–49.
88. Does this singularity also apply to, say, one of Sherry Levine's Edward Westons?
89. The term "logic" here means deductive reasoning. In his first *Critique*, Kant set himself the task of demonstrating that logic is limited, and naturally fulfilled the task to his own satisfaction. I am not concerned with whether Kant's proof stands up under the scrutiny of modern proof methods, nor even whether his theory of logic is adequate in the first place. I am merely interested in his overall project—that is, his unwavering belief that not only is (classical) logic limited, but that this limitation can be shown by the application of logic itself.

90. In a sense it doesn't even matter if no experiences are amenable to categories of understanding, for this would only extend the province of the sublime and reason to all experience, making the demand that we address the problem even more imperative. However, I agree with Kant that not all experience is sublime, because we do have an understanding governed by given categories, even if, as I believe, these are handed out by culture, rather than hardwired into our bodies. The problem then is to demonstrate that all systems of culturally given categories are limited. Though much evidence exists to suggest that this is likely, and though Gödel's theorem adds weight to the hypothesis, I suspect that in the end it comes down to a simple choice of whether we as a culture wish to begin with the premise that we will ultimately, if we all work hard enough, bring all experience into a complete and consistent, i.e., perfect system of understanding, or, as this is unlikely, whether we begin from the more humble position that it would be wise to expend some cultural capital on developing means for dealing with the stresses that arise from incomprehensions, even if these ultimately prove to be merely contingent, the product of not-yet fully perfected categories.
91. Paul Crowther, *The Kantian Sublime: From Morality to Art* (Oxford: Clarendon Press, 1989).
92. Thierry de Duve, *Kant after Duchamp* (Cambridge, MA: MIT Press, 1998).
93. Arthur Danto: *Philosophizing Art: Selected Essays* (Berkeley: University of California Press, 1999.)
94. See the essay "Why Don't Art Historians Attend Aesthetics Conferences?" in this volume.
95. Adorno, *Aesthetic Theory*, trans. and ed. Robert Hullot-Kentor (Minneapolis: University of Minnesota Press, 1997), 118.
96. *Aesthetic Theory*, 96.
97. Of the many references on this topic, a good beginning point is *Aesthetics in a Multicultural Age*, eds. Emory Elliott, Lou Freitas Caton, and Jeffrey Rhyne (Oxford: Oxford University Press, 2002).
98. See, for example, chap. 5 in my *Iconoclasm in Aesthetics* (Cambridge: Cambridge University Press, 2003).
99. See the recent collection, *Things That Talk: Object Lessons from Art and Science*, ed. Lorrain Datson (New York: Zone Books, 2004).
100. This is what I endeavored to do in "Readymade, Found Object, Photograph," published in the special edition of the *Art Journal* on the Aesthetic/Anti-aesthetic debates, ed. James Meyer, Summer 2004.
101. Jeff Wall, " 'Marks of Indifference:' Aspects of Photography in, or as, Conceptual Art," in *Reconsidering the Object of Art: 1965–1975*, eds. Ann Goldstein and Anne Rorimer (Cambridge, MA: MIT Press, 1995), 255.
102. Robert Smithson, "Donald Judd" in *Robert Smithson: The Collected Writings*, ed. Jack Flam (Berkeley: University of California Press, 1996), 6.
103. Anton Ehrenzweig, *The Hidden Order of Art: A Study in the Psychology of Artistic Imagination* (London: Paladin, 1970).
104. Smithson, "A Sedimentation of the Mind," *Writings*, 104.
105. Smithson, "A Sedimentation of the Mind," *Writings*, 111.

106. Robert Morris, "Anti Form," in *Continuous Project Altered Daily: The Writings of Robert Morris* (Cambridge, MA: MIT Press, 1993), 41–46.
107. Michael Fried, "Art and Objecthood," in *Minimal Art: A Critical Anthology*, ed. Gregory Battcock (New York: E. P. Dutton, 1968); Smithson, "A Sedimentation of the Mind," *Writings*, 103.
108. Smithson, "A Tour of the Monuments of Passaic, New Jersey," *Writings*, 68–74.
109. Stanley Cavell, *The Claim of Reason: Wittgenstein, Skepticism, Morality and Tragedy* (Oxford: Oxford University Press, 1979), 15.
110. Andy Warhol, *The Philosophy of Andy Warhol (from A to B and Back Again)* (New York: Harcourt Brace Jovanovich, 1975), 26.
111. See Alain Badiou, *Infinite Thought: Truth and the Return of Philosophy* (London and New York: Continuum, 2003).
112. See Bruno Latour's draft introduction to Bruno Latour and Peter Weibel, "*Dingpolitik: Atmospheres of Democracy*," in the catalogue of the exhibition *From Realpolitik to Dingpolitik: An Introduction to Making Things Public* (forthcoming, 2005)
113. For a history of the Warburg Institute, see: www.sas.ac.uk/warburg/institute/institute_introduction.htm.
114. See Georges Didi-Huberman, *L'image survivante: histoire de l'art et temps des fantômes selon Aby Warburg* (Paris: Minuit, 2002).
115. Even if one disagrees that beauty has a unique claim to combine experience and value, it is surely not, Austin notwithstanding, on a par with the dainty and the dumpy. Can one imagine the sort of hope and loathing we've recently seen aroused by Dave Hickey, Elaine Scarry, and so on, if they had chosen to write on the return of daintiness? And that the answer is no doesn't tell us that the dainty and the dumpy couldn't serve us as fundamental values, but only that they emphatically don't so serve us. And that tells us something crucial about "us."
116. Martin Heidegger, *The Question Concerning Technology and Other Essays*, trans. William Lovitt (New York: Harper & Row, 1977), 125.
117. Bill Readings, *The University in Ruins* (Cambridge, MA: Harvard University Press, 1996.)
118. Michael Fried, *Art and Objecthood: Essays and Reviews* (Chicago: University of Chicago Press, 1998), 170.
119. It is a joke and not a joke that in art history the tacit requirement for footnotes per article far outraces that of any other field in the university. We define ourselves, from the survey on up, through research—sheer scholarship—pretty much above all else.
120. See, among other things: Michael Ann Holly, *Panofsky and the Foundations of Art History* (Ithaca, NY: Cornell University Press, 1984) and *Past Looking: Historical Imagination and the Rhetoric of the Image* (Ithaca, NY: Cornell University Press, 1996); Joseph Koerner, *The Moment of Self-Portraiture in German Renaissance Art* (Chicago: University of Chicago Press, 1993) and *The Reformation of the Image* (Chicago: University of Chicago Press, 2004); Michael Podro, *The Critical Historians of Art* (New Haven, CT: Yale University Press, 1982); as well as various essays of my own. Other significant contributions to this general line of historiographic

reflection include Georges Didi-Huberman, *L'image survivante: histoire de l'art et temps des fantômes selon Aby Warburg* (Paris: Minuit, 2002); Margaret Iversen, *Alois Reigl: Art History and Theory* (Cambridge, MA: MIT Press, 1993); and a number of essays by Whitney Davis.

121. In choosing this word, I find myself wondering if de Duve's choice of analogy is not partially shaped by a recollection of Kant's remark about the dove that imagines its flight would be freer if it did not have to deal with the resistance of the air.

122. That Elkins is indeed able to convincingly assimilate de Duve's talk on Robert Morris to this end shows something about a disagreement I must have with de Duve despite our ability to meet in this particular remark. Diarmuid Costello's earlier remark about what is shared and unshared among the three of us seems to me just right.

123. It should be clear that I place little weight on "universal" as a positive description of this voice; I take it to mean above all that it does not appear to be the voice of a particular subject, and its surest disqualification is that discovery that it is, after all, merely such a voice. So I suppose I take it to be a voice that appears as if not ordered to the contracts and positions that otherwise order our relations, thus a test of the depth of our sociability.

124. "Die Natur war schön, wenn sie zugleich als Kunst aussah; und die Kunst kann nur schön genannt werden, wenn wir uns bewußt sind, sie sei Kunst; und sie uns doch als Natur aussieht." Translations vary, and my own would be fairly literal-minded: "Nature is beautiful when it also seems as art; and art can only be called beautiful when we are conscious that it is art and it nonetheless seems to us as nature." Immanuel Kant, *Kritik der Urteilskraft* (Wiesbaden: Suhrkamp Verlag, 1957), §45.

125. Particular arguments informing this view are developed by Ted Cohen in "Figurative Speech and Figurative Acts," *Journal of Philosophy* 72 no. 19 (197): 669–684; and Timothy Gould, in "The Audience of Originality: Kant and Wordsworth on the Reception of Genius," in Cohen and Guyer, eds., *Essays in Kant's Aesthetics* (Chicago: University of Chicago Press, 1982).

126. For example: "Formally what has been said can be expressed thus: the general nature of the judgment or proposition, which involves the distinction of Subject and Predicate, is destroyed by the speculative proposition, and the proposition of identity which the former becomes contains the counter-thrust against that subject-predicate relationship. This conflict between the general form of a proposition and the unity of the Notion which destroys it is similar to the conflict that occurs in rhythm between metre and accent." in G. W. F. Hegel, *Phenomenology of Spirit*, trans. A. V. Miller (Oxford: Oxford University Press, 1977), §61. But this is obviously more than a rhyming of Hegel's "is" and Kant's "as"—it's a reading of the deepest stakes of the *Critique of Judgment* that completely refigures their scope and consequence.

5
Afterwords

Modernism as Aesthetics and Art History

J. M. Bernstein

I

When Adorno opened *Aesthetic Theory* with his melancholic diagnosis of the disposition of contemporary art—"It is self-evident that nothing concerning art is self-evident, not its inner life, not its relation to the world, not even its right to exist"[1]—he intended that dramatic bracketing of the meaning of art, a bracketing that was nothing other than an acknowledgment of art's own troubled self-consciousness, to form the address to which any aesthetics worthy of the name would need to be a response. Aesthetics is the reflexive construction of the concepts necessary for the comprehension of the *stakes and meaning of art* in the light of the history of the dominant art of the second half of the 19th century and the first half of the 20th century: modernism. The task of aesthetics is to vindicate modernist art's *own* claim to mattering, to being significant, indeed unavoidable, for our collective self-understanding of ourselves as denizens of modernity. To imagine art history without aesthetics, on this accounting, would be to imagine art's own implicit self-consciousness, its running commentary on its presumptive necessity and threatened impossibility, being blocked from becoming explicit. By making the implicit explicit, aesthetics gives back to works, the history they inscribe and project, a cultural claim that they cannot discursively procure for themselves.

Conversely, if art does not matter, if, following the Hegelian determination of the matter, there are no needs, "mute in themselves, that await the expression that artworks fulfill by proxy,"[2] then neither aesthetics nor art history will contain enough spiritual ballast to be worth the debate about their formation, either conjugally or singly. Although there are brief hints of something other in the conversations of "The Art Seminar," especially in the remarks by Thierry de Duve, the overall trajectory has, to steal a term from Clement Greenberg, a slightly Alexandrian feel, a fine-grained formalism that lives off its avoidance of cultural substance, terminating exquisitely in James Elkins's acute and uncanny noting of nine different models or metaphors for the relation between aesthetics and art history. That Elkins lets his own wishful metaphor—that art history might be the acid that corrodes aesthetics—be the terminus of the discussion is a perhaps ungenerous but not unmotivated judgment that the conversation has failed, should fail. My hunch is that Elkins thinks that aesthetics should be dissolved by art history because art—and so art history—is, in truth, a motley, without firm borders or boundaries; works of art serve a diversity of purposes across a plethora of cultures and ages, and the attempt to define a set of constitutive features for the experience of them all violently reduces the many to the one. Conversely, the history of art in its healthiest modes is a way of acknowledging art's many voices, its plural lines of development, its distractions and curiosities, its moments of political hubris or aesthetic purity, its gross sublimities and its craft earnestness, its pedagogic fervor or religious piety, etc. Said that way, it is evident that there indeed needs to be a practice of art history that proceeds free from aesthetic interference. Nothing I want to say is meant to dispute that.

If there is a question about aesthetics and art history, it must be of narrower provenance, viz., the more or less simultaneous emergence of the philosophy of art *as aesthetics* (in Burke and Kant, say) and the kind of art that is specific to modernity, an art freed from or stripped of any external function, art that has, in that sense, become autonomous. But this is as much as to say that Elkins's acid of art history is itself a creature of modernity that hence must make necessary reference to the acid of the history of art, that disintegration of external functionality or meaning that is the ongoing condition of modern art, which, again, is the predicament Adorno is pointing to at the commencement of *Aesthetic Theory*. And what art becomes for us matters, must matter, to our interpretation of past art. How could there not be a necessary connection between the categorial comprehension of modern art, art's being without a purpose, and art historical inquiry?

One cannot get very far in locating the force fields connecting and separating art history and aesthetics unless, near the center of one's description of both disciplines, one stakes oneself as to why art matters, why anyone might care about art, why as a culture we feel ourselves bound to the arts in their glory and misery, their beauty and abjectness, their hopefulness and melancholia, and why this force field of concerns has entered into modern art itself in modes ranging from the hopelessly celebratory to the malignantly self-loathing, but always, or at least almost always, in the mode of *crisis*. How is one to bind aesthetics to art history if one leaves out of account the fact that the history of the dominant art of the past one hundred and fifty years has been a series of crises about the possibility of art? More pointedly still, one will not get very far in giving art history its due if one simply leaves out of account *the utterly aesthetic matter of fact* that we are unsure that art matters to culture at large, or rather, if we ignore culture's doubt that art matters to it, or society's crude judgment that neither art nor culture matter to how life matters any more (increasingly society relies less on the cultural reproduction of norms and values in order to secure systems integration), or, when culture does come back in, it is in the reactive forms that reflect what we thought enlightened, cosmopolitan modernity had surmounted (religion, race, vulgar nationalism) rather than the arts. If we do not care about art, or rather, if nothing about our caring about art can be vindicated as of indissoluble significance for the meaning of contemporary life, then of course the question about the fit between aesthetics and art history will idle, become formal, since nothing other than narrow disciplinary practices and investments (the endless monographs about this or that artist vs. the "this is how we philosophers talk about art: a judgment of beauty has such-and-such formal features, and will be valid if and only if it satisfies such-and-such criteria") will be at issue. I understand the Alexandrian character of "The Art Seminar" as thus symptomatic: as implying that perhaps society is right about culture and the arts, that perhaps the arts in fact lack any deep and systematic reason for existing (they carry on but without fulfilling any constitutive function—just as Hegel predicted), that disciplinary practice without overall meaning is the way a culture quietly dies. Sometimes this set of beliefs has had a name: postmodernism. I had thought that the emptiness of that program had finally lost its attractiveness. Apparently not.

From this perspective, the most pointed remark in "The Art Seminar" is Thierry de Duve's joke. After Arthur Danto inquires as to whether we would necessarily receive any more illumination from Kantian aesthetics as opposed to psychoanalysis in understanding Paul McCarthy's *Bossy Burger*, say, and de Duve concedes that of course Kant is not more useful, and Danto is about to crow in triumph, de Duve interjects: "Say you throw yourself out of the window, and you land on the sidewalk. Is Newton useful to you?

You have just obeyed the law of universal gravity, that's all." This joke moves in two directions.[3] On the one hand, the contention is that whatever aesthetics is or does, that doing need not be *useful* for the interpretation of particular works of art. To think that aesthetic terms of analysis and evaluation are significant does not entail their being routinely directly usable in either the widely art-historical or the narrowly critical interpretation of works and movements. To look at aesthetics in that pragmatic way is to look at it from the wrong direction.[4] On the other hand, in just the same way that the falling body nonetheless *perfectly* obeys the law of gravitation, so might art history receive its fundamental cultural orientation, its historical conatus, the categorial articulation of its objects' curious purposiveness without purpose from its encapsulation in aesthetic categories, or, rather, in categories that aesthetic theory elaborates. Because his account explicates both the apparent lack of direct utility of aesthetics to art history, and its underlying necessity (it reveals the categorial bearing of art history), de Duve not implausibly can regard himself as saving the phenomena without surrender.

This seems to be about right but for one crucial disanalogy between Kantian aesthetics and Newtonian theory. De Duve pointedly historicizes the meaning of art history in terms of the radical transformation in art that occurs through the collapse of tradition, that is, the waning of its traditional authority in Weber's sense of the term. Once the practice of art, its being and meaning, is no longer secured through the handing down of techniques and disciplines through schools and masters, once the baton is no longer passed down through the generations in the studio, once, that is, the carrying on of art involves a staking of the meaning of art in the production of particular works and series of works, each new work invoking another claim about what art is and how it matters (exactly as Kant depicted it in his theory of genius), then the history of art becomes something that needs to be constructed and reconstructed again and again in order that we might continue to understand the great art of the past in the light of the achievements of the present. Art history, then, becomes the guardian of the tradition in the mundane sense that there *is* anything like a tradition that *can* acknowledge both the art of the past and the art of the present as integrally mattering to one another in our experience of them is secured, at least in part, through art history's constructive efforts. Of course, all that assumes not just descriptive terms, but evaluative terms: acknowledgment of the *achievements* of the present are the record of a presumptive mattering—of art for us. The question of which works we keep and which ones we throw away is indeed an "evidential record of previous aesthetic judgments": art collections are a continuing reflection of the role of art in culture at large, and hence a cipher of cultural self-understanding. No "collection building" without cultural *Bildung*, no *Bildung* without aesthetics.

The weight of de Duve's claim turns on inserting art history into the transformed temporality of modernity in which traditional authority must cede its role to the emergent self-determining, self-authorizing mechanisms of modernity, a modernity that must perpetually reiterate its self-grounding gesture. The discontinuous temporality that constitutes art's own efforts at self-grounding is held in place, given narrative coherence, through art history's survey of the history of those efforts in relation to the practices of the recent past. This is the kind of art history that might, with some luck, not only enable us to see a broad connection between Paul McCarthy and the Grünewald altarpiece, but enable us to see the Grünewald anew through McCarthy, say by seeing the suffering Christ as enacting in religious terms what becomes the strategy of a regression to the infantile as a form of resistance to a despairing cultural nihilism. Conversely, we might find in McCarthy's carefully exuberant manufacture of disgust a last disillusioned and formless echo of the idea that in bodily suffering there existed a form of unmastered spirituality that could not be dismissed by a self-confident rational culture. Or maybe not. But it is going to be difficult to make sense of the force of disgust, its truth content, without some sense that regression (from the Oedipal to the Narcissistic, from the Paternal Law to the Maternal Body, etc.) is both a form of cultural collapse relating to the loss of authoritative forms for sublimating materiality, and a form of resistance and rebellion (against abstract culture and modernism and formalism, etc.), and hence a component of a degenerating practice of affirmation. In this respect, *in disgust's fierce repudiation of beauty's deceitful harmonizing, which is the very gesture of* Bossy Burger, *beauty shows itself to be the very stakes of the art that seems to have most radically abandoned it;*[5] but might I have not used that same description to begin accounting for the Grünewald? Is not Grünewald protesting against high Renaissance humanism and idealism in a manner precisely analogous to those governing McCarthy's protest against high modernism? Are not the violence and the grotesquery of their art necessarily understood not in terms of style or subject matter or influences or technique but as a critical rebellion against propriety and good taste, against a concurrent and dominant conception of beauty?[6] And here our art history has suddenly taken a very conventional aesthetic turn. How could it not?

Unless one is going to urge that since art is a motley, then so must be art history, de Duve's historical lesson about art history is going to be difficult to gainsay. But as my conclusion to the last paragraph suggests, we are not going to be able to easily disentangle that history from aesthetic considerations. De Duve's mistake is in supposing that the authority of Kant's aesthetic categories are fully detachable from the history of art, that we can cleave a clean separation between objective spirit (the history of art) and absolute spirit (aesthetics); that we cannot is the emphatic point of Hegel's critique of Kant. Aesthetics too needs historicizing; it is not the natural science of art since art is not a 'natural kind' (in the philosophical sense of that phrase), hence Kant is not the Newton of the art world.

The reason for the pervasive sense of the obsolescence of aesthetics that de Duve is hoping to protect it against is "that it [aesthetics] scarcely ever confronted itself with its object. By its very form, aesthetics seems sworn to universality that culminates in inadequacy to the artworks and, complementarily, in transitory eternal values."[7] Adorno is conceding here that there has been about philosophical aesthetics—as there has been about philosophy as a whole before Hegel—an abstractness and indifference to particular objects that ill consorted with the kind of sensuous particularity and hence irreducibility to conceptual grasping that is the hallmark of work of art. Yet, it is precisely against this mutual indifference of aesthetics and artworks that Adorno, and the forms of aesthetic theory and art history (to date, alas, mostly found in musicology and the history of music) he bequeathed have been rebelling against for the past thirty years. Where de Duve goes astray is in supposing that Kant's aesthetics is part of this trend of indifference rather than an incipient overturning of it. So much is hinted at in Adorno's claim that "Kant brought into thought the deepest impulses of an art that only developed in the one hundred and fifty years after his death: an art that probed after its objectivity openly, without protection of any kind."[8] For Adorno, for reasons I will come to, Kant's aesthetics is productively enacted by modernist art. This will mean that art of this kind does not serve as an illustration of this aesthetic theory, but rather this kind of art serves as a determination or elaboration or an unfolding of these aesthetic ideas, ideas that are themselves derived, at least in part, from art of this kind. So, for example, in contesting Danto's thesis that the Intractable Avant-Garde passed beyond Kantian aesthetics, above all as evidenced by McCarthy's *Bossy Burger*, Gregg Horowitz persuasively argues that even the intractable avant-garde lives off its repudiation of beauty, that art "must continue to abuse beauty ... because it cannot quite shed the memory of what beauty promised,"[9] viz., a reconciliation of culture and what must be conquered in order for culture to be possible—call it nature, the body, woman, desire. When beautiful semblance becomes not a return of the culturally repressed but a denial of that repression, a champion of cultural order, when form seems to us a lie about justice and harmony (or for Grünewald, spiritual meaning), then art must repudiate aesthetic propriety, as *Bossy Burger* "repudiates the authority of beautiful art to serve as the proper agent of the repudiated. Where art was, there disgust shall be."[10] Think of this last thought as fully and necessarily temporally indexed: the avant-garde *redetermines* beauty, harmony, and pleasure into ugliness, formlessness, and disgust—which is how the stakes expressed by the beautiful are transmitted into the present, or, what is the same, how the critical function of horror and anguish in art—from Grünewald to Soutine—come to necessitate, as their proper continuation, something like a critique of art, an anti-art, an overwhelming of the work by affect in order for the critique of deceitful beauty found in earlier art to be sustained.

Without an appropriate aesthetic theory one is not going to be able to authoritatively sketch the discontinuous line of development connecting, say, Grünewald to Rembrandt's *The Slaughtered Ox* (1655), from there perhaps to some of the uncanny and queasier still lifes, say Chardin's *The Rayfish* (1728), till we surface in Van Gogh's quivering, shuddering canvases, in Soutine's dead-and-dying beasts, in de Kooning's woman paintings, hence to Cindy Sherman's horror and inform pictures, and then to McCarthy.[11] This line of thought should remind us that Horowitz's "where art was, there disgust shall be" is not just a narrative operator, but in soldering the connection between beauty and ugliness (ugliness as unredeemed suffering) it reveals a leitmotiv in the development of modern art, the abject counterpoint to its release of beauty. If we were so minded, we could keep Diarmuid Costello happy by including Philip Guston's "clunky" paintings in thc mix, reminding ourselves of how they like other intentionally coarse moments in the avant-garde—*art brut* or Twombly's scrawls—also serve as agents for the repudiated, and hence that serving as an agent for what culture repudiates can take a diversity of artistic *and* aesthetic forms. In which case it is quite right to think of the clunky Gustons as "poignant"—their poignancy an exact acknowledgment of what they have had to forgo for the sake of preserving the memory of reconciliation. Equally however, working from the opposite direction, without these works and series of works shaping our aesthetic responses, modulating the meaning of beauty and ugliness, transience and beauty, horror and anguish, disgust and acknowledgment, and locating all the various formations and deformations of beauty beyond their original bold staking in Kant, aesthetic theory would remain an empty universal, the story of the return of the repressed in art—a tale without variation.

My hypothesis is that art history (now) and aesthetics (as the philosophical discourse appropriate to the autonomous art of modernity) are two sides of the same coin: modernism. They represent the sensuous/practical (intuitional) and reflective (conceptual) components of a broken modernity, a modernity that continues to suppose it can dispense with its material conditions of possibility, that it can sublimate happiness into consumer pleasure, that it can vanquish embodied experience as a form of authority leaving only the dull coin of habit, law, and procedure in its place, that it can fake life and no one will notice. Art's uneasy protest against all this is, of course, co-opted and dissipated at every turn (which is what makes institutional theories of art, and their cousins in the sillier reaches of the avant-garde, so attractive: if you can't beat 'em, join 'em). So the bald and obvious thought governing Adorno's aesthetic theory that aesthetics without art (history and criticism) is empty, and art without aesthetics is blind depends on construing one stretch of the history of art, modernism, as the constitutive condition for art history and aesthetics alike. For Adorno, to imagine going beyond modernism would mean simply either going beyond the point where art continued to matter to culture at all (which is what the culture industry keeps attempting to make happen to art) or that its promise was realized (which is what society keeps telling culture has happened so that it can relax). All bad readings of Warhol tend, as a convenient way of forgetting about culture and aesthetics, to suppose that one or the other of these theses must be true, maybe even that former is true because the latter is true. The radical self-loathing and spite against art that composes so much of recent art will be vacuous unless the disappointment and anger point to something real. The real thing they point to, rightly, is beauty's promise that is the promise of culture generally.

II

In order to give this claim a little more solidity, explaining a little why it is appropriate to read Kant as the expositor of modernism, and further why resistance to modernism, as evinced most notably by Elkins's, but implicit in the comments of Danto, is misguided, let me briefly take up the case of a closet third *Critique* Kantian, who is still (and now forever) unaware of his Kantianism, who generates a not unsubtle dialectical exchange of aesthetic theory and art history, of how they inform one another, depend on one another. The aesthetician is Gilles Deleuze, and his artist is Francis Bacon. Deleuze is mistaken about what he is doing (he thinks he is an ontologist) and wrong about Bacon (he is perfectly ill-suited for the purposes Deleuze recruits him); nonetheless his theoretical exorbitance will move the argument forward, above all by articulating what the meaning and stakes of Kantian beauty are. Deleuze thinks of the experience of beauty under the concept of *violence*—that is a helpful opening, an opening that is going to finally take us to the role of modernism in this argument.

Deleuze opens *Francis Bacon: The Logic of Sensation* thus:

> Francis Bacon's painting is of a very special violence. Bacon, to be sure, traffics in the violence of the depicted scene: spectacles of horror, crucifixions, prostheses and mutilations, monsters. But these are overly facile detours, detours that the artist himself judges severely and condemns in his work. What directly interests him is a violence that is involved only with color and line: the violence of a sensation (and not of a representation), a static or potential violence, a violence of reaction and expression. (FB, x)[12]

The conundrum and ambition of Deleuze's Bacon book is, precisely, to differentiate pure violence, the violence of paint, from the violence of war, the violence constitutive of modernist painting from the representation of violent events, the violence of representing from representational violence, the violence of sensation from the violence of the sensational (mutilations, monsters, crucifixions, howls, and screams). In carrying out this differentiation, it is essential that the violence of sensation be recognized as "inseparable from its direct action on the nervous system, the levels through which its passes, the domains its traverses: being itself a Figure [that is, an image without an intentional object, an image not *of* anything], it must have nothing of the nature of a represented object" (FB, 39).

However much or little it jibes with the rest of Deleuze's oeuvre, it is evident that Deleuze means this book to form an analysis and defense of artistic modernism. Bacon, Deleuze contends, is resuming "the entire problem of painting after Cézanne" (FB, xii); he is continuing the "abandonment of simple figuration" that is a general fact of modern painting, a fact which, when seen aright, is the truth of painting altogether (FB, xiv). The truth of painting altogether is that the means for representing persons and things in traditional art, above all color and line, are in fact the source of painting's power to claim at all, what makes painting a unique and irreducible form of interrogating experience and lodging a claim about it. Traditional painting's sensory claim transpires through the expressive power of color and line. Modernism is the series of painterly practices that liberates what had previously been the means of art into its subject matter; modernism is the self-presentation of painting.

But this conception of how paintings mean and claim presupposes a view about experience generally. Deleuze believes that the devices or syntactical operators of modernism, its various operations for breaking with traditional forms of perspectival representation, form a unique set of means—those intrinsic to the practice of painting itself—for releasing for experiential encounter aspects of objects and events that have, in one way or another, become blocked or repressed or veiled or excluded from ordinary modern experience. Painting matters generally because it secures access to a stratum or aspect of experience submerged in and repressed by ordinary cognitive engagements; modernism is the form of painting that itself both reveals this truth about traditional painting and carries out more explicitly painting's interrogation of the sensory order. For Deleuze the pervasive source of the repression is representational form itself.

This is the premise governing Deleuze's conception of sensation: representational form—subject/predicate forms, conceptual forms, the transcendental forms of categorial synthesis making experience possible for an univocal "I," the forms through which features of the world become identified and reidentified for instrumental and communicable purposes—these forms that turn aspects of the world into publicly identifiable objects and events, exclude from our emphatic experience of those objects and events just those material/sensuous features of them that make encounter between a material being with sensory powers and sensuously constituted material objects possible *überhaupt*. So what the reified grammar of shareable characteristics eliminates from experience are those material/sensuous features of it that can be known *only* through experience, what can be known only by being sensed, hence what is utterly singular—causally bound to the here and now of encounter—yet impersonal since not dependent upon the self-identical person.[13] Sensations in Deleuze's lexicon are what are experienced in the absence of representational forms.

Because it is representational forms that generate the categorial distinction between subjects and their objects, then Deleuze tends to think of artworks, especially modernist artworks, those objects designed for aesthetic encounter, designed to operate at the level of sensation, as simply materially connected sensations, material syntheses of sensation. By binding the idea of the artwork to the sensational experience it demands and makes possible, Deleuze in effect returns art to aesthetics and denies the dominant discourses of the past several decades which said that artworks are things or artworks are semiotic systems or artworks are constituted by their role in the institutional practices of the art world.

Adorno states that "Kant's theory is more apposite to the contemporary situation, for his aesthetics attempts to bind together consciousness of what is necessary with consciousness that what is necessary is itself blocked from consciousness."[14] I take it that what is necessary for consciousness are the subjective conditions for objective judgment as revealed through or with aesthetic reflective judgment, and hence that the blocking agent is nothing other than determinative judgment itself. The disinterested, nonconceptual, formalist stance toward the object that Kant demands is nothing other than the bracketing of the categorial functions of determinative judgment for the sake of its sensory, experiential conditions of possibility. Hence, determinative judgment, ordinary subject/predicate judgments and their progeny, what Deleuze thinks of as the forms of representation, block from consciousness subjective experience, the experiential coming-to-be of judgment, all of which Deleuze thinks within the notion of sensation.

Predicative consciousness blocks consciousness of nonpredicative experience, although as its subjective condition of possibility, the latter is necessary for the former. Art, alias aesthetic experience, is the corrective of this blockage: art as aesthetic experience performs the fit between everyday consciousness and its material conditions of possibility, *disrupting* the former for sake of the latter. Most broadly and without qualifications, we call this disruption "beauty." For Kant, for Adorno, for Deleuze, what appears in art is thus the fit, the material elective affinity between embodied subjects and the material world. More precisely, Deleuzean sensations are meant to record not the fitness itself, the purposiveness of nature for judgment which is the terminus of Kant's account, but the disorienting moment when the repressed returns, the disruption of that moment, its excess to what would resist it, and its resistance to indifferent spiritualization (form become formalism). What is presented from the highground as the necessary promise of harmony between nature and culture in Kant is offered from the point of denial and resistance in Deleuze. Nonetheless the analogical match between determinative judgment vs. aesthetic reflective judgment, and representation vs. sensation is clearly sure enough to allow us to regard the latter as the difficult, because more self-conscious, extension of the former.

If the abandonment of simple figuration is the general fact of modern painting and the uncovering of a presubjective logic of sensation is the driving orientation of Deleuze's philosophy, then there is a one-to-one correlation between such a philosophy and such an art: artistic modernism—painting from Cézanne, literature from Proust and Kafka, the uprising of the cinematic image—is itself a science of sensation, a transcendental empiricism, the productive interrogation of the prerepresentational structures of experience.[15] Deleuze's conception of art and the history of art as enacting a transcendental empiricism gets right a moment of Kant that is too easily overlooked and works in opposition to the universalist dimensions of his theory, namely his claim that judgments of beauty are, while well-founded, nonconceptual and criterionless. Judgments of beauty are nonconceptual in being not subsumable under any formal concepts, laws, or schema; hence there is no conceptually articulate clustering of sensory features that operates as a criterion for beauty or is constitutive of beauty. Beauty is always singular, always "this beauty." Hence, from knowing that one finds a particular painting or even series of paintings beautiful, one cannot deduce that the next remarkably similar work will also be found beautiful. Because sensational, because a matter of direct sensual experience, judgments of beauty, as a record of the sensory experience of particular objects, depend on the empirical presence of the objects judged: the singularity of aesthetic judgments is logically bound to their "aesthetic" character, their being nonconceptual totalities (sensory wholes without a conceptual purpose organizing them from above). Beautiful works are for Kant exemplary; but exemplarity is not universality, but rather the way in which the *authority* of a particular work is related to the authority of irreducibly particular works that come after it. Exemplarity is the form of rationality appropriate to authoritative particulars. It is through this way of considering judgments of beauty criterionless while nonetheless finding a mode of authority appropriate to unique works that Kant's aesthetics anticipates the art of modernism: its restless insistence on the transgression of past judgments in the new, its acknowledgment of the new as authoritative for the meaning of art now, and hence its declamation of the new as the site of this radical insistence upon irreducible particularity.

As the role of exemplarity makes evident, this mediation of rational authority through the particular is not a sheer empiricism, a sheer relativity of taste, but a transcendental empiricism. And it is the transcendental moment, the fact that there is indeed a logic of sensation that leads to the anxiety that aesthetics in its claim to universality occludes historical diversity and cultural difference. Appreciation of this transcendental dimension is what is missing from Keith Moxey's comment that rather than seeking "to articulate the qualities that make a work of art interesting to all people … aestheticians might attempt to analyze the bases on which different cultures privilege one set of artifacts above others." This is a case of running before we can walk. Until we have some idea of what the stakes are of *any* culture prizing the kind of artifacts we call "art" the process of interrogating their cultural systems will be idle, merely anthropological. One way of expressing this would be to say that art history without aesthetics reduces our interrogation of our own systems of such artifacts to the merely anthropological, an objectivist discounting of our own cultural life.

To say that this empiricism is transcendental is to say two things. First, that not every clustering of sensuous features of objects can generate the kind of judgment we call aesthetic; despite the fact that there is no universal criterion of beauty (or ugliness or clunkiness or elegance), only some clustering of features enable a significant encounter. And because there are such clusters, then there can be such a thing as a *history* of art that is more than one damn thing after another. There is a history because the series of works that we judge aesthetically worthy—de Duve's evidential record again—evince an empirical *logic*, a logic of sensory meaning that is not yet conceptual meaning.[16] Second, the constraint evinced in the first thesis is explained by the fact that the kinds of clustering that enable aesthetic judgments do so because they satisfy a necessary condition for the possibility of experience in general. Alexander Nehamas states the requisite notion in a narrow, individualist way when he says that "beauty … is simply the object of love … and that to love something is to desire to come to know it better than one knows it already." What this gets right is the sense in which the experience of beauty is the preparation, the anticipation, the announcement that the object is knowable, conceptualizable, representable. Nehamas is hence saying what Kant says in making aesthetic reflective judgments the presentation of the subjective conditions for objective, predicative judgments, and Deleuze says when he makes sensation the condition for representation. But why should it matter that what we know or find knowable be also something we desire and love? *Why should it matter that the world be lovable?* And the obvious answer, the one that keeps art and aesthetics alive, is that the possession of an objective culture, a culture of knowledge, skills, and morality, will be utterly antithetical to human life unless it harmonizes with the bald fact that we are embodied beings in a living, material world. If objective culture were nothing but the culture of the ascetic priest, the scientist, the bureaucrat, and the Kantian moralist, then the possession of this culture would be literally unlivable. If lovability matters, and it obviously does, it is because it signals the harmonization of objectivity, what is socially accorded the status of being there for everyone, with the needs of subjectivity, our living immersion in a material world. This is what I meant earlier when I said, following Horowitz, that beauty's promise of happiness was the promise of a reconciliation of culture with what must be conquered in order for culture to be possible.

And this is where modernism comes in, where modernism announces itself as that form of art that survives through a reiterated presentation of itself as nothing but the stakes of art and aesthetics in general. This is its wild and, for its critics, unforgivable hubris. Yet, as every critic of modernity from Rousseau through Nietzsche, Marx, Simmel, and Weber has made perspicuous, modern life evinces a continuous disarticulation of objective culture from subjective culture (to borrow Simmel's terminology): as objective culture—the forces of science, technology, industry, bureaucratic organization—grows and progresses, it does so in at least systematic indifference and at worse direct opposition to subjective culture, the cultivation of selves and political community. Modernism is the art that takes up the burden of this divorce between objective and subjective culture, their lack of harmony, the promise of reconciliation we cannot forgo without relinquishing altogether the idea of a life worth living. When in disgust McCarthy repudiates the neat formalism of high modernism, he rehearses culture's necessary promise of reconciliation as broken; no simpler modernist gesture is imaginable.

I take it that Deleuze wanted to talk about sensation and the violence of paint as the aesthetic truth of art, as opposed to pleasure and the harmony of the beautiful, because, in a wholly modernist way, he recognized that thinking about beauty as harmony, as our being at home in the world, as the enlivening experience of sensuousness in opposition to the affective neutrality of conceptual life, suppresses beauty's intransigence and unruly awkwardness. If beauty refers to the return of the culturally repressed, of the satisfactions we have had to repress for the sake of societal reproduction and advance, then within *every* experience of artistic beauty there must be presented not only the being together of form and repressed sensuousness but equally the *resistance* of form to what it informs, and the *rebellion* of the excluded material against its formal elaboration. Every moment of artistic beauty is always also about the fact that what it harmonizes is always about to collapse—collapse into a form that repulses its material conditions, or the anarchic sensuousness that has been excluded by culture's effort at self-assurance, at self-authorization (which authorization of course is routinely accomplished through the surmounting and/or repression of the authority of nature). Adorno states this thought thus:

> [Artworks] bear what is opposed to them in themselves; their materials are historically and socially preformed as are their procedures, and their heterogeneous element is that in them that resists their unity and is needed by its unity for it to be more than a Pyrrhic victory over the unresisting. *In this, aesthetic*

> *reflection is unanimous with the history of art, which irresistibly moved the dissonant into the center of the work until finally its difference from consonance was destroyed.* Art thereby participates in the suffering that, by virtue of the unity of this process, finds its way to language rather than disappearing.[17]

What Adorno here calls "the dissonant" typically appears in contemporary art history as some version of the sublime. What is pointed in Adorno's claim is that the acknowledgment of this moment of disruption, of irreconcilability, in modernist art *and* aesthetics is no longer thought of as antithetic to harmony or consonance, but rather what they have meant all along. Is not this very locating of resistance within harmony exactly the stakes in the passages that Nehamas cites, when Meyer Schapiro refers to the demon's change of appearance through "an astonishing conversion of the features into flamboyant, centrifugal, tentacular curves" or when Rosalind Krauss points to the moment when Serra's walls come to be "felt as barrier rather than as perspective, they then heighten the experience of the physical place of one's body"? I take the "astonishing conversion" and the movement from perspective to "felt as barrier" to perfectly encapsulate the dissonant coming into the center of the work in a manner that destroys its difference from consonance.

We might deepen this thought, making its connection to the main lines of development of modernist painting palpable through the consideration of a very *beautiful* National Gallery Degas, *La Coiffure* (1896)—a painting, significantly, that Matisse acquired in 1918,[18] seven years after painting *The Red Studio. La Coiffure* is a painting of a woman leaning back in a chair, her head craned horizontally along the line in which her waist-length hair is being held and combed by her maid. What distinguishes this painting, what forces us to draw back as if in defense when first seeing it, is its insistent redness: the red of the woman's gown, her hair, the wall behind her, the curtains, even her maid's hair; the same fervid red throughout. The maid offers color contrast and compositional balance to the woman: the maid's cream skirt matches the table in the right foreground, while her pale cream blouse is so drenched in the surrounding red that it appears a crushed rose-red (or is the blouse really rose? Degas keeps the visible clues ambiguous—one cuff white, the other red, etc.). The maid stands behind the woman, to her right; she is almost a column or support, her uprightness balancing the woman's near collapse into horizontality. The maid's uprightness acts like the memory of an earlier aesthetic, another modality of subjectivity and authority; she represents everything that Degas had to disavow in order to generate a fully modern mode of painting.

There is about this painting something willful, unsettled and therefore unsettling which is at one with its power. The fetishistic theme of hair combing is one that Degas had been exploiting for over a decade, but in a line continuous with the bathers, for the purpose of observing the female subject at the instant when the position of her being a subject is abandoned for the sake of a quiet moment of animal self-absorption, a luxuriating in passivity, a moment in which the woman is captured feeling herself, feeling the body she is. Degas supposes that in order to present embodiment one must capture it at the moment when it feels itself rather than when it, upright and face forward, is grasping or beholding the world. Degas knew better than anyone that the subject as agent is always about to disappear into its action, to be overtaken by meaning and narrative, and hence ready to shed the confines of embodiment (this is what the maid's "white" activity is meant to remind us of in *La Coiffure*). Attending to the body—washing itself, drying itself, combing or having its hair combed—enables it to become simultaneously subject and object, a subject absorptively immersed in its bodily objectness. (This is the reason Degas so routinely attends to dancers in repose, collapsing back into their bodies, into their exhaustion or readiness.) If one thinks of the bather series as one of bodily self-absorption in this manner, as a lapsing of subjective authority for the sake of animal embodiment, then one might think that Degas has, for all intents and purposes, discovered what Deleuze identified as "the body without organs" (FB, 45–46), recovering the material body from out of the spiritual body, finding in the luxuriating flesh another, repressed order of spirituality; dancing and bathing are material orders of meaning breaking into culture, marking it without being fully assimilable by it.[19]

I take it that Degas knew that culture needed the material body, needed ballet, needed dance, and that it almost always missed the point of these, which again is why he so routinely captures the dancer not dancing but practicing, resting, waiting, preparing (in preparation is the material excess of the body to the virtuosity of performance); or if we see them dancing it is from a odd angle—sideways on, or slightly elevated, or from below, or from too close—in order that we can see the bodily performing rather than what is performed. Degas thought we needed to tell the dancer from the dance or lose the meaning of dancing altogether. A component of Degas' discovery here is the thought that painting's "falseness," its inauthenticity, its lack of conviction and substance lay in the fact that in representing agency it inevitably tended to reify the subject, freeze it, setting up an irresolvable tension between the painterly display and the object displayed. In order to overcome this debilitating objectification, Degas found moments *in* culture in which subjects affirmed or embraced their corporeality, either displaying their material being for others or, oppositely, turning their back on sociality in order to become objects for themselves: dancing is a process of self-objectification, bathing a collapsing into embodiment. These subject matters, by locating the moment of exchange between nature and culture, between the demands of nature and the forms of cultural order, anticipate painting; they are the work of painting outside painting. Painting could hence, with such subject matter in view, mimetically repeat the work of acknowledging corporeal meaning without mastering it, without subsuming it; this makes bathing and dancing limit experiences, moments when nature appears in culture, and culture acknowledges the authority of nature without abandoning itself to it. Hence, Degas also knew that he was *using* dance and the female form as proxies for culture's acknowledgment of unassimilated nature, and that in so doing there was a costly sexual politics that he could only exploit without fully controlling. So much is evidenced in *Femme nue se coiffant* (c. 1876–77) where we have a plump nude, sitting on a puff in her bathroom combing out her long red hair. Opposite her is a fully dressed (black-tie and jacket) portly gentleman, pipe in hand, leering at her. That is the politics that the other bather pictures keep from view.

But it is not Degas' transfigurations of embodiment that interest me here, but what his work in pastels makes so vivid: his work as a colorist—his affirmation of the violence of paint. If routinely the bather pictures adopt the impressionist disregard for mimetic colors, nonetheless Degas had previously used his non-natural palette as a means for intensifying the flesh of his subjects: the echoing of the soft russet red that pervades the picture, on to the back of the women in both *After the Bath* (1885) and *Woman Drying Herself* (c. 1888–92), or, even more emphatically, the same echoing structure but now in soft, pale blue, a chilled blue, that saturates *The Bath* (c. 1894). Maybe it was the shift from pastel to oil that encouraged him to push the issue further. Whatever the source, with *La Coiffure* the innovation feels abrupt, a savage categorial violence: the radiant red, a red that seems to have been pressed through an orange dye, is no longer the descriptive means for rendering the scene but is the scene itself, as if woman, hair, room were themselves vehicles for revealing the blinding redness, a redness that rather than reflecting light becomes a vibrating source of illumination, as if in seeing the painting you might become soaked in its redness the way the maid does. The reversal or inversion of the relation between substance and color, color becoming the substance, the object painted, the figures becoming the qualifying predicates, the means or vehicle for structuring the display, contouring the color so to speak, is accomplished while leaving the original representational scene fully in place (perhaps maid and woman are more roughly and gesturally given than is usual in Degas, but still the scene is there). The balanced and therefore unresolved to-and-fro between the representational scene and its red representing as itself the scene imagines an art of pure means, to use fauvist language, an art that liberates the means of representation into what art presents, so a shift from representation to presentation. It is almost as if we cannot "see" this picture at all since form keeps collapsing into sensory experience—as if, perhaps, its exorbitant redness necessitated that we have "eyes all over" (FB, 52), as if the feeling of this picture was its lingering afterimage, the sense of it we have as we turn away, as if sensed with our backs, it looking at us. The great beauty of this painting, I am urging, unearths the excessive irreconcilability of sensuous color to form that appears *as if* reconciled elsewhere in Degas but never is. The passage through the bathers to this great painting emblematically traces the destruction of the difference between consonance and dissonance, dissonance being the truth of consonance (the painterly sublime becoming the truth of painterly beauty at the moment when we can no longer tell them apart). Degas was a passionate interrogator of form, searching out in each bend and bow, each twist or torsion of the human figure another possibility for representational coherence; to surrender form as he does here must have cost him dearly.

I could say more about Degas—a Degas that I read as a wondrous adumbration of Matisse—but the general thought should be obvious: his paintings are almost paradigmatically those castigated for their beauty, their prettiness, their easy loveliness—even nonart aficionados adore Degas. Yet, even a little attending reveals how easily his loveliest paintings can be seen to embody the painterly protocols that Deleuze gestures toward in his notion of sensation, his idea of the violence of paint. There is a prettiness about the ballet dancers and bathers that has made Degas' innovative power almost invisible—a worry I suspect that he shared and meant to defiantly correct in *La Coiffure*. With the help of Deleuze's aesthetic, something of the radicality of Degas begins to emerge, a Degas that is every bit as disorienting as the "felt barrier" of Serra's walls, who is every bit as critical of the dominant culture as McCarthy.

With modernism art becomes aesthetics (*La Coiffure*, I am urging, is best construed as an aesthetic self-reflection of Degas' own earlier work), and aesthetics bound to an art that has lost its external functionality and hence must recuperate its conditions of possibility from within. If one misreads this mutual determination, even ever so slightly, as now everyone agrees Greenberg did, then inevitably there will occur, in art and aesthetics, first trial separations, then divorce proceedings, terminating in the self-righteous and empty independence of each. On my reading, the stifled debate of "The Art Seminar" remains unconvincing because, apart from de Duve's urgings and some pointed flag-waving by Costello (he is right about the meaning of Melville's "late modernism"), it supposes that modernism is a thing of the past, and with modernism out of the way then there really is no systematic way of connecting aesthetics to art history. Or rather, there appears to be now a yawning question about the connection between aesthetics and art history because for the majority of the participants nothing is more obvious than that modernism is no longer authoritative for culture. The skirts the discussants hide behind in making this judgment is the loudly asserted irrelevance of Kant, as if the very idea of aesthetics as we now have it were not owed to him. The shallow dismissals of Kant, of his idea of beauty, in the discussion are like avant-garde dismissals of Degas' prettiness. My suggestion here has been that these are really the same judgment, the same dismissal, and in both cases I have urged the verdict is equally undeserved and wrongheaded.

The secret premise of the seminar was, finally, nothing other than the end of modernism, and by extension the end of art in its cultural-challenging sense, the sense that Greenberg and Adorno and Deleuze offered it, and which its finest practitioners have claimed for their efforts. If my diagnosis is correct, without an adequate appreciation of modernism, then truly there will be no connecting of aesthetics to art history. Thankfully, as the best aesthetic theory, the best art, and the best art history of the past several decades testify, the premise that modernism is over is false.[20]

Notes

1. Theodor W. Adorno, *Aesthetic Theory,* trans. Robert Hullot-Kentor (Minneapolis: University of Minnesota Press, 1997), 1.
2. *Aesthetic Theory*, 345.
3. My reading of the joke converges with Stephen Melville's. Indeed, at least at the formal level he and I agree that aesthetics concerns art's mattering, what he calls its provision of "orientation" for art history. For reasons that will become apparent, I doubt that we can remain quite as "low temperature" in our reckoning with Kant as he would prefer.
4. This is overstated, as I shall show below; aesthetics can be invaluable in explaining the truth content, which is to say, the force of some constitutive modernist moments of achievement, and, conversely, aesthetic considerations can prevent one from systematically misinterpreting the nature of those achievements. The negative form of the argument drives my *Against Voluptuous Bodies: Late Modernism and the Idea of Painting* (Stanford, CA: Stanford University Press, forthcoming) wherein I argue that hermeneutical errors in Greenberg's interpretation of Soutine, Cavell's of Caro, Fried's of minimalism, Clark's of Pollock, de Duve's of Duchamp, and Bois' of Ryman are, in each case, not factual but a matter of an inadequate assessment of the aesthetic stakes of the work in question. Still, de Duve's general point sticks because looking for aesthetic illumination in any particular case does mistake the nature of the relation in general: one does not systematically turn to aesthetics for narrowly hermeneutical reasons.
5. It is only this last thought that I find missing from Arthur Danto's account of *Bossy Burger* in *The Abuse of Beauty: Aesthetics and the Concept of Art* (Chicago: Open Court, 2003), 54–56; but it is just the lack of this thought that makes him think that beauty and so the "aesthetic" are detachable properties, belonging to some artworks but wholly absent in others. The

stakes of beauty are, I shall suggest below, everywhere in art. And this is equally why Diarmuid Costello goes wrong in his anti-Kantian, antibeauty comments: Gober's "silence," Whiteread's "unyielding," or Twombly's "lightness" are all ways of characterizing works that refer to aesthetic salience, and that salience will be, I shall urge, a determination of what Kant intends by his notion beauty.

6. Although I cannot here do the thought justice, it seems obvious to me that this aesthetic thought, this beginning of a thinking of the meaning of embodiment and its necessary relation to the question of pain, is utterly continuous with the emphases and governing orientations of James Elkins's *Pictures of the Body: Pain and Metamorphosis* (Stanford, CA: Stanford University Press, 1999). Indeed, to the extent that his work is not one in cognitive psychology (and it is not), it is impossible to read it as other than using art history and criticism as a way of forging the rudiments of an aesthetic theory. Do not the opening sentences of his book—"Every picture is a picture of the body. … Every work of visual art is a representation of the body" (p. 1)—belong to some version of transcendental philosophy? Is not art history here a vehicle for bringing into view something like a transcendental comprehension of the role of the human body in our having a representable world? And does not the role of pain in Elkins's work—"pain is the general condition of being alive … ." (p. 23)—parallel the use of pain in, say, Wittgenstein, where the apparently wholly epistemological issue (the skeptical problem of other minds) is tacitly revealed to embed insistent ethical stakes? And is it a mere accident that his work begins with a discussion of Alberto Giacometti's *Portrait of Isaku Yanaihara* (1956) and Balthus's *The Cherry-Picker* (1940), two works that bring into direct relation the stakes of modernism for traditional representational art? Or that abstraction is the great worry and the decisive clue to his entire story? All this seems to me about the marriage of art history and aesthetics in the light of modernism—which I am claiming is the only way that marriage can now occur. But now I am simply puzzled by Elkins's demurring in "The Art Seminar."
7. *Aesthetic Theory*, 333.
8. *Aesthetic Theory*, 343.
9. Gregg Horowitz, " 'I sat Food on my knees': The Promise of Happiness in Arthur C. Danto's *The Abuse of Beauty*," forthcoming. My reading of the McCarthy earlier was wholly indebted to Horowitz's essay, as is much else in this essay. And, as always in matters aesthetic, I am grateful to him and his work.
10. Horowitz, " 'I sat Food on my knees.' "
11. This is a slightly different genealogy than de Duve's since I think one can remain closer to the Grünewald paradigm than he does; but I would not dispute his story—different narratives locate different emphases. For a version of this story that shows how Sherman's pictures help construct it, see my *Against Voluptuous Bodies*, op. cit., chap. 9.
12. Henceforth all references in the text to FB refer to Gilles Deleuze, *Francis Bacon: The Logic of Sensation*, trans. Daniel W. Smith (London and New York: Continuum, 2003).

13. This is the point that Nehamas overlooks in his defense of aesthetic individualism and Nietzschean self-fashioning.
14. *Aesthetic Theory*, 343.
15. It would follow from this that Deleuze's philosophy as a whole is best interpreted—in the line of Wittgenstein and Adorno, say—as a form of philosophical modernism. Certainly the role that the books on Proust, Kafka, and cinema play in his work as the empirical actualization of it, would underline this hypothesis. Now, nothing could be more obvious than that this conflicts with all the extant readings of Deleuze, and, equally obviously, at least some portions of the oeuvre itself. However, if his art books provide something like empirical instantiations of the philosophy—not illustrations of it but rather the same in practice—and those works are consistently bound to the achievements of high modernism, then it makes sense to regiment the reading of the oeuvre to the provision of a philosophical modernism. This would drag Deleuze studies back from the somewhat spectacular speculative exorbitances that have dominated it to date.
16. Of course, this is not the only kind of art history that is possible—I conceded that thought at the outset. My claim is the weaker one: unless we have an art history that is simultaneously a record of our aesthetic judgments, nothing is going to make these histories art histories. The notion of art only takes on this salience when it becomes autonomous; which entails that nonautonomous art is only art to the extent that it satisfies its extra-aesthetic function aesthetically.
17. *Aesthetic Theory*, 344. (italics mine)
18. My thanks to Daniel Bernstein for bringing this to my attention.
19. Although I will not harp on it, it is evident that for Degas the human body, its materiality, is also the source or emblem of its existential solitude; this is another reason for bracketing subjectivity as agency for the sake of subjectivity as feeling. There is a great pathos in even the most radiant of Degas' dancers and bathers: their flesh is mortal, and their mortality a source of aloneness. Certainly the theme of solitude is, ironically, more salient and more aching in Degas than in Bacon.
20. The first three paragraphs of my account of Deleuze and a paragraph of my reading of Degas derive from a forthcoming essay: "In Praise of Pure Violence (Matisse's War)."

Island Mysteries

Marc Redfield

It is a rare honor for a literary critic to be allowed to offer closing reflections on a volume that studies the relation between aesthetics and art history. My mission, I presume, is to cause trouble, unleash a surprise, and make a difference—an impossible assignment (nothing is more evanescent than trouble or surprise, or more fungible than difference), yet also of course, in the present context, the only sort of task worth attempting. And though I won't be delivering my observations from a purely external vantage, my understanding of the concept of the aesthetic is indeed somewhat different from that elaborated by the other contributors to this volume, so I hope the pages that follow can at least usefully extend the range of perspectives on display.[1]

Aesthetics, for most writers or seminar participants in this collection, names an academic discipline—or subdiscipline, really: a topic usually ranged with the kind of subjects studied by members of philosophy departments. Aesthetics in this sense is a professional exploration of the nature of art, the artwork, the experience of beauty, and so on; it is an academic discourse that boasts its own journals and conferences, generates articles and books, and gives definition to a handful of named chairs, but typically does not constitute in itself a degree-granting field within the university. From a strictly institutional point of view, the relationship between the islands of Ae (aesthetics) and Ah (art history) in the vowel-rich South Seas of James Elkins's parable is somewhat lopsided: Ah is considerably the larger island, and reproduces its population—trains students, that is—more efficiently and in greater numbers. And in addition to being small, Ae would appear to be a rather foggy, bare, and rocky islet—more Easter Island than Bora Bora, at least if one goes along with the prevalent description of it in this volume. My own view is that interesting issues and obsessions lurk underneath the "dreariness" that Joseph Margolis (probably correctly) perceives as the main characteristic of professional aesthetics; and a little later I shall try to sketch out one or two ways in which aesthetics as a specific intellectual tradition repays attention.[2]

But let me first summarize why, in my view, we need to understand the academic field of aesthetics as a small—a very small—part of a much larger historical event.[3] We may call this event "the rise of aesthetics" if we understand by that phrase the emergence, over the course of the eighteenth and nineteenth centuries, of ideas and institutions of art and the artist, culture and acculturation, that little by little enabled or developed into the manifold of cultural institutions and discourses that shape present-day middle-class Western lives. Very few people become art historians, let alone aestheticians; but in the developed world only the most severely damaged, radically isolated, and desperately poor sectors of the population are functionally unaffected by the institutions and images of aesthetic culture. We take for granted that there should be certain objects called "art," a particular sort of writing called "literature," and so on. We take for granted that at least a small degree of contact with these objects and this kind of writing plays an essential role in normative psychic and social development; that in consequence, art, music, and literature classes should form part of primary and secondary mass education, and that either the state or (particularly in the U.S.) the not-for-profit sector of civil society should fund museums and concert halls, and universities with art history and literature departments; and so on. None of these phenomena existed or would have made social or intellectual sense three hundred years ago; some of them, like university-level instruction in literature or art history, only began to make enough sense to come into existence about a century ago (at most). The very notion of *recreation* as an organized complement to *work* may partly be traced back to a complex of ideas about the role of play in the fabrication of human identity that received an early and decisive articulation in Friedrich Schiller's *On the Aesthetic Education of Man* (1795).[4] From the heights of the art market to the far-as-the-eye-can-see plains of the culture and advertising industries, the aesthetic in this extended sense has left its mark on our lifeworld. Its development is inseparable from that of consumer capitalism, mass politics, and media technology; it forms a fundamental part of the vast series of transformations we call modernity.

Why summarize this protean discursive, institutional, techno-*mediatic* historical transformation as "the rise of aesthetics"? Because the notion of the aesthetic proved a fertile, if (as we shall see) deeply unstable, concept or ideologeme out of which a remarkable variety of cultural narratives and motifs could be elaborated. The aesthetic has ancient roots in Western culture (meditation on the beautiful is as old as philosophy itself); people have always made things and judged them, and the fact that our words "art" and "literature" acquired their modern meanings in the 18th century does not mean that their referents were previously nonexistent. But these words developed their new meanings as part of the development of something new: a web of speculation on the aesthetic as an experience of judgment without rule, and harmony without law: an experience, let us say, of divine order recast in human terms. In the late 18th century as now, the number of people interested in Kant's explanation of how a subjective judgment might posit universal assent was rather small; but the notion that in the aesthetic's disinterested space human beings gained a sense of their essential humanness became a leitmotiv within any number of Romantic and post-Romantic discursive contexts. This notion's cultural or ideological force derives from the aesthetic's seeming ability to marry the natural to the cultural. On the one hand, all human beings have right of access to aesthetic experience (the aesthetic is rooted in a specifically human *nature*); on the other hand, human beings, developing a sense of their own potential in and through aesthetic experience, are undergoing a certain sort of pleasurable education (the aesthetic manifests itself in and through *acculturation*). The 18th century term "taste" reduces this paradox to a single resonant metaphor. We are all born with taste, but some of us have more than others, and in any event what we have can and must be improved through education. (Thus, to take a stroll on the metaphor's literal plane, most of us, given sufficient training, can learn to distinguish Pinot Noir from other varietals; some of us can learn yet finer discriminations and become connoisseurs; the gifted and specialized few can become Masters of Wine.) The sheer fact that everyone is supposed *potentially* able to appreciate Shakespeare or Rembrandt or Beethoven allows those who have been properly schooled to claim a certain ability to *represent* the potential of those who have not. Aesthetic culture claims to prepare the consensual ground for representative democracy. Hence (for instance) the persistent emphasis in 19th century European middle-class writing on the need for the working classes to undergo (aesthetic) education as a prerequisite for political enfranchisement. By producing subjects capable of disinterested reflection, culture produces subjects capable of recapitulating the state's universality—and therefore capable of, among other things, running a nation or ruling an empire (or at least voting for those who do).

The aesthetic is thus always at some point a political discourse. It is by no means inevitably a reactionary one, and it certainly has good intentions. Thierry de Duve is not exaggerating when he claims, wryly but seriously, that "Kant's *Critique of Judgment* formulates a transcendental—I say transcendental, not utopian or anything like that—foundation for democracy and peace on earth." Whether or not de Duve is doing justice to the notorious complexities of the third *Critique*, he is unquestionably invoking the traditional ambition of modern aesthetics from Shaftesbury to Matthew Arnold and beyond. The aesthetic intends to deliver an intuition of social, epistemological, and ontological harmony. Complications set in because arguably even in Kant—and constantly, indeed, programmatically, in the less rigorous Schillerian tradition that takes off from the third *Critique*—the *sensus communis* slips away from its properly transcendental status, and becomes empirically articulated within a specific social field, and subjected to an overt or tacit version of the developmental narrative sketched a moment ago.[5] The outline of this high-aesthetic discourse is still visible behind a thin layer of rhetorical-polemical drapery in Paul Crowther's affirmation of art as "a formative aesthetic activity." (Crowther's rhetorical originality consists in denouncing any criticism or complication of this claim as a "Western"—as in: *merely* "Western"—betrayal of a truth universally to be acknowledged.)

The denunciation of aesthetics as "ideology" has been one of cultural critique's enabling gestures over the past 20 or so years, and up to a certain point, as my summary suggests, this gesture has critical force. Aesthetic discourse certainly has ideological consequence; indeed, aesthetics may be understood as offering a formalized model of ideology per se, to the extent that the singular subject of aesthetic judgment claims to become universally representative. But the cultural-studies negation of aesthetics fails to achieve full purchase on its object: underestimating the complexity of aesthetics, such criticism winds up both simplifying and repeating aesthetic discourse. For as we have seen, aesthetics is traditionally, self-consciously, and intentionally a political discourse. Its moment of disinterestedness is a recreational pause, a detour that bends back to anchor itself in the referential ground of the "human," and the empirical context of a history. Thus, to the extent that aesthetics marks off a space of disinterestedness, it incorporates into its logic a negation of itself, and is perfectly ready to survive its own reduction to politicosocial interestedness (by morphing, for instance, into the universalizing "culture" of "cultural studies"). The cultural-critique reduction does not rid us of aesthetics. It is in many ways simply yet another manifestation of a certain deep discomfort within aesthetics itself. This discomfort is visible throughout the present volume, as one contributor after another either explicitly or implicitly denounces aesthetics as dreary, dead, abstract—and does so on *aesthetic* grounds, appealing to the immediacy and singularity of an experience or judgment that is sensuous but never simply sensuous: that involves in some fashion possibilities of human thought, identity, and formation.

My own belief is that the endless dissatisfactions and anxieties that aesthetics generates—not just in this volume, and not just over the last two decades, but over the last two hundred years—stem from an instability at its heart. Aesthetics is not simply an ideology, at least not in the ordinary sense. It is a complex and historically consequent discourse that figures as disinterested pleasure—an experience that I shall risk calling an "experience of shock" in Walter Benjamin's sense.[6] Committed to the possibility that meaning could become indistinguishable from sensory apprehension, aesthetics discovers the difference and deferral that makes signification possible; committed to the promise that the singular and the subjective could discover a passage to the universal, aesthetics uncovers the subject's fragmentation. I cannot reproduce here the analyses that would properly document these claims—I have tried to do so elsewhere—but in the rest of this essay I shall look closely at a few moments in the texts assembled in this volume and glance at a couple of passages from other texts in the aesthetic tradition, in an effort to provide at least some sense of the tensions inhabiting aesthetic speculation.[7]

Aesthetics, according to this account, is not, or at least not primarily, an island named Ae; it is rather the ocean that allows the outcroppings of Ae and Ah to become islands in the first place. The discursive and institutional history of modern aesthetics stands behind every sentence composing the present collection of texts, and has made possible not just the thoughts and words, but the professional careers of all of this volume's contributors. Traces of the aesthetic's uncontainability are legible now and then. Dominic Willsdon's call for an "aesthetics-at-large" inspires Arthur Danto to contrast aesthetics "as an academic discipline" to aesthetics "as a living thing"—and it is arguably no accident that this positively valorized expansion of the aesthetic seems to flower out of manifestations of damage, loss, and mourning ("the shrines that were set up all over New York City the day after 9/11"). I shall come back to that point. But first let me underscore the proliferation of terms, discriminations, and metaphors we encounter over the course of "The Art Seminar" and in "Assessments." "Aesthetics has almost been a material substance in this conversation," Elkins summarizes; "it has hardness or softness, broadness or narrowness, it flows … it melts, it is flexible and can be folded and even placed inside something else, like art history." We may add that in this context it is not always easy to tell one quality from its opposite. De Duve, for instance, referring to Danto's remarks about the 9/11 shrines, first contrasts his own "narrow" notion of the aesthetic with Danto's "broad" one—"I confine aesthetics to the domain of art, whereas you take aesthetic qualities, predicates, attributes, and feelings, out of art and into the domain of everyday life"—but then tells us that narrowness is breadth: Danto is "in fact narrowing aesthetics, while I am broadening it, because the field of art includes anything and everything today. Once a urinal or a Brillo box can be art, anything can be art." What is it to be narrow or broad when the one is the other, and vice versa? But we remark a pattern: from a variety of viewpoints and polemical vantages, again and again the aesthetic "broadens" to include "anything and everything"—before (or after) being denounced as dreary and lifeless, fit only for the "library" to which, according to Danto, Kant ought to be confined. At the same time (and this is, I think, really just another version of the same problem), the participants worry about the difference and the borderlines between aesthetics and art history. Which contains which? Is art history the "evidential record of previous aesthetic judgments" (de Duve) or are "judgments about art-historical significance" fundamentally different from "judgments about aesthetic quality" (Rampley)? And since one can never know whether or not someone else's judgment was or was not strictly aesthetic in the Kantian sense—was or was not contaminated by intellectual or sensual interest—how could this argument ever resolve itself? Aesthetics seems everywhere, yet at the same time one can never quite put one's finger on it.[8]

A similar kind of slippage is at work in Elkins's institutional parable. Elkins is describing a clearly perceptible socio-institutional difference (aestheticians and art historians, barring a few crossover figures like Elkins himself, go to different conferences, publish in different journals, and so on), and he is keenly aware that this difference straddles and to some extent conceals far less stable ones ("Art-historical texts that bristle with details can still depend on the most broad assumptions about artworks; and conversely, aesthetics texts that keep to the language of metaphysics can still turn on unique encounters with unique works"). Still, like most contributors to this book, Elkins seems at least in principle to favor art history (the discipline dedicated to "what is taken to be either irreducibly visual or ungeneralizably singular about artworks") over aesthetics ("the discipline that abstracts or otherwise generalizes" the irreducibly visual or singular). One has the suspicion that, like Margolis, he finds aesthetics "dreary" (though apparently aestheticians, as a social aggregate, are not: Elkins closes his paper remarking "the level of noise at last year's [American Society for Aesthetics] conference," and seems to approve of the "good-natured" proposition-driven arguing to which, in his estimation, aestheticians are more inclined than art historians).[9]

But let us take a closer look at the islands of Ah and Ae, and their comedy of misunderstanding. Traders go back and forth between them, which is a good thing, since these communities, Hegelian enough to require the recognition of the other in order to become what they are, like to commission representations of themselves—though of course they don't like the result, to the point of not recognizing the other's representation *as* a representation, which is to say as an act of recognition: "No one on either island has a theory that encompasses the practices of the other." Nor is there an external vantage—a third island, let us say, with the whispery name of Ph, inhabited by philosophers—from which these differences can be resolved. The question remains, however, whether the difference of this difference is a stable one—whether, as Elkins seems to suggest, we can at least say, clearly and once and for all, that there *is* a difference, and we perceive it *there*. His island allegory encourages the idea that the institutional difference between art history and aesthetics mirrors a fundamental and secure ontologico-discursive difference, but I think the allegory crumbles as Elkins begins putting pressure on what he calls the "proposition" of the "aesthetician," described as "a logical proposition—something like, 'Immanent materiality is separated from the conceptual by an aporetic gap.'" The aesthetician's proposition implies "that the uniqueness, or the particularity, or the nonverbal, undescribed, innarrable, 'purely visual' portions of an artwork are conceptualized in the same sense as the phrase 'domain of concepts.'" And the art historian in Elkins objects: "It is not clear that a phrase such as 'immanent materiality' does justice to what happens in the studio or in the viewing of a work, when the artist is just plain confused about the work, or when an art historian is absorbed in a single object . . . ."

Elkins hints here at a kind of performative enrapture, an entrancement inseparable from a singular moment, a specific motion of thought or hand. He thus suggests (without, of course, saying so: to use the terms I am about to use is manifestly to repeat the philosophical abstraction that is being criticized) that the aporia that the aesthetician imagines to be between conceptuality and materiality is "really" one between conceptuality and performance. For the objection is that the aesthetician falls short of the aporia by misstating it in conceptual language. What goes missing, then, in the aporia is the singular, unique, nonverbal element to which the aporia gestures in order to come into being as an aporia: the aporia betrays itself in forming itself. Now on the one hand, the art historian on Ah, trying to draw Ae, repeats the terms of the aporia by rephrasing it as one "between something known (the domain of concepts) and something *else* unknown, and that other thing cannot be known without giving up what is known." (One depends just as much on conceptual language to say "something else unknown" as to say "material.") But on the other hand, something has been gained: the aporia has been rephrased more rigorously and now involves the reader/thinker/artist in its toils, for to conceive of it is now manifestly to betray it. "Materiality" (or "absorption in an object," etc.) cannot be rendered in conceptual language but must and can only be *performed*. "Performance" is certainly as abstract a term as "material," but to rekey the aporia as one between cognition and performance is at least to register the reader or writer or thinker's participation in its contradiction. Strangely enough, therefore, the artists and art historians of Ah turn out to be better aestheticians than the aestheticians of Ae—at the expense, however, of losing consciousness of their accomplishment.

In order, for example, to value the chronicling of that act, it is necessary *not* to see the relation as such; so artists who begin to take some version of the proposition as philosophers do, might be tempted to give up art and start doing philosophy. And conversely, aestheticians who start to perceive the problems entailed in claiming that the proposition is a well-formed sentence might be likely to begin writing something that resembles history, at least in its skepticism about the value of the proposition as a logical claim.

More skeptical than any philosopher, and more skeptical in a quite academically savvy and self-conscious mode—they clearly could hold their own in any common room or lecture hall at Oxford, or for that matter on Ae—the artist-historians put into question "the value of the proposition as a logical claim." Yet their skepticism—their philosophical triumph over philosophy—seems to require a blindness: "it is necessary *not* to see the relation as such" if one wishes to remain on Ah.

And in that case, can anyone be sure what island one is on, or which is which? Of course in a socio-institutional sense one knows; but as soon as one begins, like Elkins, to parse the grammar of aesthetic reflection and performance, it becomes harder and harder to draw lines. Is Elkins himself writing as an art historian or an aesthetician here? Or is that ultimately the wrong question to ask; would it not perhaps make more sense to understand him as writing within a complex and conflicted discourse that might as well, for reasons given earlier, be called "aesthetics": a discourse that on the one hand seems driven to mistrust itself to the point of (ambivalently) desiring its own negation, and on the other hand seems fated to violate the borders it compulsively draws? One of the odder aspects of the Ah and Ae parable is that, as my summary above records, at a certain point Ah begins to acquire a population of artists as well as art historians. The arrival of the artists confuses the institutional allegory (many good art historians may paint or sculpt seriously, as Elkins has observed elsewhere, but still: artist and art historian are two extremely different social roles),[10] and causes trouble on a disciplinary-conceptual level as well (that historians should share space with the object of their analysis is in a sense a contradiction in terms—an obliteration of distance that would make history-writing impossible). The artists' arrival makes sense, though, if we understand the seascape of Ah and Ae as a trope for aesthetics. There are other islands in the "University" sector of the archipelago populated by literary critics and literary historians and creative writers and so on; a shade farther off are islands boasting writers' and artists' colonies, and museums and art galleries; then things get hazy and the islands multiply, populated by entertainers and educators of all sorts. The artists obviously paddled over from somewhere; they are important members of this cultural Oceania, and are to some extent welcome wherever they visit, since they represent the authority and authenticity of human self-performance—the revelation of human *being* for its own sake. (Still, one does not really want to live with them either. Better that they stay on their art studio and creative writing islands, for, after all, a picture of them, painted perhaps on Ah, will normally do just as well.)

All the various citizens of the archipelago—art historians, artists, literary critics, curators, etc.—know what island they live on because they get their paycheck there and have certain assigned tasks to perform. But as to what they are "really" doing when they perform these tasks—of that no one can ever be entirely sure. Those who ask even the most basic questions rapidly find themselves adrift, swimming in deep waters. Now and then people get together and blame this problem on Ae, which is a respected but not a popular island, and one that even some of its own inhabitants profess to find dreary.

Earlier I claimed that something like an experience of shock lies at the heart of aesthetic speculation—a claim that is not as shocking as it might appear at first glance. The experience of the beautiful or the sublime is commonly understood to befall or overcome us. Though it demands acculturation, we cannot reliably prepare for it; in some respects aesthetic experience thus strangely and paradoxically recalls that trauma. Let me offer here one canonical example: in Edmund Burke's *A Philosophical Enquiry into the Origin of Our Ideas of the Sublime and the Beautiful* (1757), the thematic association of the sublime with astonishment as terror is only the most prominent instance of a deeper association of the aesthetic in general (that is the beautiful as well as the sublime) with an experience of shock. The aesthetic is that which *strikes* us.[11] Burke's remarks on beauty emphasize the aesthetic specificity of the experience of the beautiful: it is not an experience conditioned by habit, or by rational thought, mensuration, or any other activity of the understanding. With the casualness of a man of letters who, unlike the professional Kantian philosopher, can always smuggle God back in when he wishes, Burke separates aesthetic judgment radically from ethical and teleological judgment. Beauty is the pleasure of contemplation, as distinct from a desire to possess (p. 91); "the beautiful strikes us as much by its novelty as the deformed itself" (p. 103), and does not wait for us to grow accustomed to the object, measure it, integrate it into custom and habit. It has no link to fitness or use: in his goodness the Creator has "frequently joined beauty to those things which he has made useful to us," but this is a sheer metonymy (p. 107). The Creator's true wisdom was rather, Burke suggests, to invent the aesthetic as a force that strikes:

> Whenever the wisdom of our Creator intended that we should be affected with any thing, he did not confide the execution of his design to the languid and precarious operation of our reason; but he endued it with powers and properties that prevent

> the understanding, and even the will, which *seizing upon the senses and imagination, captivate the soul before the understanding is ready either to join with them or oppose them.* It is by a long deduction and much study that we discover the adorable wisdom of God in his works: when we discover it, the effect is very different, not only in the manner of acquiring it, but in its own nature, from *that which strikes us without any preparation from the sublime or the beautiful.* (p. 107–08; emphasis mine)

Burke's speculation here offers a version of a claim that one can find almost anywhere one looks in writing on aesthetic experience. That the aesthetic *befalls* us is audible even in the German word Kant uses to describe aesthetic pleasure, *Gefallen*; that the shock of this experience has to do with its being in some way not precisely *mine*—even though it happens only to me, here and now, in its irreplaceable singularity—is a leitmotiv legible throughout the aesthetic tradition, from the 18th century to the present. In his introduction to a recent special issue of *Diacritics* on "Rethinking Beauty," for instance, Simon Jarvis characterizes "the true judgment of beauty" as "the moment at which shock or awe break into utterance."[12] (One may think here of Diarmuid Costello's and Stephen Melville's insistence on the "Wow!" of aesthetic interjection—a breaking-into-utterance that perhaps even resonates in the "Ah" and "Ae" of Elkins's parable). In the same issue, Peter de Bolla, drawing on writings of Philippe Lacoue-Labarthe, suggests that "art experiences are singular in the sense that they can only occur to the perceiving subject—they are subjective in the way Kant describes—but they do not belong to the subject, nor are they made by the subject. … [T]he particular quality of an encounter with art is our coming to understand what we cannot live, what is outside the domain of experience."[13] And as I suggested earlier, a particularly subtle meditation on aesthetic experience is discoverable in Walter Benjamin's analysis of the "shock experience" in relation to

Baudelaire's poetry: though for Benjamin the experience of shock is not specifically aesthetic (it is perhaps better summarized as the quintessential experience of modernity), it brings into focus the strange character of a singular undergoing (*Erlebnis*) that is inassimilable to a traditional definition of experience (*Erfahrung*) (p. 163). The syncope of action or performance, as we elucidated it in Elkins's text, may be taken as a version of this marking or scoring of subjectivity—a rapture that can manifest itself as bliss or as pain or as some other, less nameable affect—by a force at once intimate and alien to it.[14]

Shock requires management, and the aesthetic tradition is itself in a sense a giant shock absorber. Dislocation becomes harmony; self-loss becomes self-formation; the strange, biting, entrancing pleasure of aesthetic judgment becomes acculturation. Yet the aesthetic remains a source of anxiety, to the extent that loss and difference haunt the intuition of harmony and the narrative of self-realization that aesthetic experience is supposed to deliver. Aesthetics can never guarantee any identities, least of all its own; its harmonies are always ready to turn false and tinny. The beautiful, as Diarmuid Costello notes early in "The Art Seminar," can be—must at a certain point be—another word for kitsch. The aesthetic hates and negates itself, becomes the "anti-aesthetic" for the sake of itself—hence the negative dialectical spiral played out by modern and avant-garde art from the late 19th century to the present. And because of the aesthetic's unstable, self-corroding nature, texts focused on aesthetic issues often yield hints of an ongoing, mostly unacknowledged work of mourning, now and then relieved by violent fantasies of purgation and renewal. Earlier I claimed it to be no accident that Arthur Danto should have turned to 9/11 shrines as he reflected on aesthetics as a "living thing"; as I close these remarks, let me direct attention to a few other moments in the seminar when loss, damage, and mourning seem to be called up and to some extent managed. For it is really quite remarkable how many scenes of risk, death, and dismemberment flicker into view over the course of this thoroughly proper academic conversation. Probably everyone's favorite example will be the moment when Thierry de Duve, defending the relevance of Kant as a theorist of aesthetic experience, stages aesthetic *Gefallen* for us as a literal fall: "Say you throw yourself out of the window, and you land on the sidewalk. Is Newton useful to you? You have just obeyed the law of universal gravity, that's all." One can pay homage to the brilliance of a *mot* while pressing the phantasmatic contours of its logic: so aesthetic judgment is like falling? Or indeed, like landing, since the moment of anagnorisis is that of contact, possibly lethal contact, with a hard urban surface? But the interest of this moment thickens as Stephen Melville, in his "Assessment" essay writes of de Duve's "flung professor": in the original anecdote, "you" threw "yourself" out the window, but Melville's version allows a more sinister interpretation: were you flung? Have we been clueless Watsons all this time, overlooking a murder?

Such questions would be pointlessly extravagant if the flung professor were the only potential corpse in this conversation, but we encounter another hint of mystery and ambiguous murder-suicide when Elkins expresses his doubts "about how aesthetic terms might survive within historical contexts—like those little cyanide capsules spies supposedly keep in their mouth." Here the seminar's ongoing debate about inside and outside, solidity and liquefaction, borders and contamination, becomes for a moment a lurid story—yet nonetheless once again a teasingly ambiguous one: do the aesthetic terms "survive"? And if not, is their death intentional or accidental, self-produced or caused by an external force? We have sufficiently belabored the anxiety-producing potential of the aesthetic to understand why aesthetic terms should be figurable as poison pills; all that need be stressed at this point is the way in which Elkins's imagery simultaneously invokes and undermines ethical and epistemological certainty. The pills are poison, but their role is ambiguous: Elkins's question "how aesthetic terms might survive within historical contexts" is asking counter-intuitively whether the *pills*, not the spies, can survive—though the "death" of the one would also presumably be that of the other. And presumably the spy—"art history," in the allegory—would have chomped down on the pill deliberately (though presumably under duress). A bit of embalmed death, entombed like a melancholic lost object within the body of art history, yet by definition oriented toward its own rupture and overflow, the cyanide pill is a rich figure for the play of inside and outside, containing and flooding, that drives the seminar's conversation.

Elkins nicely develops and extends the motif of the ambiguous murder of (and by) aesthetics in his closing comments:

> Aesthetics has almost been a material substance in this conversation: it has hardness or softness, broadness or narrowness, it flows (there are "confluences" of aesthetics and other disciplines), it melts, it is flexible and can be folded or even placed inside something else, like art history. I will add one more metaphor, which also produces a ninth model: it can be opened. It can be opened and Kant can be taken out: not wholly, of course, but in pieces. The possibility of an operation in which parts of Kant are removed from the body of aesthetics might be the not-so-hidden theme of this conversation. So let me propose, in ending, a ninth model and a metaphor to go with it: art history might be the acid that corrodes aesthetics. Has it ever happened the other way around?

Throughout the seminar, "Kant" has served as a personification of aesthetics per se. "By my count 'Kant' or 'Kantian' appears no less than 37 times in the transcript," Ladislav Kesner observes—disapprovingly, of course. Barring a few exceptions such as de Duve and Melville, the scholars assembled here tend to express the kind of energetically ambivalent feelings about Kant that, according to Freudian narrative, sons are supposed to feel for fathers.[15] (We may note parenthetically that the seminar participants and the present volume's contributors are almost without exception male.) Here, at the end of the day, the dead father, lodged in "the body of aesthetics," is chopped into "pieces," extracted and fetishized, castrated and killed all over again—after which "operation" the "body of aesthetics" is disposed of in good murder-mystery fashion: "art history might be the acid that corrodes aesthetics."[16] Like the stories of the flung professor and the spies with cyanide pills, this one simultaneously offers us the lure of a lurid plot line and the opacity of ambiguous agency: Elkins's verbs are passive; who is doing this deed? And is this deed murderous, or merely necrophilic: is the body—either the body of aesthetics or the body of Kant, lodged within that first body—alive or dead? Could the seeming victim actually be the murderer? ("Has it ever happened the other way around?") And will conversations about the aesthetic ever be able to steer entirely clear of such ambiguity-laced scenes of fragmentation, incorporation, and mourning?

Probably not, to judge from the record. These dramas of uncertain agency work to transform into oedipal aggression the less manageable, more haunting anxieties of self-loss and uncontainability to which the shock of the aesthetic at once gives rise and responds. It is to the seminar participants' credit that they press their conversation about aesthetics and art history to the point at which such scenes become tempting.

Notes

1. Most but not all of the texts composing this volume were available to me as I composed this afterword. The pages that follow respond to the "Starting Points" by Joseph Margolis and James Elkins; to "The Art Seminar" transcript; and to "Assessments" by Paul Crowther, Harry Cooper, Ladislav Kesner, Matthew Rampley, Stephen Melville, Keith Moxey, and Alexander Nehamas.
2. I share Margolis's opinion that writing on aesthetics "cannot fail to be dreary" if it is supposed that "our best beginnings (in Aristotle, in Hume, in Kant) have pretty well hit very near to the fixed and essential mark." Nothing indeed is duller than pious repetition, and if our relation to these

or other canonical texts is that of pedagogues directing attention to a "fixed and essential mark," the lesson is certainly going to be a boring one. But I do not think that invoking the Zeitgeist in order to prescribe for aesthetics a set of determined and determining themes ("a world of flux," and so on) is a cure for dreariness. Quite the contrary: the dreariness of aesthetics, like that of any other humanistic field, is caused by just this sort of abstraction from the specificity of texts to the generality of theme. It is caused, in other words, by a failure to read strongly and carefully (and the failure to read, here, may be thought of as broadly akin to a failure to "see" strongly and carefully when producing art history or art criticism). Arguably the best aesthetic speculation of our time has emerged in and through an engagement with the texts of the aesthetic tradition.

3. For a fuller account of the developments summarized in this and subsequent paragraphs, see my *Politics of Aesthetics: Nationalism, Gender, Romanticism* (Stanford, CA: Stanford University Press, 2003), 9–14, passim; also my *Phantom Formations: Aesthetic Ideology and the Bildungsroman* (Ithaca, NY: Cornell University Press, 1996), 1–12, passim.
4. For a study taking this line, see David Lloyd and Paul Thomas, *Culture and the State* (London and New York: Routledge, 1998).
5. I argued the case for this interpretation of Kant in *Phantom Formations*, 12–20.
6. Walter Benjamin, "On Some Motifs in Baudelaire," in *Illuminations: Essays and Reflections*, ed. Hannah Arendt, trans. Harry Zohn (New York: Schocken Books, 1969).
7. I shall be discussing some peculiarities of aesthetic experience in what follows, but a full examination of this matter would require a careful study of the role of form in aesthetic discourse and aesthetic judgment. For readings that seek to show how, in the most rigorous texts in the aesthetic tradition, the notion of aesthetic form becomes a strange, nearly illegible figure, see, in addition to my own books, Samuel Weber, *Mass Mediauras: Form, Technics, Media* (Stanford, CA: Stanford University Press, 1996).
8. The seminar's argument about disciplinary boundaries thus repeatedly assumes an ethical tone. John Hyman tells us that "a confluence or intersection of art and art history" is something "we really don't want"—the implication being that disciplinary contamination is thoroughly possible; it is simply that we should remain "firmly on our own patch." Martin Donougho's riposte is similarly axiological: "interaction is good," besides the fact that "it happens anyway." As Stephen Melville comments, the entire discussion needs to be understood in relation to the "disciplinary scattering" effected by the modern university. But the slippage among terms and roles in these texts seems particularly characteristic of aesthetic discourse. I am thinking here of Harry Cooper remarking that "it was refreshing to see a philosopher (Arthur Danto) decrying transhistorical judgments while an art historian (Thierry de Duve) made absolute claims like 'Kant got it right'"; Matthew Rampley calling Danto an "art critic"; Diarmuid Costello defining himself as an "art theorist rather than either an art historian or an aesthetician"; and so on.

The seminar discussion is further complicated by the different ways in which seminar participants use words like "beauty," and by overabbreviated invocations of Kant. Keith Moxey, for instance, quoting Nicholas Davey, believes that aesthetic judgment in Kant is "based upon a shared intersubjective *a priori* framework of aesthetic judgments which are unaffected by tradition, history, or social circumstance." Davey's is an improvised remark and I pause to iron out its wrinkles only because later in this essay I shall be suggesting that "Kant" plays a symbolically important role in the seminar's conversation, and it is worth documenting at least one instance in which he is being called up and denounced with importunate haste. One cannot speak of a "shared intersubjective a priori framework of aesthetic judgments" for at least two reasons: 1) aesthetic judgments are singular and subjective; 2) they respond to empirical occasions and thus, as acts of judgment, are not a priori. They are, to be sure, enabled by the subjective a priori principle of the sensus communis. Precisely to the extent that it is a priori, the common sense or fundamental communicability presupposed by aesthetic judgment is not reducible to the empirical consensus of a community (or to a "shared intersubjective framework"). Yet precisely because judgments of taste occur in empirical contexts, they do in fact find themselves conditioned by what Davey and Moxey call "tradition, history, or social circumstance." Kant claims, for instance, that different societies have different ideals of beauty: because "the standard idea of the [figure or] shape of an animal of a particular kind has to take its elements from experience," and because these elements have to inform an ideal that has to be "exhibited as an aesthetic idea fully in concreto in a model image," Kant believes that "a Negro's standard idea of the beauty of the [human] figure necessarily differs from that of a white man, that of a Chinese from that of a European." Immanuel Kant, *Critique of Judgment*, trans. Werner S. Pluhar (Indianapolis: Hackett, 1987), 81, 82 (par. 17). Such passages doubtless raise more interpretive questions than they answer, but let that suffice as my point here: Kant's writing on aesthetic judgment deserves slow scrutiny.

9. The conversation of art historians, Elkins says, is "less deliberate" (which is probably good: it suggests the spontaneity of aesthetic consciousness) than that of aestheticians, but the latter nonetheless seem a jovial crew: their arguing is marked by "pervasiveness," "naturalness," and "inexhaustibility."

10. See James Elkins, *Our Beautiful, Dry, and Distant Texts: Art History as Writing* (University Park: Pennsylvania State University Press, 1997), 48. This finely intelligent study offers a powerful examination and example of the ways in which art historical writing inevitably engages "aesthetic" issues of representation, exemplarity, performance, and so on.

11. Edmund Burke, *A Philosophical Enquiry into the Origin of Our Ideas of the Sublime and the Beautiful*, ed. James T. Boulton (Notre Dame, IN: University of Notre Dame Press, 1986). A full reading of the treatise would have to discuss Burke's sensationist-physiological musings in Part IV: the sublime as the result of a literal "striking," repeated as "another and another and another stroke" on the eye (p. 137). Or on the ear, which is

"struck"; "if the stroke be repeated pretty soon after, the repetition causes the expectation of another stroke"; thus the "tension of the part" increases "with every blow" (p. 140). Similarly (Burke returns obsessively to striking and being struck in these pages), the sublime arises from seeing a succession of objects, e.g., columns, which, "each in its order as it succeeds, repeats impulse after impulse, and stroke after stroke," generating the sublime (p. 141). Whatever one makes of the suggestion of masochistic beating and the importance of repetition, difference and sameness here, one might well conclude that the "dreariness" of aesthetics conceals peculiar and interesting rhetorical agitation.

12. Simon Jarvis, "An Undeleter for Criticism," *Diacritics*, 32:1 (2002): 12. Jarvis does not comment on his phrase's resemblance to the name the U.S. military gave its bombing operation in Iraq ("Shock and Awe"), but there would be much to say about the aestheticization of war in the modern era. For a rich, if brief, commentary, see Walter Benjamin, "The Work of Art in the Age of Mechanical Reproduction," in *Illuminations*. I have discussed the intimacy between aesthetics and technics in *The Politics of Aesthetics*, 14–22, passim.
13. Peter de Bolla, "Toward the Materiality of Aesthetic Experience," *Diacritics* 32:1 (2002): 34–35. He has been invoking remarks by Philippe Lacoue-Labarthe in *Poetry as Experience*, trans. Andrea Tarnowski (Stanford, CA: Stanford University Press, 1999).
14. One could link what is being said about performance here to the blindness thematized in Jacques Derrida's *Memoirs of the Blind: The Self-Potrait and Other Ruins*, trans. Pascale-Anne Brault and Michael Naas (Chicago: University of Chicago Press, 1993). In a very different mode, Elkins explores the "blind experiment" of the act of painting in *What Painting Is* (London and New York: Routledge, 1999): "Painting is alchemy. Its materials are worked without the knowledge of their properties, by blind experiment, by the feel of the paint. A painter knows what to do by the tug of the brush as it pulls through a mixture of oils, and by the look of colored slurrics on the palette" (p. 9).

    It should be added that the motif of shock or surprise in aesthetic experience can manifest itself in somewhat comical modes. "I have read that Clement Greenberg would cover his eyes as a painting was set up and then abruptly uncover them in a gesture equivalent to dropping the veil: the work was then what struck the eye as an instant of pure vision, before the theoretical intellect could go to work." Arthur C. Danto, *Beyond the Brillo Box: The Visual Arts in Post-Historical Perspective* (New York: Farrar, Straus, Giroux, 1992), 17.
15. "Forget Kant," might be the motto of much of this volume. I would not except John Hyman's remarks from this pattern. His aggressively territorial riposte to de Duve ("then let me speak as a philosopher") claims a whole, unviolated and unfragmented Kant for philosophy, but arguably does so in order to embalm Kant in philosophy's history, as a "very systematic thinker" inextricable from a bygone context ("his philosophy as a whole is founded on the idea that geometry and arithmetic are a priori bodies of knowledge about space and time, and if you want to understand his

thought rather than picking out attractive quotations that have resonance in new contexts, then your first responsibility is to say what significance the idea has in Kant's philosophy"). One must certainly respect the complexity of Kant's text, as I insisted in a previous footnote, but one must also accept that fragmentation and dissemination beset all texts, particularly those that claim us. Put in mock-Freudian terms: the philosopher's dream of a collected and complete Kant expresses the wish that Kant be declared dead and properly buried.

16. A certain scene of dismemberment and recollection seems part of the phantasmatics of Kant's reception, at least at the present time: a sketchy version may be discerned in Jarvis's text, for instance, as Jarvis argues the case for "detaching" certain parts of Kantian philosophy from other parts of it.

NOTES ON CONTRIBUTORS

Ján Bakoš is Professor of Art History at Comenius University Bratislava. He is the author of *Umelec v klietke* [*Artist in the Cage*] (Bratislava, 1999); *Štyri trasy metodológie dejín umenia* [*Four Routes of Art Historical Methodology*] (Bratislava, 2000); *Periféria a symbolický skok* [*The Periphery and the Symbolic Jump*] (Bratislava, 2000); and *Intelektuál & Pamiatka* [*Intellectuals and Historical Monuments*] (Bratislava, 2004). He also edited *Contemporary Art and Art History's Myths* (Bratislava, 2002) and *Artwork through the Market* (Bratislava, 2004). (dejubaja@savba.sk)

Ciarán Benson is Professor of Psychology at University College Dublin. His books include *The Cultural Psychology of Self: Place, Morality and Art in Human Worlds* (London, 2001); and *The Absorbed Self: Pragmatism, Psychology and Aesthetic Experience* (London, 1993). He was appointed Chairman of the Arts Council of Ireland by the Irish Government (1993–1998). He was also Founding Chairman of the Irish Film Insititute (1980–1984) and of The City Arts Centre, Dublin (1985–1991). (cbenson@eircom.net)

J. M. Bernstein works at the Department of Philosophy at the New School for Social Research. His publications include *The Fate of Art: Aesthetic Alienation from Kant to Derrida and Adorno* (Cambridge, 1992); and *Adorno: Disenchantment and Ethics* (Cambridge, 2001). He edited and wrote the introduction to *Classic and Romantic German Aesthetics* (Cambridge, 2003); and *Against Voluptuous Bodies: Late Modernism and the Idea of Painting* (Stanford, CA, 2005). (Department of Philosophy – GF, 65 Fifth Avenue, New York, NY 10003, USA)

Harry Cooper is Curator of Modern Art at the Fogg Art Museum. His exhibitions there include *Frank Stella 1958* (forthcoming in 2006), *Medardo Rosso: Second Impressions* (2003), and *Mondrian: The Transatlantic Paintings* (2001). In addition to the catalogues for these shows, his publications include "Kelly's Selvage" in *Ellsworth Kelly: Self-Portrait Drawings 1944–1992* (New York, 2003); "Recognizing Guston" in *Philip Guston: A New Alphabet* (New Haven, 2000); and "Mondrian, Hegel, Boogie," *October* 84 (Spring 1998): 119–142. (hcoooper@fas.harvard.cdu)

Diarmuid Costello is Senior Lecturer in the Theory of Art at Oxford Brookes University. Recent publications include "Aura, Face, Photography: Re-Reading Benjamin Today," in *Walter Benjamin and Art*, edited by Andrew Benjamin (London, 2005), 164–84; "On Late Style: Arthur Danto's *The Abuse of Beauty*," *British Journal of Aesthetics* 44 no. 4 (October 2004), 424–439; and "Museum as Work in the Age of Technological Display: Reading Heidegger Through Tate Modern" in *Art and Thought*, edited by Dana Arnold and Margaret Iversen (Oxford 2003), 174–196. (dcostello@brookes.ac.uk)

Paul Crowther is Professor of Art and Philosophy at the International University Bremen. His major publications include *Philosophy after Postmodernism: Civilized Values and the Scope of Knowledge* (London, 2003); *The Transhistorical Image;*

Philosophizing Art and Its History (Cambridge, 2002); *The Language of Twentieth-Century Art: A Conceptual History* (New Haven, CT and London, 1997); *Art and Embodiment: From Aesthetics to Self-Consciousness* (Oxford, 1993; and *Critical Aesthetics and Postmodernism* (Oxford, 1993). (p.crowther@iu-bremen.de)

Arthur Danto is Emeritus Professor of Philosophy at Columbia University. His books include *Nietzsche as Philosopher* (New York, 2005); *Mysticism and Morality* (New York, 1972); *The Transfiguration of the Commonplace* (Cambridge, MA, 1981); *Narration and Knowledge* (New York, 1985); *Connections to the World: The Basic Concepts of Philosophy* (New York, 1989); and *Encounters and Reflections: Art in the Historical Present* (Berkeley, CA, 1990).

Nicholas Davey was educated at the Universities of York, Sussex, and Tübingen. He has lectured at the City University London, the University of Manchester, and the University of Wales Institute, Cardiff, and he is currently professor of philosophy at the University of Dundee. His principal teaching and research interests are in aesthetics and hermeneutics. He has published widely in the fields of Continental philosophy, aesthetics, and hermeneutic theory (www.universityofdundee.edu/philosophy). His new book, *Unquiet Understanding: Reflections on Gadamer's Hermeneutics* is forthcoming from the State University Press of New York in 2006. (J.R.N.Davey@dundee.ac.uk)

Thierry de Duve is professor at the University of Lille 3. His books include *Pictorial Nominalism: On Marcel Duchamp's Passage from Painting to the Readymade* (Minneapolis, MN, 1991) and *Kant after Duchamp* (Cambirdge, MA, 1996); he curated *Voici—100 ans d'art contemporain* at the Brussels Palais des Beaux-Arts in 2000 (in English as *Look! One Hundred Years of Contemporary Art* [Ghent, 2001]), and the Belgian pavilion at the 2003 Venice Biennale (shared by Sylvie Eyberg and Valérie Mannaerts). (thierry.de.duve@skynet.be)

Anna Dezeuze is Research Fellow at the AHRB Research Centre for Studies of Surrealism and its Legacies, University of Manchester. Her publications include "Tactile Dematerialization, Sensory Politics: Hélio Oiticica's *Parangoles*," *Art Journal* 63 (Summer 2004): 58–71; "Do-it-Yourself Artworks: A User's Guide," in *Dead History, Live Art? Spectacle, Subjectivity, and Subversion in Visual Culture Since the 1960s,* edited by Jonathan Harris (Liverpool, forthcoming); "1960–1970," in *A Companion to Contemporary Art since 1945,* edited by Amelia Jones (Oxford, forthcoming). (anna.dezeuze@manchester.ac.uk)

Martin Donougho teaches in the Department of Philosophy, University of South Carolina, Columbia. His publications include a translation of and introduction to Hegel's 1823 *Lectures on the Philosophy of Art*, forthcoming from Oxford; "Stages of the Sublime in North America," MLN 115 (December 2000) 909–940; "Hegel and the 'End of Art,'" forthcoming in an anthology on Hegel and the arts, edited by Stephen Houlgate (Northwestern University Press); and entries on "Louis Kahn," "Mies van der Rohe," and "Rudolf Wittkower" in the *Thoemmes Encyclopedia of Twentieth-Century American Aesthetics*. (donougho@sc.edu)

James Elkins teaches at the University College Cork, Ireland, and at the School of the Art Institute of Chicago. His most recent books include *Visual Studies: A Skeptical Introduction* (New York, 2003), *On The Strange Place of Religion in Contemporary Art* (New York, 2004), and *What Happened to Art Criticism?* (Chicago, 2003).(jelkins@artic.edu)

Robert Gero works at the Department of Art and Design at the University of Michigan, Ann Arbor. He holds a MFA in sculpture in addition to a Ph.D. in Philosophy from the New School for Social Research. His dissertation title is *Strategies of the Artificial Sublime: Vacant, Obscure and Rude* (April 2004). His publications include "The Post-Medium Condition," in *Prospettive sul*

Postmoderno, edited by N. Limnatis and L. Pastore (Milan, 2005). (rgero@umich.edu)

David J. Getsy is Assistant Professor in the Department of Art History, Theory, and Criticism at the School of the Art Institute of Chicago. His publications include *Body Doubles: Sculpture in Britain, 1877-1905* (New Haven, CT, 2004); *Sculpture and the Pursuit of a Modern Ideal in Britain, c.1880-1930* (Aldershot, 2004); "Privileging the Object of Sculpture: Actuality and Harry Bates's *Pandora* of 1890," *Art History* 28 (2005): 74–95; and "Tactility or Opticality, Henry Moore or David Smith: Herbert Read and Clement Greenberg on the Art of Sculpture, 1956," in *Imagination Seizes Power: Papers from the Herbert Read Conference*, edited by M. Paraskos (London, 2005). (dgetsy@artic.edu)

Michael J. Golec is Assistant Professor of Art and Design History in the Department of Art and Design and the Department of Architecture at Iowa State University. His publications include "'Doing it Deadpan': Venturi, Scott Brown, and Izenour's Learning from Las Vegas," *Visible Language* 37 no. 3 (2004): 266–287; and "A Natural History of a Disembodied Eye: The Structure of Gyorgy Kepes' Language of Vision," *Design Issues* 18 no. 2 (Spring 2002): 3–16. (mjg402@iastate.edu)

Francis Halsall is lecturer in art history at Limerick School of Art and Design, and occasional lecturer in art history at University College Cork. He was one of the conveners of the conference that ended in the roundtable in this book, and he is a coeditor of the book *Re-discovering Aesthetics* (forthcoming) and the accompanying research project www.rediscoveringaesthetics.com. He is completing a book on art history and systems-theory. Recent publications include: "One Sense is Never Enough," *Journal of Visual Art Practice* (October, 2004); and "Niklas Luhmann," in *Art: Key Contemporary Thinkers*, eds. Diarmuid Costello and Jonathan Vickery (Berg Publishing, 2006). (francishalsall@yahoo.co.uk)

Gregg M. Horowitz is Associate Professor of Philosophy at Vanderbilt University. His publications include *Sustaining Loss: Art and Mournful Life* (Stanford, CA, 2001); and, with Arthur Danto and Tom Huhn, *The Wake of Art: Criticism, Philosophy, and the Ends of Taste* (New York, Gordon and Breach, 1998). He is currently writing on the use of archaic media in contemporary art and, separately, on Freud.

John Hyman is Chairman of the Philosophy Faculty at the University of Oxford and a Fellow of The Queen's College. His recent publications include "The Urn and the Chamber-Pot," in *Wittgenstein, Culture and the Arts*, edited R. Allen (London, 2001); "Subjectivism in the Theory of Pictorial Art," *The Monist: Art and the Mind* 86 (October 2003); and "Realism and Relativism in the Theory of Art," *Proceedings of the Aristotelian Society*, 105 Part 1 (2005). A new book is entitled *The Objective Eye: Colour, Form and Reality in the Theory of Art* (Chicago, forthcoming). (The Queen's College, Oxford, OX1 4AW, UK. www.queens.ox.ac.uk/fellows/hyman/)

Margaret Iversen is Professor in the Department of Art History and Theory at the University of Essex. Her work on historiography includes *Alois Riegl: Art History and Theory* (Cambridge, MA, 1993). Publications concerning psychoanalysis and contemporary art include *Mary Kelly* (London, 1997); "What is a Photograph?" *Art History*, 17 no. 3 (September 1994); "Readymade, Found Object, Photograph," *Art Journal* (Summer 2004); and "Hopper's Melancholy Gaze," in *Edward Hopper*, edited by Sheena Wagstaff (London, 2004). She co-edited *Art and Thought* (Oxford, 2003).

Michael Kelly is chair of the Philosophy Department at the University of North Carolina at Charlotte. Former Executive Director of the American Philosophical Association and managing editor of the *Journal of Philosophy* (Columbia University), he is the author of *Iconoclasm in Aesthetics* (Cambridge University Press,

2003) and editor of the *Encyclopedia of Aesthetics* (Oxford University Press, 1998). Before moving to Charlotte in 2005, he also taught philosophy and art history at the University of Delaware. His current work is on art and aesthetics in the 1960s.

Ladislav Kesner was curator of Chinese art, head of Asian Art Department, and deputy general director of the National Gallery in Prague. He is currently director of Cultropa, a museum planning and consulting company. He teaches at Charles University, Prague. (lkesner@cultropa.cz)

Joseph Margolis is Laura H. Carnell Professor of Philosophy at Temple University. His most recent publications include *Moral Philosophy after 9/11* (University Park, PA, 2004); and *The Unraveling of Scientism* (Ithaca, NY, 2003). He has just completed *The Arts and the Definition of the Human* and *Intentionalism and Piecemeal Reductionism in the Analysis of Art and Culture.*

Stephen Melville works at the Department of History of Art at the Ohio State University. His publications include *Philosophy beside Itself: On Deconstruction and Modernism* (Minneapolis, MN, 1986); *Seams: Art as a Philosophical Context* (New York, 1996); and, with Philip Armstrong and Laura Lisbon, *As Painting : Division and Displacement* (Cambridge, MA, 2001). He is editor of *The Lure of the Object* (Williamstown, 2005); co-editor, with Bill Readings, of *Vision and Textuality* (London, 1995); and co-editor, with Philip Armstrong and Erika Naginski, of *Res* 46, *Polemical Objects*, (Autumn 2004). (Melville.3@osu.edu)

Keith Moxey is Ann Whitney Olin Professor of Art History at Barnard College/Columbia University. His publications include The *Practice of Theory: Poststructuralism, Cultural Politics and Art History* (Ithaca, NY, 1994); *The Practice of Persuasion: Politics and Paradox in Art History* (Ithaca, NY, 2001); and the following anthologies: *Visual Theory: Painting and Interpretation* (1991);

Visual Culture: Images and Interpretations (1994); *The Subjects of Art History: Historical Objects in Contemporary Perspective* (1998); and *Art History, Aesthetics, and Visual Culture* (2002). (pm154@ columbia.edu)

Alexander Nehamas teaches philosophy and comparative literature at Princeton University. He is the author of *Nietzsche: Life as Literature*; *The Art of Living: Socratic Reflections from Plato to Foucault*; *Virtues of Authenticity: Essays on Plato and Socrates*; and several essays on aesthetics and the philosophy of art. *Only a Promise of Happiness: The Place of Beauty in a World of Art* is forthcoming.

Michael Newman is associate professor of art history, theory, and criticism at the School of the Art Institute of Chicago. He was educated at Oxford, the Sorbonne, the Courtauld Institute, and the Catholic University of Leuven. He has published in *Artforum, Art in America*, the *British Journal of Aesthetics, Kunst and Museum Journal, Parachute, and Research in Phenomenology*.

Matthew Rampley is Director of the Graduate Research School at Edinburgh College of Art. His publications include *Nietzsche, Aesthetics and Modernity* (Cambridge, 2000); *The Remembrance of Things Past: On Aby M. Warburg and Walter Benjamin* (Wiesbaden, 2000); and *Exploring Visual Culture* (Edinburgh, 2005). (Graduate Research School, Edinburgh College of Art, Lauriston Place, Edinburgh EH3 9DF; m.rampley@eca.ac.uk)

David Raskin is Associate Professor in the Department of Art History, Theory and Criticism at the School of the Art Institute of Chicago. His publications include "Donald Judd's Moral Art," *Donald Judd*, edited by Nicholas Serota (London, 2004), 79–95; and "Specific Opposition: Judd's Art and Politics," *Art History* 24 (November 2001): 682–706. (draskin@artic.edu)

Mary C. Rawlinson is Associate Professor of Philosophy at Stony Brook University in New York. She is co-editor of *Derrida and Feminism* (Routledge, 1997); and editor of five issues of the *Journal of Medicine and Philosophy*, including *Foucault and the Philosophy of Medicine; The Future of Psychiatry;* and *Feminist Bioethics*. Her publications include articles on Proust, literature and ethics, Hegel, French feminism, and a forthcoming volume on detective fiction as moral philosophy. (Mary.Rawlinson@sunysb.edu)

Marc Redfield is Professor of English and holds the John D. and Lillian Maguire Distinguished Chair in the Humanities at Claremont Graduate University. His publications include *Phantom Formations: Aesthetic Ideology and the Bildungsroman* (Ithaca, NY, 1996); and *The Politics of Aesthetics: Nationalism, Gender, Romanticism* (Stanford, CA, 2003). He co-edited *High Anxieties: Cultural Studies in Addiction* (Berkeley, CA, 2002); and edited two special issues of *Diacritics*: "Addictions" (1997), and "Theory, Globalization, Cultural Studies, and the Remains of the University" (2001). Most recently he edited a special issue of the online journal *Romantic Praxis*, "Legacies of Paul de Man" (2005).

Adrian Rifkin is Professor of Visual Culture at Middlesex University, UK. His publications include *Ingres Then and Now* (London, 2003); and "Waiting and Seeing," *Journal of Visual Culture* 2 no. 3 (December 2003): 325–339. An overview of his work and work in progress may be found on www.gai-savoir.com. (info@gai-savoir.com)

Crispin Sartwell is Associate Professor of Political Science at Dickinson College in Carlisle, PA. He is a syndicated opinion columnist and author, most recently, of *Six Names of Beauty* (Routledge, 2004). (c.sartwell@verizon.net)

INDEX